The New Generation of
Country Music Stars

The New Generation of Country Music Stars

Biographies of 50 Artists Born After 1940

DAVID DICAIRE

McFarland & Company, Inc., Publishers

Jefferson, North Carolina, and London

LIBRARY OF CONGRESS CATALOGUING-IN-PUBLICATION DATA

Dicaire, David, 1963–
    The new generation of country music stars : biographies of
50 artists born after 1940 / David Dicaire.
        p.   cm.
    Includes bibliographical references and index.

    ISBN 978-0-7864-3787-0
    softcover : 50# alkaline paper ∞

    1. Country musicians — United States — Biography.   I. Title.
    ML394.D54   2008
    781.642092'273 — dc22 [B]   2008022998

British Library cataloguing data are available

Cover photograph ©2008 Shutterstock

Manufactured in the United States of America

McFarland & Company, Inc., Publishers
    Box 611, Jefferson, North Carolina 28640
        www.mcfarlandpub.com

Contents

v

Introduction

For the first fifty years of its recorded history, from 1920 to 1970, country music was the predominant creation of the working class, white, mostly poor, rural folk. The style evolved from its humble roots in the foothills and backwoods of rural America to cosmopolitan centers around the country and around the world without sacrificing its cherished, traditional sound. In the late 1970s, the facts-of-life music changed direction when it was delivered to a new audience — one that was educated, middle class and urban.

The seeds of change had been planted in the 1960s, but would take a decade or more to blossom. At the time, the dominant trend in recording practices belonged to the Nashville studios. In an effort to compete in the cutthroat music industry, the executives in Music City, U.S.A., decided to incorporate elements of pop into the pure strain of country. The results of this strategy would dictate the course of the genre for the next forty years.

The country-pop Nashville Sound began to make serious inroads into mainstream radio, blurring the lines between styles. Popular music acts such as John Denver and Olivia Newton-John scored hits on both the country and Top 40 radio charts; they also won Country Music Association awards. As the decade wore on the style became increasingly polished, further alienating a segment of its fan base.

The rebellious nature of performers provided an alternative to country-pop as many challenged the Nashville techniques of song production. This trend began in the 1960s and would be fittingly dubbed the "Outlaw movement." Initially considered a passing fad and the simple reaction of disgruntled musicians, it dominated the country music charts and awards during the 1970s. It also won the hearts of many rock and roll fans for its use of electric guitars and drums producing a hard-core sound.

It was only logical that the two most popular styles of country music to dominate the 1970s — outlaw and country-pop — would merge into one sound. It occurred with the movie *Urban Cowboy*, which ushered in a new craze and age. Suddenly country dances and fashion, riding mechanical bulls, and hanging out in roadhouse nightclubs were all the rage. Although the

1

Urban Cowboy trend endured throughout much of the 1980s, and influenced many, it never produced a single major artist. However, it did bring one major change in that country no longer belonged solely to the rural populace; it was a form that city dwellers could and did embrace.

By the early 1980s, country music was at a crossroads. The style needed to rediscover its roots, its tradition, its simplicity, and it needed a hero to point it in the proper direction. George Strait emerged with his *Strait Country* album and ignited the New Traditionalist movement.

By the mid–1980s, the New Traditionalist movement was in full swing as a whole crop of fresh artists emerged and dominated the charts. They received the most airplay, pushing aside the more established artists. The back-to-basics, non-pop approach to arrangements and instrumentation celebrated the folk roots of the music. Many fans who had drifted away from the genre returned to enjoy the gifts of Strait, Randy Travis and Clint Black.

The Outlaw movement continued throughout the 1980s as some of the aging practitioners fought to keep it alive. There were those who took the basics of the sub-genre and pushed it further away from the mainstream to create an alternative to the mainstream. The nonconformist sound provided another dimension to the diversified country music fan base.

The New Traditionalists dominated the latter half of the 1980s before they gave way to so-called New Country artists. Clint Black and Travis Tritt were at the forefront, but Garth Brooks was the superstar. An avid fan of the Eagles, Kiss and Billy Joel, he retained the basic elements of country music and mixed them with rock and roll, pop, and singer-songwriter elements that catapulted him to the top.

Black represented a new breed of singers who cut a clean, handsome, softer image compared to that of Merle Haggard, Waylon Jennings and Hank Williams, Jr. Most important, Brooks and his followers were groomed for crossover success and would push the genre into unprecedented record sales at the multi-platinum level. They appealed to the country side of the music industry as well as the pop crowd.

The first half of the 1990s saw a boom in the genre and produced an interesting array of artists. There were one-hit wonders and alternative artists as well as mainstream acts. New Country pushed aside George Jones, Dolly Parton, Willie Nelson, Johnny Cash and Merle Haggard as fresh audiences had little patience with their seemingly outdated music. Country radio stations played music for their contemporary audience and phased out old favorites and alternative artists.

By the middle of the 1990s, New Country completely dominated the charts and radio. Shania Twain, the biggest star of that era, enjoyed huge success with her country-pop stylings and blazed the trail for other female artists, including LeAnn Rimes, the Dixie Chicks, Faith Hill and Trisha Yearwood, among others, to follow. In the latter half of the decade the women ruled the industry.

In the late 1990s and the early part of the next decade, country music supporters were treated to a variety of styles providing something for every fan's taste. The usual styles — bluegrass, honky tonk and western swing — were still popular and sounded fresh when recorded with updated techniques. Alternative, mainstream, and country-pop styles continued to hold their respective audiences.

Today, the genre is a powerful industry with a rich and diverse talent base that still provides something for every taste. The term "modern country," like "modern blues" and "modern jazz," encompasses a variety of styles as well as sub-styles. For example, alternative country can be broken down into alternative country-rock, Americana, and neo-traditional folk. The blending of the old and the new ensures a very bright future.

Despite all of the new trends in country music, the old styles have not been forgotten. There are western swing enthusiasts who have built upon the foundation laid by Bob Wills. There are also dedicated bluegrass players who champion the efforts of Bill Monroe. Honky tonk formed the bedrock of the New Traditionalists movement and remains quite popular.

There remains a core group that celebrates the achievements of the early string bands like Gid Tanner and His Skillet Lickers and the Possum Hunters. The major difference between the outfits of yesteryear and today is that the modern groups don't feature a leader but emphasize the equal responsibility of all members. There have also been a number of duos in the last forty years that have made their mark on the industry.

The cowboy songs featured in the old westerns of the 1930s and 1940s that became part of the national psyche have also weathered the test of time. Although not as sophisticated as the slick, special effects-loaded movies of today, the remastered versions on DVD of the old films have won over a new audience, preserving the memories of an era long gone but not forgotten. Many of today's action heroes owe a great debt to those actors of an earlier era.

Many of the country-pop vocalists of today claim a connection to the greatest voice in country music history, Patsy Cline. She injected her songs with a pop flavor that had a strong influence on Shania Twain, LeAnn Rimes, the Dixie Chicks, Trisha Yearwood and Faith Hill, among others.

The slick techniques that brought many aspiring singers to Nashville to record their songs remain intact. Today's CDs are produced with a definite technological skill and mastery to sound modern and contemporary. The legacy of Chet Atkins lives on.

Like every other style, country music is constantly evolving in order to appeal to a new generation of fans. However, mainstream twang, a simple music at its core, has always been about tradition. The gap between the traditionalists who cherish the older sound and the new enthusiasts who push the boundaries ensures that the genre will forever remain exciting and dynamic.

The music has strived to appeal to an audience that grew up on rock and roll, MTV (as a video channel), soul, blues funk, punk and early rap. Interesting marketing strategies have been put in place to encourage appeal to the new fans. Country is no longer solely the music of a certain demographic of the population, but one that appeals to a cross-section of the listening audience.

There are three networks devoted to the genre: CMT, VH-1 Country, and GAC. Originally, The Nashville Network (TNN) was the premier American country music video channel; it was launched in the early 1980s. In 2000, it was renamed The National Network to accommodate its reformatted programming. The renamed TNN competed against USA Network, TNT, and superstations TBS and WGN.

This book features the modern country artists who have kept the tradition of the genre alive in a contemporary setting. The first section, "The New Traditionalists," features those that re-established the mainstream country sound in the 1980s by delving into the past. They returned the genre back to its roots and delivered the music to urban America. "Alternative Country" highlights those that made country music on their own terms. "Groups" features those acts that carried on the tradition of the Skillet Lickers, the Carter Family, the Possum Hunters and many others prominent in the 1920s and 1930s while making contributions to every new style of the genre. "Country-Pop" celebrates those that were able to spin gold by combining country with pop stylings. "New Country" champions a cross section of country singers from the United States, Canada, Australia and New Zealand.

There are hundreds of country music associations that preserve every aspect of the style. There are also thousands of festivals that take place all over the globe. The venues provide something for everyone from the casual listener to the rabid fan.

The changes to country music have not affected its popularity or power; in fact, they have kept the style fresh and appealing to a new generation of fans who have discovered the beauty, magic, depth and intensity of the genre. The once regional sound of the Appalachian people has grown into a billion-dollar industry and is an integral part of the pop culture scene. However, in the end, country music remains country music.

PART ONE

The New Traditionalists

In the early 1980s, country music was at a crossroads. The Urban Cowboy craze was in full swing. There were country-pop crooners, a handful of aging Outlaws and the country-rock group Alabama. The genre needed to rediscover its roots and draw upon the classic styles of the past.

In 1981, an unassuming hero emerged from his native Texas with the song "Unwound." George Strait had no crossover desires and delivered a back-to-basics, neo-traditional sound that didn't include any pop elements. The arrangements and instrumentation reflected the celebration of his rural roots.

Others would soon take up the cause. Ricky Skaggs, an instrumental prodigy, owed his sound to traditional bluegrass. The Judds, a mother and daughter duo, sang simple songs with mass appeal and were the direct opposite to the country-pop stylings of Barbara Mandrell and Dolly Parton. Reba McEntire dominated the 1980s with her mainstream sound. In 1986, Randy Travis released his debut album that put the New Traditionalist style squarely at the forefront of country music.

The New Traditionalists built their sound on classic honky tonk, yet had all the advantages of updated production techniques and equipment, making the music sound authentic and modern. By the mid–1980s, they had taken over the country airwaves and charts. Strait, Skaggs, Travis and Vince Gill only added to the dominance of the style and became the leading figures.

Eventually, others such as Alan Jackson, Clint Black, Keith Whitley, and Travis Tritt arrived on the scene. Each had his own distinct style and branched out from the New Traditionalist format. The sub-genre had established a launching pad for the superstars of the early 1990s who would take country music to a commercial universe never thought possible.

From the New Traditionalist movement sprang the Neo-Traditionalists, a group of artists that also played in the hard-core country style but were revivalists. The biggest difference between the new and neo camps was that the latter operated on the fringes of the industry while the former were strictly mainstream. Some of the main proponents of the neo-trad movement were Iris DeMent, Lorrie Morgan, Michael Martin Murphey, Diamond Rio, Jamie O'Hara, Carlene Carter and Rosanne Cash.

Some of the names associated with the New Traditionalist style but not featured in this book include John Anderson, the O'Kanes, Joe Diffie, John Michael Montgomery, Marty Stuart, Trace Adkins, Suzy Bogguss, Marty Brown, Tracy Byrd, Mark Collie, Skip Ewing, Radney Foster, Hank Flamingo, Sammy Kershaw, Tracy Lawrence, David Lee Murphy, Collin Raye, Aaron Tippin, Clay Walker, Larry Boone, Mark Chesnutt, Doug Stone, and Ty Herndon.

The following artists featured in this book returned country music to its roots, but used modern recording techniques, proving that the style could sound contemporary and authentic:

- George Strait, who is credited with igniting the entire New Traditionalist movement.
- Ricky Skaggs, a bluegrass enthusiast and one of the best instrumentalists of the modern era.
- Reba McEntire, who was the most important female singer of the 1980s and 1990s even after she pursued a television and film career. She could also be classified as part of the Neo-Trad movement.
- Keith Whitley, who had a short but powerful career that had a major impact on the future direction of the genre.
- Vince Gill, one of the major mainstream performers in the early 1990s going against the grain during the Garth Brooks era.
- Alan Jackson, who took the established parameters of the New Traditionalist movement and expanded on it without wavering from the mainstream.
- Randy Travis, who broke wide open with his first album and quickly became the poster boy for the style.
- Toby Keith, a patriotic country musician who came into prominence in the 1990s. He has not shied away from controversy.
- Clint Black, who ignited the mass-market appeal of country music that exploded in the 1990s.
- Travis Tritt, a prime voice projecting an Outlaw image without the big hat.

George Strait (1952–)

Strait Style

The influence of honky tonk, bluegrass and western swing on today's country music is immeasurable. The new artists have taken the best of mainstream country to forge something fresh and exciting. One of these modern performers managed to weld traditional roots with contemporary elements to create his own style. His name is George Strait.

George Strait was born on May 18, 1952, in Pearsall, Texas. He was raised in the state on a ranch that had been in the family for nearly a century. Although his mother would leave, taking his sister along, young George remained behind with his father and brothers. When not helping out with chores on the farm, he played music in a local rock and roll garage band.

However, his musical dreams seemed far away at this point in his life. He attended college briefly before dropping out and eloping with his high school sweetheart. Later he joined the army and was stationed in Hawaii, where during his posting he played on a base band. The outfit also performed in civilian venues under a different name.

In 1975, he gained his honorable discharge from the army and relocated back to Texas hoping to complete his college education. He studied agriculture at Southwest Texas State University, and during this time he formed his own country band, Ace in the Hole. The group developed a local following in the south and central parts of Texas and as far away as Huntsville and Houston. Sometimes they opened for Strait's idol, Bob Wills and His Texas Playboys. Although the amateur group recorded, they never gained enough attention to sustain a long term venture.

Strait moved to Nashville in an effort to ignite his career, but because he lacked connections in the music business the venture was a negative one. Upon his return home, he was determined to correct this shortcoming and hooked up with a Texas club owner who had once worked for MCA records. In 1980, the company signed him to a recording contract after executives listened to his marketable sound.

In 1981, his first album, *Strait Country*, appeared. His first single, "Unwound," was released and climbed into the Top Ten. However, the second song pulled from the album, "Down and Out," was less successful. The record broke open with "If You're Thinking You Want a Stranger (There's One Coming Home)," which went all the way to number three on the charts. More importantly, Strait's record drew deeply from the honky tonk tradition, bypassing the trappings of lush country-pop crossovers, Outlaw, Urban Cowboy swagger and country-rock; it pointed the genre to a new future direction.

For the remainder of his career, he would release a string of consistent, quality albums and CDs that were a blend of hardcore honky tonk, western swing and Bakersfield country with some melodic ballads. Each contained at least one number one hit. Over twenty-five years later, he holds the record for more number one songs (41) than any other country singer, surpassing Conway Twitty by one.

The 1980s belonged to him as he dominated the singles charts, and all of his albums reached platinum or gold status. While many of the superstars of the 1980s watched their careers fizzle, Strait, because of his dedication to traditional styles, was able to survive the early 1990s when a more commercial approach ruled in Nashville. His consistency was the key to his success.

At various intervals he released greatest hits packages, including a four-disc career retrospective entitled *Strait Out of the Box* in 1995. Whether the product was new or repackaged material, fans could not get enough of King George, a moniker that had been rightfully bestowed upon him.

In 1982, he began his movie and television career. He had bit parts in *The Soldier* and *Mystery*. Later, he played Dusty, the lead in the film *Pure Country*, which included a successful soundtrack. He also appeared as himself in the movies *The Horse Whisperer* and *Grand Champion*. In addition he provided the voice of Cornell on the animated television show *King of the Hill*.

The performance side of his career also made the news. From 1997 through 2001, he headlined the George Strait Country Music Festival, which included appearances by Tim McGraw, Faith Hill, Kenny Chesney, Alan Jackson and other stars. Since 1983, one of his regular concert venues has been the Houston Livestock Show and Rodeo. This resulted in an album, *Last Time: Live from the Astrodome*, recorded during the final show at the Astrodome in 2002, which set a paid attendance record.

In 2003, the Rodeo moved to Reliant Stadium where a year later he would set a new attendance record. In his more than twenty appearances at the Houston Rodeo, he has played to a total of a couple of million fans, making him one of the most visible country artists on the scene. His appeal never faltered over his career and remained steady throughout every new trend.

In 2006, he released *It Just Comes Natural*, a CD of new material that included the hit singles "Give It Away" and the title track. Many of these songs were written with longtime collaborator Dean Dillon. But the biggest news of the year was his induction into the Country Music Hall of Fame. He performed "Give it Away" and became only the second artist (aside from Eddy Arnold) to become a member of the prestigious institution while still recording number one songs.

In 2007, he launched a tour with Ronnie Milsap and newcomer Taylor Swift as his opening acts. He performed at the Houston Rodeo where his son worked as a roper. There are also more future releases marked for an audience with an insatiable appetite for his music. Strait continues to perform and record.

George Strait is a country music rock. For over twenty-five years he has been one of the most solid performers on the circuit. His albums have ranged from excellent to very good and the fact that some of his recorded efforts seem weaker than others is because so many were simply outstanding. It was evident from the very first release that he was something special when he shot to the top of the charts where he has remained throughout his distinguished career.

With his smooth, emotive voice he has crafted a sterling career. There is an effortless ability to his vocal delivery that has enabled him to stay on top of the charts for three decades. Part of his genius exists in his skill to record in the hard-core country tradition, yet give it a fresh, contemporary feel, giving his albums an even balance and mood. His certification according to music industry standards ranks him just behind Elvis and the Beatles.

The greatest influences on Strait were the traditional country artists Merle Haggard and George Jones. Another was the western swing enthusiast Bob Wills. Strait managed to borrow heavily from all of these performers and fashion something that was his own without sacrificing anything. It is an essential component of his very successful career.

In turn, Strait has made an impact on a number of artists including Clint Black, Brooks & Dunn, Garth Brooks, Billy Ray Cyrus, Pirates of the Mississippi, Steve Wariner, John Berry, Ace in the Hole Band, Kenny Chesney, Daryle Singletary, Mark Wills, Gil Grand and George Canyon. His earnest approach, which has seen him uphold the harder sounds of Haggard, Wills and Hank Williams, Sr., has often been compared to the slickly-produced country-pop material. But King George has blazed a path for the new generation proving that a singer can stick to roots and enjoy celebrated success.

Strait has been nominated for more CMA Awards than anyone else and has won sixteen of them. He was Entertainer of the Year in 1989 and 1990. As well, he was acknowledged as the top touring country act of the 1990s and remains a staple of U.S. radio. *Strait Out of the Box* is the number two box set on the all-time best selling parade.

He has given the world a wealth of songs to enjoy. A partial list includes "Marina Del Rey," "You Look So Good in Love," "Right or Wrong," "Let's Fall to Pieces Together," "Does Fort Worth Ever Cross Your Mind," "The Fireman," "You're Something Special to Me," "Nobody in His Right Mind Would've Left Her," "All My Ex's Live in Texas," "Am I Blue," "Ocean Front Property," "Baby Blue," "Famous Last Words of a Fool," "If You Ain't Lovin', You Ain't Livin'," "Ace in the Hole," "Baby's Gotten Good at Goodbye," "What's Going on in Your World," "You Know Me Better Than That," "If I Know Me," "I'd Like to Have That One Back," "I Know She Still Loves Me," and "Carried Away." The aforementioned tunes are just some of his number ones. He has also enjoyed many other songs that placed in the top ten.

While his albums and singles have sold over sixty million copies, the performance side of his career has also been an important part of his grand success. He has set numerous attendance records across venues throughout the United States. He is a cherished live artist because he is able to reproduce his songs to sound exactly the way they are found on record.

George Strait is a country music legend who has fashioned a very powerful career because of his savvy and talent. His dedication to traditional country combined with a contemporary edge enabled him to stay ahead of the pack.

DISCOGRAPHY:

Let's Get Down to It, MCA MCAC-53648.
Strait Country, MCA 31087.
Strait from the Heart, MCA 31117.
Right or Wrong, MCA 31068.
Does Fort Worth Ever Cross Your Mind, MCA 31032.
Something Special, MCA 5605.
#7, MCA 5750.
Merry Christmas Strait to You, MCAD-5800.
Ocean Front Property, MCAD-5913.
If You Ain't Lovin' (You Ain't Livin'), MCA MCAD-42114.
Beyond the Blue Neon, MCA-42256.
Livin' It Up, MCA-6415.
Chill of an Early Fall, MCAD 10204.
Holding My Own, MCAD-10532.
Pure Country, MCAD-10651.
Easy Come, Easy Go, MCAD-10907.
Lead On, MCA 11002.
Blue Clear Sky, MCA 11428.
Carrying Your Love with Me, MCA 11584.
One Step at a Time, MCA 70020.
Always Never the Same, MCA 70050.
Merry Christmas Wherever You Are, MCA 700093.
George Strait, MCA 170143.
The Road Less Traveled, MCA 170220.
For the Last Time: Live from the Astrodome, MCA 170119.
Honkytonkville, MCA 000011402.
Somewhere Down in Texas, MCA 000444602.
How About Them Cowgirls, MCA Nashville 02805.
Ace in the Hole, MCAC-53693.
Strait Country/Strait from the Heart, MCAD-5871.
Greatest Hits, MCAD-5567.
Greatest Hits, Vol. 2, MCAD-42035.
Ten Strait Hits, MCA 10450.
Strait Out of the Box, MCA 11263.
The Very Best of Strait, Vol. 2: 1988–1993, MCA Nashville 19397.
Latest Greatest Straitest Hits, MCA 170100.
20th Century Masters — The Millennium Collection: The Best of George Strait, MCA 170280.
20th Century Masters — The Christmas Collection, MCA 000091202.
The Very Best of Strait, Vol. 1: 1981–1987, MCA 19367.
50 Number Ones, MCA Nashville 000045902.
Greatest Collection [2004], Platinum Disc 3342.
Love Collection, Madacy 51070.
Greatest Collection [2005], Platinum Disc 3610.

Chronicles, MCA Nashville 000461102.
Livin' It Up/If You Ain't Lovin' (You Ain't Livin')/#7, Madacy 51662.
Christmas Collection, Madacy 251558.
The Ultimate Collection [Madacy 3 Disc], Madacy 52278.
The Ultimate Collection [Madacy 2 Disc], Madacy 52490.
Strait Hits, Universal 5060001272139.

Ricky Skaggs (1954–)

Kentucky Thunder

When Bill Monroe consolidated various musical elements — the fast-paced tempos, unique rhythms, and lonesome sound — into one cohesive unit to create bluegrass, he ignited a movement that is still vibrant today. In the modern era there have been many who continued to carry the bluegrass torch. Preeminent among them is Ricky Skaggs.

Ricky Skaggs was born on July 18, 1954, in Cordell, Kentucky. Like Alison Krauss and Barbara Mandrell, he was a child prodigy. At five, his father gave him a mandolin, and Ricky taught himself how to play the instrument. That same year he performed on stage for the first time at a Bill Monroe concert, reeling off a driving version of "Ruby Are You Mad at Your Man?"

He continued to develop as a musician by adding the fiddle and guitar to his blossoming musical arsenal, as well as playing in the Skaggs Family group. At seven, Ricky appeared with Flatt & Scruggs on television. He absorbed the honky styles of George Jones and Ray Price, and showed an interest in the British Invasion bands the Beatles and the Rolling Stones. Although his taste was eclectic, he remained devoted to bluegrass and traditional country that formed the basis of his sound.

At fifteen, he was a member of Ralph Stanley's bluegrass band, the Clinch Mountain Boys, which also included Keith Whitley. The two young virtuosos became good friends since they were both exciting fiddlers, and it was only natural for them to jam together. Sometimes these sessions included Keith's brother Dwight on banjo and the trio played on radio opening for Stanley, who was truly impressed with them.

Skaggs, a multi-instrumental performer on the guitar, mandolin, fiddle, and banjo, was an invaluable member of the group. During his three-year stint with Stanley, he played at numerous bluegrass concerts and shared the stage alongside many country music legends who were always in awe of the Kentucky kid with the wild-eyed licks. He also played on Stanley's *Cry from the Cross* album and did session work on Whitley's solo album, *2nd Genera-tion Bluegrass*.

In 1972, he left the Clinch Mountain Boys and worked a regular job at the Virginia Electric Power Company, but music was in his blood. When the Country Gentlemen invited him to join the group, Skaggs jumped at the chance and remained with them for two years. Later, he moved on to the more progressive bluegrass band J.D. Crowe & the New South, adding his talent and experience to that outfit.

He did more studio work with Whitley on the album *That's It*, and later formed his own proper bluegrass outfit, Boone Creek. They played honky tonk, western swing and bluegrass to enthusiastic audiences, but never really made a major impact. Because of his multi-instrumental abilities, Skaggs was asked to join a number of groups, but turned down all offers.

Finally, in 1977, after much badgering, he took Rodney Crowell's place in Emmylou Harris's Hot Band. For three years he helped the country diva rev up her career through concert appearances and recorded material. Skaggs was featured prominently on her album *Roses in the Snow*. Also during this time he had a great influence on his boss as he instilled more of a traditional bluegrass element in her alternative sound.

During his stint with Harris, he was involved in many different projects including a final effort with Boone Creek, *One Way Track*, as well as two duet albums with Tony Rice, *Take Me Home Tonight in a Song* and *Skaggs and Rice*. However, his most satisfying project was the recording of his first solo album, *Sweet Temptation*.

Sweet Temptation became a bluegrass hit featuring three songs from Ralph Stanley, "I'll Take the Blame," "Could You Love Me One More Time," and "Baby Girl," as well as the Lester Flatt tune "I'll Stay Around." His then-boss, Harris, contributed guest vocals. But perhaps the most encouraging element of the album was the fact that Skaggs was championing bluegrass and New Traditionalism while others were caught up in the Urban Cowboy fad.

It was with great enthusiasm and confidence that he entered the studio to work on his second album, *Waitin' for the Sun to Shine*. The effort was his first for Epic Records and spawned two number one hits, "Crying My Heart Out Over You," and "I Don't Care." Despite the fact that it contained many remakes and boasted a simplistic approach, the record caught the attention of the country music press as well as rock and roll publications.

He would go on to enjoy three more number one hits including "Heart-broke," "I Wouldn't Change You If I Could" and "Highway 40 Blues." His personal success was rewarding, but his overall impact on the course of country music was even more important. Along with George Strait, he opened doors for acts like Randy Travis to solidify the New Traditionalist movement leaving the Urban Cowboy craze behind as a bad memory.

His next album, *Highways & Heartaches,* displayed a maturity in his bluegrass sound combined with a strong traditionalist sensibility. It would boast four top songs and clearly established him as a major voice on the circuit. Skaggs had rekindled an interest in the style Bill Monroe had pioneered, influencing dozens of outfits to take up the cause.

It was only a matter of time before he was recognized for his achievements. In 1983, he won a Grammy for Best Country Instrumental Performance; in 1984, for Best Country Instrumental Performance ("Wheel Hoss"); and in 1986, for Best Country Instrumental Performance ("Raisin' the Dickens"). The CMA would make him Male Vocalist of the Year in 1982 and Entertainer of the Year in 1985. His group, the Ricky Skaggs Band, would win Instrumental Group of the Year three consecutive times from 1983 to 1985. But the best prize was becoming the youngest member of the Grand Ole Opry, in 1982.

Throughout much of the decade he remained a dominant artistic and commercial force in the genre. With the string of Top Ten hits and albums including *Don't Cheat in Our Hometown, Country Boy, Live in London, Love's Gonna Get Ya, and Comin' Home to Stay,* Skaggs carried the torch that Bill Monroe had lit so long ago. He was an icon and one of the most popular country music performers on the scene.

In the latter part of the 1980s, his career began to wane. His records still amassed respectable sales, but his songs spent less time on the charts. However, the respect he commanded in the country music community was reflected in the number of musicians he recorded with including Rodney Crowell, the Bellamy Brothers, Johnny Cash, Jesse Winchester and Dolly Parton.

Skaggs suffered through a dry period in the early 1990s as his New Traditionalist/bluegrass mixed sound was pushed aside by the slick contemporary style of Garth Brooks and others. In 1992, Columbia Records dropped him from their label due to poor sales. He concentrated on the performance side of his career and played at many festivals and concerts. He also hosted his own syndicated radio program, *The Simple Life,* starting in 1994.

In 1995, he returned to the recording studio and released *Solid Ground* on Atlantic Records. It was a comeback effort for Skaggs and included "Cry Cry Darlin'," "Every Drop of Water," as well as a remake of Harry Chapin's "Cat's in the Cradle." The title song was also a hit. It was not an adventurous effort, but sparked renewed interest in his career. Alison Krauss (acoustic guitar), Jerry Douglas (Dobro), Glen D. Hardin (piano), Vince Gill (background vocals), and Brad Ahern (guitar, vocals) guested on the album.

Life Is a Journey, released in 1997, continued the momentum. While the effort lacked the fresh excitement of his early records, his breathtaking musical skills made up for it. He was still an instrumental force to be reckoned with, and there remained an exuberance that made the listening adventure worthwhile. Highlights included "Hillbilly Highway," "When Life Hits Hard," and "Let's Put Love Back to Work."

Fifteen years after his last true bluegrass album, Skaggs returned with a genuine and heartfelt effort called *Bluegrass Rules!* A dynamite record that featured his backing band, Kentucky Thunder, it restored him at the forefront of the genre. Bryan Sutton, Bobby Hicks, Dennis Parker, Paul Brewster, Marc Pruett and Mark Fain all played superbly on the CD as did their fearless leader. Songs of note included the self-penned "Amanda Jewel" and "Somehow Tonight," as well as "Little Maggie," "Ridin' That Midnight Train," and "Get Up, John."

In 2000, he released *Big Mon: The Songs of Bill Monroe* that featured an all-star lineup of Mary Chapin Carpenter, the Dixie Chicks, Charlie Daniels, John Fogerty, Bruce Hornsby, Joan Osborne, Dolly Parton, Travis Tritt, Dwight Yoakam and Patty Loveless among others. Other tributes to his idol included *Sing the Songs of Bill Monroe* and *Uncle Pen*.

Although Skaggs remained a prolific recording artist, the performance side of his career was much stronger. He toured many different venues with his band, Kentucky Thunder, with a staple of their circuit schedule being bluegrass festivals. A true force on stage, he always gave the enthusiastic crowd their money's worth.

In 2004, *Brand New Strings* was released. Three of the four songs Skaggs wrote for the album were instrumentals: "I Corinthians 1:18," "Appalachian Joy," and "Monroe Dancin'." He played seven different instruments on the album, sang harmony vocals and was also credited as the engineer. The work was a balance between traditional and progressive bluegrass.

He broke tradition with his next effort, *Instrumentals*, which was composed of numbers without lyrics. Some of the highlights included "Going to Richmond," "Crossing the Briney," and "Gallatin Rag," which featured a guest appearance by Andy Statman on clarinet. Despite the inclusion of this unorthodox instrument in a bluegrass band, they make it work.

Ricky Skaggs is a modern bluegrass icon. He has expanded the appeal of the style, building on the work of his prime influences, Bill Monroe, Lester Flatt, Earl Scruggs and Ralph Stanley. He is a country music institution and is one of the most favorite sons in the genre.

Ricky Skaggs is a dynamic instrumentalist and arguably the most important one in the modern era of country music. His dexterity, speed and taste are supreme. His musicianship is found on the works of many contemporary artists including Eddie Adcock, Rhett Akins, Mike Auldridge, the Battlefield Band, Jerry Douglas, Keith Whitley, Dolly Parton and a host of others. He was also a part of Emmylou Harris's group as well as Boone Creek, the Country Gentleman, the Clinch Mountain Boys, and J. D. Crowe & the New South. Of course, his most famous association is with his longtime outfit,

Kentucky Thunder. He has left his fingerprints throughout the country music world.

Kentucky Thunder is a group of highly skilled individuals who take their cue from their leader. Bryan Sutton plays guitar, fiddle, mandolin, and banjo. He left the band in 1999 but returns occasionally. Bobby Hicks, the energetic fiddle player from North Carolina, joined the original Ricky Skaggs band that evolved into Kentucky Thunder. He remains with the group, adding his rollicking instrumental ability. Jim Mills, the banjo player, worked with the Brass Mountain Boys and Doyle Lawson & Quicksilver before joining the group. He has gone on to release a solo album. Darrin Vincent, the fiddler, was also a child prodigy, playing with his family's band. He worked with dozens of country acts before joining Skaggs's outfit. Andy Leftwich, a young fiddler, joined the band and immediately raised eyebrows. Mark Fain is a guitar player with a wealth of experience and was a fine addition to the talented lineup. Cody Kilby, a guitarist, and Paul Brewster round out the group. Other members have included Dennis Parker (bassist) and Marc Pruett.

The leader of Kentucky Thunder has passed on his love of bluegrass to all members. The greatest influences on Skaggs were Bill Monroe, Lester Flatt, Earl Scruggs and Ralph Stanley. The bold, innovative music of these pioneers made a lasting impact and instilled his musical drive. In many of his albums he paid homage to the musicians who ignited the initial spark in him and provided the fire that allowed him to carry on during the tough parts of his distinguished career.

Ricky Skaggs had a positive effect on a number of acts. A partial list includes Emmylou Harris, Alison Krauss, Vince Gill, Wade Hayes, Keith Whitley, George Strait, Randy Travis, and Clint Black. Although not everyone followed in his bluegrass footsteps, he touched many with his instrumental skill and dedication to the style.

Ricky Skaggs is a vital modern country musician with a long, colorful career. From his early days as a child prodigy to the dues-paying years as a sideman and on to his solo career, he has always displayed a love of the country style in his heart, especially bluegrass. His instrumental abilities, his choice of material, the awards, the prestige — all are part of the package that make up the leader of Kentucky Thunder.

DISCOGRAPHY:

Sweet Temptation, Sugar Hill 3706.
Skaggs & Rice, Sugar Hill 3711.
Waitin' for the Sun to Shine, Epic 37193.
Family & Friends, Rounder 0151.
Highways & Heartaches, Epic 37996.

Don't Cheat in Our Hometown, Epic 38954.
Country Boy, Epic 26170.
Live in London, Epic 93546.
Love's Gonna Get Ya!, Epic 40309.
Comin' Home to Stay, Epic 40623.
Kentucky Thunder, Epic 45027.
Radio Special, Epic 2022.
My Father's Son, Epic 47389.
Ricky Skaggs & Jerry Douglas, Rounder 81.
Solid Ground, Atlantic 82834.
Country Pride, Sony Special Products 24204.
Crying My Heart Over You, Camden 745.
Life Is a Journey, Atlantic 83030.
That's It, Rebel 1550.
Bluegrass Rules!, Rounder 801.
Ancient Tones, Skaggs Family 1001.
You May See Me Walkin', Platinum Disc 17862.
Soldier of the Cross, Skaggs Family 5001.
Big Mon: The Songs of Bill Monroe, Skaggs Family 1002.
History of the Future, Hollywood 901003.
Sing the Songs of Bill Monroe, Hollywood 165030.
Uncle Pen, Music Hill 71009.
Live at the Charleston Music Hall, Skaggs Family 901004.
Brand New Strings, Skaggs Family 9010006.
Rejoice, Shabach 5451.
Favorite Country Songs, Epic EK-39409.
Super Hits, Epic EK-57199.
Country Gentleman: The Best of Ricky Skaggs, Epic/Legacy 64883.
Greatest Hits, Platinum Disc 17852.
Ricky Skaggs, Platinum Disc 1770.
16 Biggest Hits, Epic/Legacy 61640.
The Essential Ricky Skaggs, Epic/Legacy 89068.
Solid Ground/Life Is a Journey, Collectables 7800.
Waitin' for the Sun to Shine/Highways & Heartaches, Gott Discs 25.
Favorite Country Songs Collectables 8127.
Heartbroke, Rajon 0547.

Reba McEntire (1955–)

Feel the Fire

The first generation of country musicians instilled much passion into their music, a lesson that has not been lost on the contemporary set. Many of the modern figures have followed the path blazed by their predecessors, injecting the same intensity and enthusiasm into their songs. One female singer put so much emotion into her entire catalog that she made her listeners feel the fire. Her name is Reba McEntire.

Reba Nell McEntire was born on March 28, 1955, in Chockie, Oklahoma. Her father was a professional rodeo rider who taught all of his children — his three daughters and one son — how to ride; her mother taught them music. The four children formed a family group and enjoyed a regional hit in 1971 with "The Ballad of John McEntire," a tribute to their grandfather. It was good training ground for Reba.

In 1974, when Reba sang the national anthem at the National Rodeo Finals in Oklahoma City all thoughts of a family group evaporated. It was evident that she possessed the most talent of all the McEntire children and a solo career in music loomed over the horizon. Country singer Red Steagall, after hearing her perform, urged her to head to Nashville to cut a demo. The young girl heeded the advice and packed her bags for Music City U.S.A. armed with big dreams.

In 1975, McEntire signed to Mercury Records and released her first record that same year. Unfortunately, her traditional hard sound was out of style with the audience's tastes and the singles received very little airplay. A fiery individual, she was determined to make it in the music business and juggled marriage, school and her fledging singing career.

In 1978, the single "Three Sheets in the Wind" b/w "I'd Really Love to See You Tonight" reached the Top Twenty. Despite this slight encouragement, it would be two more years of hard paying dues before she placed another song on the charts. Finally, in 1980, "(You Lift Me) Up to Heaven" made it to number eight in the country singles chart.

In an effort to appeal to a great portion of the listening audience, she waxed more ballad-oriented material. The third album, *Feel the Fire,* was another failure, but she received encouragement when the next single, "Today All Over Again," reached the Top Five. As well, the fourth studio album, *Heart to Heart,* was her first record to chart.

Her fifth effort, *Unlimited,* included the number three hit "I'm Not That Lonely Yet" as well as "Can't Even Get the Blues" and "You're the First Time I've Thought About Leaving," back-to-back number one hits. It was just the beginning of her assault on the country music charts, and she was definitely a star on the rise.

On the performance side of her career, she left behind the nightclubs and honky tonks for a regular gig opening for the Statler Brothers, as well as Conway Twitty, Ronnie Milsap and Mickey Gilley. The concert performances at the better venues helped push record sales, and the record sales encouraged people to see her live.

In 1984, she departed Mercury Records, bitter over their musical approach, promotional and overall vision for her career. She recorded one last album, *Behind the Scene*, before moving on to MCA Records. "Just a Little Love," the first single for her new label, reached the Top Five; however, it was not quite magic time.

She wanted to make country music on her own terms and convinced the top brass at MCA who gave into Reba's demands. She released *My Kind of Country*, which included "How Blue," a number one hit. More importantly, the album covered old favorites from Ray Price, Carl Smith, Connie Smith and Faron Young that placed her firmly within the New Traditionalist movement spearheaded by George Strait. After years of being out of sync with the current trends of country music, she was finally leading the way. This was reflected in her winning the prestigious Female Vocalist of the Year Award by the Country Music Association in 1984. Passed over that year were Dolly Parton, Barbara Mandrell and Charly McClain; all had better years than McEntire.

The rest of the decade would belong to McEntire as she established herself as the top country music female artist. Her songs often reached number one and the albums were certified gold. One of her self-penned efforts, "Only in My Mind," was a Top Five hit. She began to headline her own concerts and won a second Female Vocalist of the Year award from the CMA. On January 14, 1986, she became a member of the Grand Ole Opry.

Her next release, *Whoever's in New England*, was a very successful, especially the title cut which marked a change in her recorded material. McEntire had begun to write and release feminist songs in a traditional country style that spoke to women of her generation. The song "Whoever's in New England" was also the subject of her first video and began a run of top singles that would stretch for three years.

She found time during her heavy tour schedule to record *What Am I Gonna Do About You*, which went gold and produced two number one singles, the title track and "One Promise Too Late." She claimed her third CMA Female Vocalist of the Year Award and was also named Entertainer of the Year. Her position as the top female country music vocalist was solidified.

In 1987, McEntire won her first Grammy, divorced her husband, and moved to Nashville. She also released *The Last One to Know*, which included the number one "Love Will Find Its Way to You" as well as the title track which became a top hit. The album went platinum and won her a fourth CMA award as Female Vocalist of the Year. The seasonal effort *Merry Christmas to You* would go on to sell a couple of million copies.

In 1988, with the album *Reba* she switched gears stylistically. For the past few years she had been firmly established as a leader of the New Traditionalist camp, but her self-titled record included more country-pop flavored songs. "Sunday Kind of Love" peaked at number three, and the album stayed on top of the charts for eight weeks. Two more singles, "I Know How He Feels" and "New Fool at an Old Game," helped the effort go platinum. Later McEntire formed Starstruck Entertainment, a company that handled all aspects of her career including booking, publishing and promotion. The agency would go on to represent other artists.

In 1989, her fourteenth studio album, *Sweet Sixteen*, spawned four hit singles including "Cathy's Clown" (the old Everly Brothers hit), "Till Love Comes Again," "Little Girl," and "Walk On." On a personal note, she married Narvel Blackstock, who had been her road manager as well as steel guitarist in her backing band since 1980. The couple would later have a son. That same year she made her feature acting debut in the comic horror film *Tremors*. *Live*, a concert performance, appeared on shelves for the Christmas rush.

In May 1990, she returned to touring, and by the fall released *Rumor Has It*, which contained the number one "You Lie." Three other songs, the title track, "Fancy," and "Fallin' Out of Love," also placed in the Top Ten. The album would sell a few million copies, and her concert performances were by now major events. However, tragedy struck on March 16, 1991, when seven members of her band and her road manager were killed in a plane crash.

It hit McEntire hard, and she dedicated her next studio effort, *For My Broken Heart*, to them. The album would go gold and platinum, spawning two massive singles, the title song and "Is There Life Out There?" She would later co-star in the television mini-series *The Gambler Returns: The Luck of the Draw*. Her tours continued to sell out as devoted fans could not get enough of her first-rate performances.

The album *It's Your Call* went triple platinum and also became her first Top Ten pop record. It included the single "The Heart Won't Lie," a duet with Vince Gill that would eventually go to number one. Her next hit, another duet, with Linda Davis, "Does He Love You," would be found on the *Greatest Hits, Vol. 2* effort, selling a few million copies. The aforementioned single would give her a second Grammy and a CMA award for Vocal Performance. She later appeared in the television movie *The Man from Left Field*.

Her career continued to roll on. *Read My Mind* went triple platinum and spawned the usual array of top hits including "The Heart Is a Lonely Hunter" as well as "She Thinks His Name Was John," a controversial song about AIDS. She had a speaking role in the movie *North* and a cameo in *The Little Rascals* movie. McEntire was the executive producer of a television movie based on her song "Is There Life Out There?" She also published her autobiography, *Reba: My Story*. The book became a best-seller and gave fans insight into her personal life.

The album *Starting Over* marked the twentieth anniversary of her recording career. Although it topped both the country and pop charts, it yielded only one Top Ten hit, "Ring on Her Finger, Time on Her Hands." The compilation of cover songs from the past was a bit of a disappointment, but she would rebound with her next effort.

What If It's You spawned four Top Twenty hits: "How Was I to Know" (a number one), "The Fear of Being Alone," the title track, and "I'd Rather Ride Around with You," peaking at number two. The album would to gold and platinum. That year she also starred in the television mini-series *Buffalo Gals,* where she portrayed sharpshooter Annie Oakley.

Her next top single, "If You See Him/If You See Her," was recorded with Brooks & Dunn. It enabled her next album, *If You See Him,* to reach the top of the charts. Three other singles from the album were hits. She expanded her star appeal with numerous guest-star appearances on television series and in the television movie *Forever.* By this time she had long been a household name among pop culture audiences.

Her second memoir, *Comfort from a Country Quilt,* was released in May 1999. She found time to record two outstanding albums, *Secret of Giving: A Christmas Collection* and *So Good Together.* Her first effort initiated a television movie, *Secret of Giving,* while the second one boasted the singles "What Do You Say," "I'll Be," and "We're So Good Together."

In 2000, McEntire stepped outside the country music realm to tackle and conquer the Broadway stage. Brought in to star in the musical *Annie Get Your Gun* because of her famous name, she far exceeded expectations with her performance. With her flair for entertaining, television and film experience, ability to sing, and rodeo background she was a natural. The role garnered her many awards including one from Drama Desk, the Outer Critics Circle and Theatre World.

In October 2001, all of her acting experience was poured into her television show *Reba.* It featured her as a single mother of four children whose ex-husband lives next door with his new love interest. A sitcom with potential, it quickly became the focus of her career. She would manage to release one single, "I'm a Survivor," that peaked at Top Five and preceded the release *Greatest Hits, Vol. 3: I'm a Survivor.*

She would devote more time to her recording career in 2003 with the release of the single "I'm Gonna Take That Mountain." As well, her studio album *Room to Breathe* was released and would eventually go platinum. The single "Somebody" went to number one and was followed by "He Gets That from Me" and "My Sister"; both were Top Ten hits. Although her music production was much smaller in scale than in previous years, it remained pure quality.

In 2005, she appeared in a special concert version of the musical *South Pacific* that was performed at Carnegie Hall. It contained an all-star production team that included Brian Stokes Mitchell and actor Alec Baldwin. Later it appeared on PBS as part of the Great Performances series. That same year the catalogs of Mercury Records and MCA Records were combined under the label of Universal, which led to many of Reba's records being repackaged. The Reba album release from Universal first, *#1's*, went gold and platinum.

In 2006, she provided a voice in the animated film *Charlotte's Web*. In February 2007, her television show ended its successful five-year run, which meant that she could now concentrate more on her music career. She continues to record and perform.

Reba McEntire is a country music icon. She was the most dominant female voice in the genre during the 1980s and for much of the 1990s. She had a plethora of number one songs and many of her albums went gold, platinum and triple platinum. She was a solid concert headliner who toured all over the world entertaining legions of her adoring fans.

Any discussion of Reba McEntire begins with her deep vocal talents. Her voice can wrap itself around a tender ballad and wring every ounce of emotion from it. The passion and fire unleashed on up-tempo numbers demonstrates the rock side of her singing prowess. The smoothness, professional edge and maturity in her abilities provided the soundtrack for a generation of country music fans.

She has utilized her superior singing ability in a variety of media including records, movies, television and theatre to expand her career. With a sureness, a confidence and a positive attitude she developed into a powerful actress able to deliver high drama and quality comedy. Her Broadway stage appearances became events and earned her more awards to add to her impressive collection.

She was able to project a strong stage presence in concert, and as a performer she became a world class entertainer. There was nothing quite like Reba on tour because she was able to deliver a total package to the audience that included music, personality and fun. Her knack for working a crowd beckoned to years gone by and is reminiscent of the Carter Family's skills.

McEntire has given the world a number of great songs. A partial list includes "Three Sheets in the Wind" b/w "I'd Really Love to See You Tonight," "(You Lift Me) Up to Heaven," "Today All Over Again," "I'm Not That Lonely Yet," "Can't Even Get the Blues," "You're the First Time I've Thought About Leaving," "Just a Little Love," "How Blue," "Somebody Should Leave," "Only in My Mind," "One Promise Too Late," "Love Will Find Its Way to You," "Sunday Kind of Love," "I Know How He Feels," "New Fool at an Old Game," "Till Love Comes Again," "Little Girl," "Walk On," "You Lied," "Fancy," "Fallin' Out of Love," "Is There Life Out There," "The Heart Won't Lie," "Does He Love You," "The Heart Is a Lonely Hunter," "She Thinks His Name Was John," "What If It's You," "How Was I to Know," "The Fear of Being Alone," "I'd Rather Ride Around with You," "If You See Him/If You

See Her," "What Do You Say," "I'll Be," "We're So Good Together," "I'm a Survivor," "I'm Gonna Take That Mountain," "Somebody," "He Gets That from Me," and "My Sister." Her immense and diverse catalog speaks volumes of her incredible talent.

As the leading female country vocalist for more than a decade it is understandable that she would have a large influence on a number of artists. A partial list includes Linda Davis, Faith Hill, Stephanie Bentley, Terri Clark, Lila McCann, Danni Leigh, Meredith Edwards, Trisha Yearwood, LeAnn Rimes, Sara Evans, Ashley Monroe, Shania Twain, Carrie Underwood, Catherine Britt, Chely Wright, the Dixie Chicks, Danielle Peck, Jo Dee Messina, Kathy Mattea, Kellie Pickler, Lindsey Haun, Lee Ann Womack, Miranda Lambert and Taylor Swift.

The Reba McEntire story is about a very talented singer who was determined to make it in the music business and overcome many obstacles to accomplish her dreams. She not only became a star but dominated the charts and the industry for over a decade. She conquered many media with her spectacular talent and her ability to feel the fire.

DISCOGRAPHY:

Reba McEntire, Mercury 836330.
Out of a Dream, Mercury 836331.
Feel the Fire, Mercury 822887-2.
Heart to Heart, Mercury 826283-2.
Unlimited, Mercury 822882-2.
Behind the Scene, Mercury 812781-2.
Just a Little Love, MCA MCAD-31081.
My Kind of Country, MCA MCAD-31108.
Have I Got A Deal for You, MCA MCAD-31109.
Reba Nell McEntire, Mercury 822455-2.
What Am I Gonna Do About You, MCA MCAD-5807.
Whoever's in New England, MCA MCA-5691.
Merry Christmas to You, MCA MCAD-42031.
The Last One to Know, MCA MCAD-42030.
Reba, MCA MCAD-42134.
Reba Live, MCA MCAD-8034.
Sweet Sixteen, MCA MCAD-6294.
Rumor Has It, MCA MCAD-10016.
For My Broken Heart, MCA MCAD-10400.
It's Your Call, MCA MCAD-10673.
Read My Mind, MCA MCAD-109.
Starting Over, MCA 11264.
What If It's You, MCA 11500.
If You See Him, MCA 70019.
Secret of Giving: A Christmas Collection, MCA 70092.
So Good Together, MCA Nashville 170119.

I'll Be, MCA 1701442.
Room to Breathe, MCA Nashville 000045102.
Duets, Humphead 020.
Reba Duets, MCA Nashville 000890302.
Greatest Hits, MCA 5979.
You Lift Me Up to Heaven, Special Music 846496.
Forever in Your Eyes, Special Music 836692.
Greatest Hits, Vol. 2, MCA 10906.
Oklahoma Girl, Mercury 522711.
The Best of Reba McEntire (1994), Mercury 824342.
American Legends: Best of the Early Years, PSM 520287.
Moments & Memories: The Best of Reba [Australia], MCA International 73096.
Moments & Memories: The Best of Reba [Canada], MCA International 81075.
Greatest Hits, Vol. 3: I'm a Survivor, MCA 170202.
I'm Not That Lonely, Delta 5118.
20th Century Masters — The Christmas Collection: The Best of Reba McEntire,
    MCA Nashville 000064802.
Greatest Collection, Platinum Disc 3337.
Love Collection, Madacy 51066.
Whoever's in New England/Sweet Sixteen/What Am I Gonna Do About You,
    Madacy 51663.
Christmas Collection, Madacy 251559.
Reba's #1's, MCA Nashville 5386.
Reba McEntire at Her Very Best, Humphead 006.
What Am I Gonna Do About You/It's Your Call, Madacy 52495.
20th Century Masters — Millennium Collection, MCA Nashville 000192802.
Just a Little Love, Xtra 26521.
Have I Got A Deal for You/My Kind of Country, MCA 5893.

Keith Whitley (1955–1989)

Hard Act to Follow

The history of country music is filled with two types of acts: those who enjoyed a long, colorful career and those that left us much too early. Often, the impact a musician made can't be measured by longevity, but by creativity, talent and power. One such singer who held great promise died too young and proved a hard act to follow. His name was Keith Whitley.

Keith Whitley was born on April 1, 1955, in Sandy Hook, Kentucky. He was a child prodigy: he won a singing contest before he was five years old; learned how to play guitar before his tenth birthday; and sang on the radio a few years before he was a teenager. As a teen, he formed his first group, the Lonesome Mountain Boys, mainly a bluegrass outfit, with high school friend

Ricky Skaggs. The band played Stanley Brothers tunes and found quick success performing at local venues.

In the 1960s, bluegrass legend Ralph Stanley re-formed his band after the death of his brother. Some time later, he discovered the talented duo of Whitley and Skaggs and invited them to join his Clinch Mountain Boys, an invitation which they readily accepted. Keith stayed with the group for two years and appeared on several albums including the 1971 offering *Crying from the Cross*, which was named Bluegrass Album of the Year. He also picked up valuable performance lessons from the veteran entertainer.

From 1973 to 1975, Whitley drifted from one band to another looking for a new direction. He was still very much in the bluegrass phase of his career, and the style had enjoyed a renaissance of sorts but was slowly settling to an even level of popularity. He returned to the Clinch Mountain Boys and remained there for two more years, recording five more albums.

In 1978, he joined J. D. Crowe & the New South, an established bluegrass outfit where he remained until 1982. Years later, a compilation of songs during this period would be released as *Sad Songs & Waltzes*. At this point in his career, he had acquired a sufficient amount of experience and boasted strong credentials, but his musical travels were about to take on a more personal path.

After years of lending his talents to others, he finally embarked on a solo career. Whitley signed to RCA Records and released his debut record, *Hard Act to Follow,* a collection of pure honky tonk. Although it was a commercial and critical failure it marked the beginning of his switch from bluegrass-based material to a more traditional sound. Some of the highlights included the title track as well as "Turn Me to Love," "If a Broken Heart Could Kill," and "If You Think I'm Crazy Now (You Should Have Seen Me When I Was a Kid)."

In 1985, he released *L.A. to Miami*, which yielded the Top Twenty single "Miami, My Amy," igniting his ascent. He enjoyed three Top Ten hits: "Ten Feet Away," "Homecoming '63," and "Hard Livin'." He impressed many in the country music community who had written him off after the first album but were now reconsidering his special sound.

Although his career seemed in perfect working order, his personal affairs were a shambles. He attempted to right this wrong by marrying Lorrie Morgan. She was a country star in her own right and the union seemed like the steady, firm influence he needed in his life to help him combat alcoholism.

In 1988, his third album, *Don't Close Your Eyes,* was released and became a smash hit. The title track, "When You Say Nothing at All," and "I'm No Stranger to the Rain" were number one hits. He not only solidified his position as one of the top New Traditionalist artists on the circuit but also as a leader and a major influence. He was poised to move on to the next level of superstardom.

However, fate has a way of dealing bad hands to those who tempt it. On May 9, 1989, he suffered a fatal case of alcohol poisoning and died at the age of forty-three. His last studio work, *I Wonder Do You Think of Me*, completed before his death and posthumously released, contained the number one singles "It Ain't Nothin'" and "I Wonder Do you Think of Me." A later single, "I'm Over You," peaked at number three.

Keith Whitley was a rising country music star before he died. After years of paying dues in a variety of outfits and contributing to the careers of many others, he had finally devoted his bountiful talents in order to benefit his own career. As an artist he was a complete package of voice, musicianship and songwriting.

He had a twang in his vocal delivery that made him sound like a genuine country artist. Although not the most original singer, he did have the ability to know his limits, and this is one of the major attributes to his style. He never attempted anything that was out of his range and stayed within the parameters of what he could do, earning him much respect.

Whitley had a large impact on a number of artists. A partial list includes Ricky Skaggs, Ricky Van Shelton, Travis Tritt, Randy Travis, Jimmie Dale Gilmore, Joe Ely, Steve Earle, Garth Brooks, Tim McGraw, Keith Urban, Toby Keith, and Kenny Chesney. Not only did he touch those in the New Traditionalist camp, but he also was a guiding light to others plying different styles. His influence would have been much more profound if he had lived longer because he was just hitting his peak when he died.

During his short career he gave the world a number of interesting songs. A short list includes "Miami, My Amy," "Ten Feet Away," "Homecoming '63," "Hard Livin'," "Don't Close Your Eyes," "When You Say Nothing at All," "I'm No Stranger to the Rain," "I Wonder Do You Think of Me," "It Ain't Nothin'," and "I'm Over You." Certainly if he had lived his catalog would have been much larger. The many gems that the country audience missed out on due to his untimely death are a painful thought.

Few artists with such a slim catalog and short time in the spotlight continued to have an impact long after their death. An electronic duet with his wife, Lorrie Morgan, reached the Top Twenty. Another duet with Earl Thomas Conley, "Brotherly Love," peaked at number two. The *Keith Whitley—A Tribute Album*, issued in 1994 and including rare tracks that had been previously unreleased, further expanded on his growing posthumous fame. When Alison Krauss & Union Station had a hit with "When You Say Nothing at All," which rose all the way to number three, it only added to the Whitley legend.

But why should someone who had such a small discography and a short time in the sun be considered such an important artist in country music circles?

There is no denying his talent. He possessed a style that was easily accessible and a true natural wonder. Perhaps the answer lies in the promise that was only starting to surface in Whitley's career before his untimely death. Many believe that if he would have continued to release quality material like "I'm Over You," and "Talk to Me, Texas," over a period of time, he would have reached the stratosphere of George Jones and Merle Haggard. Since he died without ever fulfilling this potential, the fantasy is fueled.

Whitley was a New Traditionalist and one of the leaders of the movement to return country back to its roots. Along with George Strait, his good friend Ricky Skaggs, and Randy Travis, Keith was an integral cog in the development and popularity of the style. Interestingly, the movement faded soon after Whitley's unfortunate passing.

The Keith Whitley story was that of a talented individual with a voice that resonates to this day. The quality music he left behind, the talent, the potential, the frustrating death are all part of the package. He proved that he was a hard act to follow and as the years drift by the legend has grown even wider.

DISCOGRAPHY:

Tribute to the Stanley Brothers, Jalyn 129.
Sad Songs & Waltzes, Rounder 610399.
Hard Act to Follow, MCA 8225.
L.A. to Miami, RCA 5870-2-R.
Don't Close Your Eyes, RCA 6494-2-R.
I Wonder Do You Think of Me, RCA 9809.
Kentucky Bluebird, RCA 3156-2-R.
Wherever You Are Tonight, BNA 66762.
Greatest Hits, RCA 2277-2-R.
Second Generation Bluegrass, Rebel 1504.
The Best of Keith Whitley, RCA 86242-2.
Super Hits, RCA 66850.
The Essential Keith Whitley, RCA 66853.
Remembered, BMG Special Products 44677.
RCA Country Legends, RCA 65103.
Platinum & Gold Collection, RCA 55165.
All American Country, BMG Special Products 40731.
16 Biggest Hits, RCA Nashville/Legacy 78247.
Collections, Sony BMG 82876820432.

Vince Gill (1957–)

Oklahoma Swing

Many of the early country music artists hailed from the Appalachian region — Virginia, North Carolina, Tennessee, and Kentucky. In modern times, new singers emerged from every part of the nation including metropolitan areas and the suburbs. Another region that has produced contemporary country music talent is the American heartland, the home of the man responsible for Oklahoma Swing. His name is Vince Gill.

Vince Gill was born on April 12, 1957, in Norman, Oklahoma. His first taste of country music came from local bluegrass and his father, a judge who played country banjo and guitar. The young Vince picked up both instruments, honing his skills until he was proficient enough to play in local bands. He later added fiddle, Dobro, mandolin, and bass to the sound of his first group, Mountain Smoke. The highlight of the band's life was to open for the established recording group Pure Prairie League.

After high school graduation, he moved to Kentucky and joined the Bluegrass Alliance and stayed for about a year playing alongside band members Sam Bush and Dan Crary. After a brief stint in Ricky Skaggs's Boone Creek, Gill relocated to Los Angeles, hardly a country music hotspot. He found work in Byron Berline's group, Sundance. It seemed that Gill's career wasn't progressing very quickly.

In 1979, he gathered his courage and auditioned for Pure Prairie League, whose members remembered him from the high school concert. To his surprise they hired him as their lead singer, and Gill remained with the group for three years. He recorded a few albums with them and they scored a Top Forty hit with the song "I'm Almost Ready." He began to write material for them but departed in 1981 because of family duties.

After his wife, Janis Oliver, a well-known member of the Sweethearts of the Rodeo duo, located on the West Coast, gave birth to a daughter, he contacted Rodney Crowell who jumped at the chance to have Vince in his band, the Cherry Bombs. It was while a member of this outfit that Gill met Emory Gordy, Jr., and keyboardist Tony Brown who possessed enough contacts to land a Vince a solo recording contract with RCA Records. After paying his dues for a decade and a half, it was the break that he had been looking for his entire career and made the most of it.

Gill moved his small family to Nashville and cut his first EP, *Turn Me Loose,* with Gordy as producer. The EP yielded the single "Victim of Life's

Circumstances," which slipped into the Top 40 of the country charts. It began a run of hit singles that reached into the 2000s and made him a star.

His first full length studio effort, *The Things That Matter*, included a duet with Rosanne Cash, "If It Weren't for Him," which became his first Top Ten hit. A second song, "Oklahoma Borderline," was another Top Ten hit.

The album *The Way Back Home* was a solid effort and yielded the Top Five hit "Cinderella." When not concentrating on his own career, he sat in on dozens of sessions with a variety of singers including Rosanne Cash and later toured in Emmylou Harris's back-up band in the late 1980s.

In 1989, his solo career began another chapter when he signed with MCA Records. The first album for his new label, *When I Call Your Name,* yielded the hit "Never Alone," a song he had co-written with Cash. The record also included a duet with Reba McEntire, "Oklahoma Swing." The title track peaked at number two and broke everything open. It earned Gill his first Grammy and another single, "Never Knew Lonely," reached the Top Five as the record would go on to sell over a million copies.

He became one of the most popular artists on the country music circuit as a live performer. He also carried on the momentum with his next offering, *Pocket Full of Gold*. It boasted four Top Ten singles including "Liza Jane," "Look at Us," the title track, and the number one hit "Take Your Memory with You." A year after its release, the CD went platinum. On the strength of the smash record he joined the Grand Ole Opry.

Although he had made great strides in just three short years, it was the 1992 studio album *I Still Believe in You* that made him a superstar. It went platinum within two months of its release. The title ballad became another number one hit and the second single, "Don't Let Our Love Start Slippin' Away," was another chart topper. Later, one album would yield "One More Last Chance" and "Tryin' to Get Over You," both top songs, and the number three hit "No Future in the Past."

In 1993, his best-of album went gold, as did his Christmas offering, *Let There Be Peace on Earth*. He also performed a duet with Reba McEntire, "The Heart Won't Lie," from her CD *It's Your Call*; the song went to number one. At this point in his career, despite the stiff competition, he was one of the most celebrated and popular male country artists on the circuit.

In 1994, he released *When Love Finds You*, which topped the country charts and crossed over to the pop listings. It would sell over four million copies on the strength of a number of Top Five hits including "What the Cowgirls Do," the title track, "Whenever You Come Around," "Which Bridge to Cross (Which Bridge to Burn)," and "You Better Think Twice." In the era of Garth Brooks, Gill managed to hold his own and carve his own niche in the very competitive industry.

Often, when a superstar such as Gill reaches a certain plateau, he begins to coast. However, the Oklahoma native wasn't about to rest on past performances. He fashioned an American roots album, *High Lonesome Sound*, which yielded three Top Five hits, "Worlds Apart," "Pretty Little Adriana," and "A Little More Love." Although not quite as successful as some of his other works, it proved that he still had the magic touch.

In 1998, amidst a divorce from his wife Janis Oliver, he released *The Key*, which announced his return to a more hardcore country sound. It produced one Top Five hit, "If You Ever Have Forever in Mind," and the album went platinum on its way to becoming his first to top the charts. He remained one of the top acts on the circuit, and his performances were events.

Like many other artists, his personal life found its way into his songwriting. *The Let's Make Sure We Kiss Goodbye* celebrated his new romance with pop singer Amy Grant; the couple were married in 2000. Although it yielded a Top Ten hit in "Feels Like Love," the critics and fans weren't enamored with this effort, and it was shut out at the Grammys. The record was special to him for a very important reason because it featured his daughter Jenny on backup vocals.

He returned to favor with the 2003 release *Next Big Thing*, which marked his first foray as full-time record producer. The CD featured guest appearances by Emmylou Harris, Lee Ann Womack, Michael McDonald, Kim Keyes, Andrea Zonn, Leslie Satcher, and Gill's wife, Amy Grant. Highlights included "We Had It All," "Young Man's Town," "These Broken Hearts," "Real Mean Bottle," and "The Sun's Gonna Shine on You." It was one of his strongest efforts in some time because he finally took the helm and decided how the record should be made.

He followed three years later with *These Days*, an ambitious four-disc set of new material proving that he was still a force in the country music wars. The multiple disc set featured different sides of his musical personality: acoustic bluegrass, rock and roll, traditional country & western, and modern soul and jazz. "Workin' on Big Chill," "Love's Standin'," and "Cowboy Up" were highlights from the rock disc. "The Reason Why," "What You Don't Say," "Rock of Your Love," "The Memory of You," and "Time to Carry On" (sung with his daughter) made up the pop side. The country & western disc featured "Some Things Never Get Old," "Sweet Little Corrina," "If I Can Make Mississippi," and "Take This Country Back." The acoustic bluegrass disc included "Little Brother," "Cold Gray Light of Gone," "A River Like You," and "Ace Up Your Pretty Sleeve."

The depth and range of his entire set of musical skills were utilized to create this very interesting work. A number of artists were involved in the project including Gretchen Wilson, Amy Grant, Jenny Gill, Bonnie Raitt, Rodney Crowell, Sheryl Crow, Diana Krall, Buddy Emmons, Phil Everly, Rebecca Lynn Howard, the Del McCoury Band, Patty Loveless, Emmylou

Harris, John Anderson, Katrina Elam, Lee Ann Womack, LeAnn Rimes, Guy Clark, Trisha Yearwood, Bekka Bramlett and Michael McDonald.

Vince Gill is a country music institution. He has been one of the most successful artists of the modern era, enjoying a string of top hits and platinum albums. His concerts are well received, and his work on the efforts of others has only enhanced his reputation. He has fulfilled many roles as a songwriter, picker, producer, singer, and recording and performing artist.

He possesses a voice that is tailor-made for the traditional material that has made him famous. However, there are different shades in his delivery that allow him to sing in any style. Gill's high lonesome vocals always ring true and are the force that makes all of his songs instantly recognizable.

Vince Gill is a traditional country music artist, and for most of his career he has explored every inch of this path. He has never followed trends and has remained faithful to the people that influenced him — Ray Price and Jim Reeves. Others who shaped his music include country-rockers the Eagles, Emmylou Harris and bluegrass practitioner Ricky Skaggs.

He has been heavily rewarded for the wealth of country music he has delivered to the world. He has won eighteen Grammy Awards including Best Male Country Vocal Performance for his song "The Reason Why," taken from the *These Days* CD. He was the CMA Entertainer of the Year in 1993, and again in 1994. He is one of the most honored singers in the modern music era.

He is a noted songwriter and has penned many tunes for various artists. A partial list includes "Take This Country Back" (John Anderson), "The Rock of Your Love" (Bonnie Raitt), "Faint of Heart" (Diana Krall), and "Sweet Little Corrina" (Phil Everly of the Everly Brothers). In addition, Emmylou Harris recorded "Some Things Never Get Old." His originality, cleverness and attitude as a songwriter shine through every tune.

He has also sung a number of his own songs including "Victim of Life's Circumstances," "If It Weren't for Him," "Oklahoma Borderline," "Cinderella," "Never Alone," "Oklahoma Swing," "Never Knew Lonely," "Pocket Full of Gold," "Liza Jane," "Look at Us," "Take Your Memory with You," "I Still Believe in You," "Don't Let Our Love Start Slippin' Away," "One More Last Chance," "Tryin' to Get Over You," "No Future in the Past," "When Love Finds You," "What the Cowgirls Do," "Whenever You Come Around," "Which Bridge to Cross (Which Bridge to Burn)," "You Better Think Twice," "Worlds Apart," "Pretty Little Adriana," "A Little More Love," "If You Ever Have Forever in Mind," "Feels Like Love," and "The Reason Why." Whether performing an original or a cover of someone else's material he has always been able to interject a personal appeal to it.

The Vince Gill story is the portrait of one of the most successful country artists of the modern era. His songs have constantly charted, and his albums have gone gold and platinum. His Oklahoma swing with its sensibility, originality, dedication, and sincerity has proven to be a winning formula.

DISCOGRAPHY:

Turn Me Loose, RCA MHLI-8517.
The Things That Matter, RCA 6914-2-R9.
The Way Back Home, RCA 5923-1.
When I Call Your Name, MCA 42321.
Pocket Full of Gold, MCA 10140.
I Still Believe in You, MCA 10630.
Let There Be Peace on Earth, MCA 10877.
When Love Finds You, MCA 11047.
Vince Gill & Friends, MCA 66432-2.
High Lonesome Sound, MCA 11422.
The Key, MCA 70017.
Breath of Heaven: A Christmas Collection, MCA 70038.
Let's Make Sure We Kiss Goodbye, MCA 170098.
Next Big Thing, MCA 170286.
These Days, MCA Nashville 0006021.
Songs from the Heart, MCA 200952.
The Best of Vince Gill, RCA 9814-2-R.
I Never Knew Lonely, RCA 61130.
The Essential Vince Gill, RCA 66535.
Souvenirs, MCA Nashville 11394.
Super Hits, RCA 66944.
Vintage Gill, BMG Special Products 44528.
Double Barrel Country: The Legends of Country Music, Madacy 5336.
Masters, Eagle Rock Entertain 028.
Platinum and Gold Collection, RCA 54211.
20th Century Masters: The Millennium Collection: The Best of Vince Gill, MCA Nashville 0000923302.
All American Country, Collectables 9515.
The Encore Collections, BMG Records 44528.
Christmas Collection, Madacy 52273.
Vince Gill, KRB Music 1109.

Alan Jackson (1958–)

High Mileage

In the 1940s, a decade of great experimentation in country music, the honky tonk style was first established. Since then countless musicians, including many modern performers, have built their careers on its grit and power. One of the New Traditionalists incorporated honky tonk elements of the past in order to gain high mileage out of his contemporary sound. His name is Alan Jackson.

Alan Jackson was born on October 17, 1958, in Newnan, Georgia. He began his musical career singing in church and at home. He continued to hone his skills at selected parties, as well as in choirs and as part of a country duo. However, he was still years away from a professional career. He had more dues to pay before achieving success.

He left school to sell cars and then worked construction for a few years, but the burning desire to become a professional musician remained. In his spare time, he carefully polished his talents in order to realize his ambitions. At the age of twenty, he turned professional as he was finally confident enough to sit in with other musicians.

After woodshedding in a number of groups for some time, Jackson started his own band, Dixie Steel, which played in local bars and clubs to enthusiastic reviews. He continued to write songs in his spare time in an effort to work up enough material for a solid demo. He was waiting for the one big break that would open opportunities for him.

Like many other aspiring musicians, Jackson boasted the invaluable support of an ambitious mate, in this case, his wife, Denise. She worked as a flight attendant, and in a chance meeting with country music legend Glen Campbell, she mentioned that her husband was a songwriter. It led to a major break as she received the phone number and address of Campbell's publishing company. The organization was impressed with Alan's material but urged him to continue improving his skills.

Nevertheless, Jackson and his wife moved to Nashville armed with a demo tape that opened doors for him. But it wasn't instant stardom in country music town, as the budding singer was forced to work in a mailroom and do other odd jobs. He eventually found work in a musical setting when he joined the staff of Glen Campbell Music where he contributed songs.

On the side, Jackson played in local clubs where he met Keith Stegall, and the pair worked on a second demo to take around to the various record companies in town. It was this recording that led to a contract with Arista Records. In 1990, his debut album, *Here in the Real World,* was released and, a year later, the effort had gone platinum.

On the strength of the two hit singles, "I'd Love You All Over Again" and "Someday," his album *Don't Rock the Jukebox* went double platinum. Jackson, with his matinee good looks, his solid country sound and first rate material, was heralded as a new rising force. The industry had always been eager to champion someone with his strong credentials.

In 1991, Jackson joined a long list of distinguished country music figures when he became a member of the Grand Ole Opry. It had taken six years since his arrival in Nashville, but the hard-paid dues proved to be worth it. He rose to national prominence and his future appeared very bright.

In 1992, he released *A Lot About Livin' (And a Little About Love)*, which spawned five Top Five singles. The first two, "She's Got the Rhythm (And I Got the Blues)" and "Chattahoochee," went to number one. "Mercury Blues" stalled at the second spot, and "Tonight I Climbed the Wall" and "Who Says You Can't Have It All" peaked at the fourth spot on the charts.

The holiday album *Honky Tonk Christmas* was sandwiched between his previous effort and the next album, *Who I Am*. The latter went double platinum very quickly and boasted the number one singles "Summertime Blues," "Gone Country," "Livin' on Love," and "I Don't Even Know Your Name." With each successful effort, he was expanding his star status as one of the top male country acts on the circuit.

For the rest of the decade, Jackson balanced strong studio releases with an increasing heavy touring schedule. *The Greatest Hits Collection* went triple platinum and was one of the most successful country albums to appear in 1995. By this time he was a well-established musician and one of the few who was able to hold his own during the Garth Brooks era.

In 1996, *Everything I Love* surfaced and commenced a new era of his recording career since the material from this point on would eventually find itself on a second greatest hits package. The effort became his fourth straight release to top the country album charts, and it gave him five Top Ten hits, including the number ones "Little Bitty" (a Tom T. Hall cover), "There Goes," "Everything I Love," "Who's Cheatin' Who," and "Between the Devil and Me."

The follow-up, *High Mileage*, released two years later, once again occupied the top spot and became Jackson's highest-charting album on the pop side when it reached the fourth position. This effort contained the Top Ten singles "Right on the Money," "I'll Go On Loving You," "Gone Crazy," and "Little Man." He possessed the ability to churn out classic collections of songs with relative ease.

In 1999, he released *Under the Influence*, a tribute to his favorite country singers that featured material from George Jones, Merle Haggard, Charley Pride, Jimmy Buffett, Hank Williams, Jr., Don Williams and Jim Ed Brown. A successful endeavor, the album just missed topping the charts, breaking his string of number one albums. Jackson was not deterred because he returned to the studio determined to reclaim his high perch.

A year later, *When Somebody Loves You* raced to the top of the charts upon its release on the strength of the number one single "Where I Come From." That same year, he teamed up with George Strait for the duet "Murder on Music Row," a defense of traditional country in the face of a new wave of pop crossover stars. His tough stance only added to his popularity in purists' circles.

Like so many other artists, he was greatly moved by the September 11 tragedy and relied on his musical abilities to make his statement. He wrote and recorded the poignant single "Where Were You (When the World Stopped Turning)," which easily topped the country charts and became his first single to crack the pop Top Forty. It took on anthem-like proportions in the post-attack period.

In 2002, he emerged with the *Drive* album, which spawned another number one hit, "Drive (For Daddy Gene)," a tribute to his late father. The album was his seventh to top the country charts, and it also became his first to reign on the pop charts. Despite increased competition and more than a decade in a tough business that often casts many artists aside, Jackson managed to maintain the momentum in his startling career.

In 2003, his second greatest hits collection appeared and featured a crossover duet with Jimmy Buffett, "It's Five O'clock Somewhere." A year later the well-received *What I Do* became the purest country album from Jackson in years. It also included the songs "Too Much of a Good Thing" and "Monday Morning Church," with both songs reaching the Top Five. The latter was a duet with Patty Loveless.

In 2006, *Precious Memories*, a collection of fifteen hymns originally recorded as a Christmas gift for his mother, was released. That same year, the album *Like Red on a Rose* appeared and featured the Top Five hit "A Woman's Love." He continues to record and perform.

Alan Jackson is a country music fixture. He has cleverly created a strong career based on superb songwriting, playing and material selection. He is one of the most recognizable figures in country music and a very important artist of the modern era. There are many aspects to his very successful career.

He is a competent guitarist but has always been able to add an extra dimension of excitement to his rock-steady playing that gave his music an edge. For example, his workout on "Mercury Blues" gave the song energy without distancing himself from his well-known and beloved personal style. Although never confused with Chet Atkins as a guitarist, Jackson laid down some of the tastiest country licks over the years that others incorporated into their musical vocabulary.

His distinctive vocals complement his good guitar work. Although not considered to be one of the great voices of country music, Jackson has a soothing appeal in his vocal delivery that speaks to each listener on an individual level. When combined with his easy instrumental skills it provides a total package that is a proven seller.

His musical style is the amalgamation of his two prime influences: George Jones and Waylon Jennings. Although unable to match Jones's calibre of singing, Jackson has drawn on the strength of his idol's phrasing skills. He incorporated Jennings's gritty, bare, electrified elements, yet managed to retain a personal and individual identity.

Along with Travis Tritt, Tim McGraw, George Strait, Garth Brooks, Clint Black and Ricky Van Shelton, Jackson is one of the top male stars of modern country music. He has continued the grand tradition of the genre while taking the genre in a new, exciting direction. This ability to preserve and create on an equal basis is a special skill that has always been a major highlight of his style.

Alan Jackson's band, better known as the Strayhorns, has always comprised a solid crop of musicians able to complement their leader on many different levels. They include fiddle player Dan Kelly, guitarists Tom Rutledge and Danny Groah, drummer Bruce Rutherford, fiddler Mark McClurg, keyboardists Monty Parkey and Robbie Flint, bass player Roger Willis and harmonica player Tony Stevens. Many of the members have been part of the outfit for years. For example, Rutherford joined the group in 1990.

Jackson has provided the world with a number of classic songs. A short list includes "Summertime Blues," "Livin' on Love," "Little Bitty," "Who's Cheatin' Who," "Here in the Real World," "I'd Love You All Over Again," "Someday," "Love's Got a Hold On You," "She's Got the Rhythm (And I Got the Blues)," "Chattahoochee," "Gone Country," "I Don't Even Know Your Name," "All I Want for Christmas Is You," and "Mercury Blues." Whether he covered someone else's song or played an original, there was a definite touch in Jackson's delivery.

Jackson's popularity has always been about more than just his catalog. His appearance on television shows like *Home Improvement* displayed an enhanced artistic dimension. The Ford commercial where he gave "Mercury Blues" a good workout endeared himself to a cross section of the public. His song "Where Were You (When the World Stopped Turning)," dedicated to the victims and the aftermath to the 9/11 tragedy, demonstrated his large heart. Many of his tunes hold a special place in the annals of country music.

He remains one of the most durable country music stars of the last twenty years. He is, after Garth Brooks, one of the best recognized figures of the 1990s, a solid supporter of the New Traditionalist movement. Perhaps of his multitude contributions and abilities the most important has been the consistency that has seen him write much of his material and never hit a dry period, a claim very few can make.

The Alan Jackson story is about a very talented individual who made the most of his one major break. His wholesome, down-to-earth image made him one of the most accessible performers on the circuit. Combined with his abilities as musician, singer and songwriter he was able to carved out a permanent niche for himself in the hearts of country music fans. He has gained high mileage out of every aspect of his career.

DISCOGRAPHY:

Here in the Real World, Arista 8623.
Don't Rock the Jukebox, Arista 5714.
A Lot About Livin' (And a Little 'bout Love), Arista 18711.
Honky Tonk Christmas, Arista 19736-2.
Who I Am, Arista 19759.
Everything I Love, Arista 18813.
High Mileage, Arista 18864.
Under the Influence, Arista 18892.
When Somebody Loves You, Arista 69339.
Drive, Arista 60735.
Let It Be Christmas, Arista 67062.
What I Do, Arista 63103.
Precious Memories, Arista 80281.
Like Red on a Rose, Columbia 88172.
Live at Texas Stadium, MCA Nashville 005894.
Greatest Hits Collection, Arista 18801.
Super Hits, Arista 18886.
Greatest Hits, Vol. 2, Arista 53097.
Very Best of Alan Jackson, BMG International 60112.
The Collection [Madacy 3 Disc], Madacy 52239.
Collections, Sony 8287682034.
The Collection [Madacy 2 Disc], Madacy 52484.

Randy Travis (1959–)

Full Circle

In the early 1980s a trend began in country music called the New Traditionalist movement, a back-to-basics style that drew upon honky tonk. More importantly, it bypassed the Urban Cowboy fad and pop elements that had dominated the genre at the turn of the decade. One of the leading proponents of the new style who proved that everything comes full circle was Randy Travis.

Randy Bruce Traywick was born on May 4, 1959, in Marshville, North Carolina. He was encouraged to pursue his musical ambitions and picked up the guitar when he was eight years old in order to imitate his heroes Hank Williams Sr., George Jones and Lefty Frizzell. At ten, he and his brother

Ricky formed the Traywick Brothers, a country western duo that played in local talent contests.

Although music was one of their main interests, so was challenging the local authorities. Ricky went to jail in his teens, and Randy ran away from home when he was sixteen. He ended up in Charlotte and won a talent contest at Country City Bar that turned into a regular gig. He also worked as a cook and remained there for a few years despite repeated confrontations with the law.

Although he might have ended up in prison like his brother, Randy escaped such a fate due to the relationship with his boss and manager, Lib Hatcher. Travis remained focused on his burgeoning musical career and landed a recording contract with the help of Joe Stampley of Paula Records. In 1978, he released a few singles, of which "She's My Woman" was the best of the lot, scraping the bottom of the charts. It was evident that he had more dues to pay.

In 1982, Travis and his manager Hatcher moved to Nashville where they found work in the restaurant business. Randy worked hard to hone his musical skills and managed to release one album, *Randy Ray Live*, which was a regional hit. In 1985, he caught a break and was signed to Warner Brothers Records around the same time that he changed his last name to Travis.

One year later, *Storms of Life* was released, and things would never be the same for him again. The album included the hits "On the Other Hand," "Diggin' Up Bones," "No Place Like Home" "Forever and Ever, Amen," and "1982"; it went multi-platinum, making him the first country artist to achieve that distinction. But there was more to his breakthrough effort than record sales and chart topping hits; the effort defined the new direction that country music would take for the next few years. Travis had delivered a solid traditional set of songs, returning the genre back to its roots.

His second release, *Always & Forever*, proved even more successful as he began a streak of seven straight number one singles. The album also had crossover appeal that resulted in more sales and earned him in 1987, and again in 1988, the Country Music Association title of Male Vocalist of the Year. In a very short time, he had raced to the top of the country music heap.

He would follow up with the albums *Old 8x10* and *No Holdin' Back* at the end of the decade. The former contained the hits "Honky Tonk Moon," "Deeper Than the Holler," and "Is It Still Over?" The latter included a cover of Matraca Berg's nugget "Mining for Coal," Melvin Endsley's "Singing the Blues," Allen Shamblin's "He Walked on Water," Brook Benton's "It's Just a Matter of Time," as well as "Hard Rock Bottom of Your Heart," which was a smash tune.

In the 1990s, he continued to rule as one of the top country male vocalists; however, others like Clint Black and Garth Brooks would surpass him later in the decade. Travis remained popular and continued to deliver top albums and hit singles. By this point in his career he possessed an established fan base.

In 1992, "Wind in the Wire" was written to go along with a television show of the same name. His next proper album, *Heroes and Friends*, was a collection of duets which included obvious choices — George Jones, Conway Twitty and Tammy Wynette — all important influences on Travis. Surprisingly, he sang a tune with the King of the Blues, B. B. King, and actor, tough guy Clint Eastwood. The singles "A Few Ole Country Boys" and the title track, "Heroes and Friends," were hits. It was an interesting experiment and projected a different side to his musical personality.

High Lonesome was a very traditional album released during a time when the country-pop, rock stylings of Garth Brooks had taken over the airwaves and concert halls. "A Better Class of Losers," "We're Not the Jet Set," "I'd Surrender All," "Forever Together," and "Allergic to the Blues" were the highlights. However, by 1992, he took a sabbatical from music to concentrate on his acting career. He appeared in a few films, but his fans wanted him to return to churning out twang.

In 1994, *This Is Me* put him back on top on the strength of "Whisper My Name," his first number one single in two years. Other highlights included "Honky Tonk Side of Town," "Before You Kill Us All," "Runaway Train," and "That's Where I Draw the Line." His status as one of the main voices in country music was reinforced. Many of his longtime faithful were happy to see him attempt a comeback.

In 1996, *Full Circle*, his last effort for Warner Brothers, featured a return to his honky tonk roots combined with a more contemporary appeal. The songs "Are We in Trouble Now" and "King of the Road," the old Roger Miller chestnut, were just some of the highlights. Although it was a good record there were no outstanding singles, and it fared less successfully than his previous releases.

In 1997, he switched to DreamWorks Records, and his first release for his new label, *You and You Alone*, was a solid work that featured guest appearances by Alison Krauss, Vince Gill and Melba Montgomery. The CD boasted three Top Ten singles: "Out of My Bones," "Spirit of a Boy, Wisdom of a Man," and "The Hole." It was an interesting collection of material from an artist who had once ruled the charts.

In 1999, *A Man Ain't Made of Stone* was released and underlined Travis's problem. He had always been a traditionalist, and when he broke in during the mid–1980s he returned country back to its roots. However, a decade later he was out of step with the current trends that doomed his albums. By this time country-pop artists such as Shania Twain and Faith Hill ruled the airwaves and sold millions of albums.

In 2000, *Inspirational Journey*, a collection of traditional and contemporary religious songs, was released. Although it was not the usual material that his fans expected, he was one of many country artists, including Johnny Cash, Loretta Lynn, Tammy Wynette, Merle Haggard, and Dolly Parton, who recorded albums for the Christian set. It was an interesting adventure and foreshadowed a future direction.

After the release of *Live: It Was Just a Matter of Time*, he continued with his gospel direction on *Rise and Shine*, *Worship & Faith*, *Passing Through*, and *Glory Train: Songs of Faith, Worship and Praise*. Each album was recorded in a traditional country music setting and explored different sides of spiritual themes; in a sense Travis revived his career. He continues to record and perform.

Randy Travis is a country music natural. His easy vocals were tailor-made for super success, which he achieved and maintained for over twenty years. The accessibility of his style has made him a fan favorite during his entire career. He started out as a New Traditionalist and became one of its most important artists, only to abandon the genre in favor of gospel-flecked material later in his career.

The Travis voice is instantly recognizable from the first couple of notes of any song. There is a reassurance, a calmness, a durable quality in his vocal delivery that reminds one of past greats like George Jones and Eddy Arnold. He has always been able to hook listeners from the country music side as well as pop and rock with his warm timbre.

Randy Travis is a direct descendant (musically) of George Jones, Merle Haggard, Jim Reeves and Ernest Tubb. He was always a staunch supporter of hard-core country throughout much his career until his recent venture into gospel. However, even during his current phase, he remains a mainstream performer having no intentions of moving over to the glitzier side of the spectrum as many of the modern artists have done.

Travis arrived on the scene during a period when the New Traditionalist movement was just taking hold, and his importance in the sub-genre rivals that of George Strait and Ricky Skaggs. He fit in perfectly with the style and returned country back to its honky tonk roots and won back a large number of fans who had drifted away disinterested with the Urban Cowboy fad and watered down pop-twang.

Travis gave the world a number of great songs. A partial list includes "On the Other Hand," "Diggin' Up Bones," "No Place Like Home," "Forever and Ever, Amen," "1982," "Hard Rock Bottom of Your Heart," "Honky Tonk Moon," "Deeper Than the Holler," "Is It Still Over?" "Mining for Coal," "Singing the Blues," "He Walked on Water," "It's Just a Matter of Time," "A Few Ole Country Boys," "A Better Class of Losers," "We're Not the Jet Set," "I'd Surrender All," "Forever Together," "Allergic to the Blues," "Honky Tonk

Side of Town," "Before You Kill Us All," "Whisper My Name," "Runaway Train," "That's Where I Draw the Line," "Are We in Trouble Now," "Doctor Jesus," "Don't Ever Sell Your Saddle," "Jerusalem's Cry," "Keep Your Lure in the Water," "Three Wooden Crosses," "Farther Along," "Blessed Assurance," "In the Garden," "Peace in the Valley," "Angels," "Running Blind," "Pick Up the Oars and Row," "Shout to the Lord," "Here I Am to Worship," "Since Jesus Came into My Heart," and "O How I Love Jesus." Whether singing one of his own gems or a cover version, the mainstream king has always been able to interject his own personality.

The Randy Travis story is the heartwarming tale of a talented individual who remained dedicated to his own musical vision. Although his popularity waned later in his career, he was still recognized as one of the most important modern artists because he changed the direction of country music. He proved that country music could return full circle to recapture its past glory.

DISCOGRAPHY:

Too Gone Too Long, Warner 7-28286.
Storms of Life, Warner Bros. 2-254355.
Always & Forever, Warner Bros. 2-25568.
Old 8x10, Warner Bros. 2-25738.
Old-Time Christmas, Warner Bros. 2-25988.
No Holdin' Back, Warner Bros. 2-25972.
Heroes and Friends, Warner Bros. 2-26310.
High Lonesome, Warner Bros. 2-26661.
Wind in the Wire, Warner Bros. 45319.
This Is Me, Warner Bros. 45501.
Full Circle, Warner Bros. 46328.
You and You Alone, Dream Works 50034.
A Man Ain't Made of Stone, Dream Works 50119.
Inspirational Journey, Warner Bros. 47893.
Live: It Was Just a Matter of Time, Image 1036.
Rise and Shine, Warner Bros. 886236.
Worship & Faith, Word Entertainment 886273.
Passing Through, Word Entertainment 886348.
Glory Train, Word Entertainment 88642.
Songs of the Season, Word Entertainment 87146.
Greatest Hits, Vol. 1, Warner Bros. 2-45044.
Greatest Hits, Vol. 2, Warner Bros. 2-45045.
Forever & Ever ... The Best of Randy Travis, Warner Bros. 33461.
Greatest #1 Hits, Warner Bros. 47028.
Super Hits, Vol. 1, Wanner Bros. 47065.
Trail of Memories: The Randy Travis Anthology, Rhino 78184.
The Essential Randy Travis, Warner Bros. 76165.
The Very Best of Randy Travis, Warner Bros./Rhino 78996.

The Platinum Collection, Warner Platinum 74050.
Greatest Hits, Rhino 8122799960.

Toby Keith (1961–)

Red, White and Blue

Country music is about tradition. From the very beginning, even before there was an industry, the practitioners of the old-timey sound guarded the sacred music with a fierce sense of preservation. That custom was renewed with the New Traditionalist movement. In the 1990s, long after the sub-genre had faded, one young, brash individual carried on with his red, white and blue style.

Toby Keith Covel was born on July 8, 1961, in Clinton, Oklahoma. His introduction to country music was a family affair. His grandmother ran a supper club in nearby Oklahoma City, and the young lad was intrigued by the number of acts that passed through. His parents encouraged his enthusiasm by buying him a guitar when he was eight. His father was a huge fan of Bob Wills, the Father of Western Swing. From that starting point he discovered others including his idol, Merle Haggard.

During his high school career, he worked as a rodeo hand and played football. He continued to hone his musical skills and after graduation found employment in the booming oil fields. On the side, he formed the Easy Money band that played in area honky tonks, which proved to be a dead-end to the advancement of his potential career.

When a severe recession impacted the oil industry, Keith found himself without a job. He fell back on his football training and played semipro ball for a USFL farm team after unsuccessfully trying out for the parent club. With music the only real profession he was interested in, he focused all of his energies, and eventually a polished demo tape found its way to Mercury Records via the producer for the country-rock band Alabama.

In 1993, his self-titled debut album broke him out as one of the new rising stars on the circuit. It contained the number one "Should've Been a Cowboy" and the Top Five "Wish I Didn't Know Now," "A Little Less Talk and a Lot More Action," and "He Ain't Worth Missing." The record would go on to sell over two million copies. But more importantly than the sales and top hits was the fact that his sound was traditional country in a time when crossover hits ruled the airwaves.

His sophomore CD, *Boomtown*, produced a second number one, "Who's

That Man." Other highlights included "Upstairs Downtown" and "You Ain't Much Fun." With a second strong record he was clearly proving that the first was no fluke. His concerts began to attract larger audiences, and he was one of the fastest rising stars on the circuit. His workingman sound was one that millions of country fans could relate to.

After the holiday offering *Christmas to Christmas,* he returned with *Blue Moon.* Another winner, it went platinum and spawned the number one "Me Too," as well as "A Woman's Touch" and "Does That Blue Moon Ever Shine on You." He continued to uphold the traditional country flag with pride and distinction on his studio work and live concerts.

The year 1997 was a pivotal one in his career. The album *Dream Walkin'* was released, and it provided him with three hit singles: the title track, "We Were in Love," and "I'm So Happy I Can't Stop Crying," a duet with Sting. It also marked the first time he worked with producer James Stroud, a relationship that would continue into the 2000s. He also switched labels, growing tired of Mercury's way of doing business and moving to DreamWorks.

In 1999, *How Do You Like Me Now?* was released and spawned two number one hits, the title cut and "You Shouldn't Kiss Me Like This." There was also the Top Five hit "Country Comes to Town." The songs only tell half of the story; Keith projected a tougher, stronger sound that earned him more fans and for the first time crossover success as well as industry honors. The Academy of Country Music named him Male Vocalist of the Year, and he also received an award for Album of the Year. His star magnitude was enlarged with appearances on the television shows *Touched by an Angel* and a *Dukes of Hazzard* reunion. He also made a series of telephone commercials.

In 2001, *Pull My Chain* was the first of his studio releases to top the country charts. It yielded three number one singles: "I'm Just Talkin' About Tonight," "I Wanna Talk About Me," and "My List." By this time he was a well-known name, but soon his fame would spread even wider in a very controversial manner.

The song "Courtesy of the Red, White & Blue (The Angry American)" was released in the summer of 2002, a response to the 9/11 attacks. It was a song of pure patriotism from someone who had made a good living in his native homeland. However, like other such strong statements, it drew different responses from various sections throughout the country. The patriotic side thought it was a great song and pushed it to the top of the charts. The critics thought otherwise, and the ensuing battle was good for his career.

The album *Unleashed* debuted at number one on both the country and pop charts. "Who's Your Daddy?" gave him another number one, and "Beer for My Horses" became a Top Ten hit. The latter was a duet with another red, white and blue American, Willie Nelson. Keith was now one of the brightest (if not most talked about) artists on the circuit.

In 2003, *Shock'n Y'All* connected with the American heartland, ensuring that he would remain on top of the charts. It contained the number one single "I Love This Bar," and the fans championed it like his previous works.

Although his career was about the music, there always seemed to be obstacles in his path. During this period his ongoing feud with the Dixie Chicks made as many headlines as his music. When Natalie Maines, lead singer for the group, denounced the president and the impending war in Iraq she ignited an incredible amount of backlash. Later, the brash vocalist made derogatory comments about Keith's "Courtesy of the Red, White & Blue," which prompted him to attack Maines's talent (or lack of it). He went further by posting a picture of her standing with Iraqi dictator Saddam Hussein as a backdrop to his concerts. At the ACM awards, she wore a controversial T-shirt that was a direct shot at Keith. The feud has grown cold over the past few years but the smoldering ashes could be reignited at any time.

Keith brushed aside the controversy and continued on with the business of making records. *Honkytonk University* was another winner and produced the number one hit "As Good as I Once Was," as well as the Top Five "Big Blue Note." Other highlights included the title track. Despite all of the publicity, he remained one of the most popular singers on the circuit.

He parted ways with longtime producer Stroud to establish his own company, Show Dog Nashville. The first record on the new label was *White Trash with Money*, which yielded the top singles "Get Drunk and Be Somebody," "A Little Too Late," and "Crash Here Tonight." He continued to tour and did some USO shows in support of the troops.

In 2007, the CD *Big Dog Daddy* appeared with the single "High Maintenance Woman." He remained one of the top drawing acts on the circuit and stayed away from the controversy that has plagued his much of his career. He continues to record and perform.

Toby Keith is a country music patriot. He has constantly churned out traditional songs with an ease and skill that so few possess. His abilities are apparent in the fact that he rose from obscurity to prominence very quickly. Although he has been dogged by controversy throughout his career, he has always responded with his music.

He possesses a classic honky tonk voice. There is a depth to it, as well as a plaintive element that is not weakness but a true aspect of the style. Hank Williams, Sr., contained a similar timbre in his vocal delivery. Keith also boasts a patriotic slant in his phrasing that gives his lyrics authority and strength.

He is one of the most visible artists on the circuit. He has done television work including the ads for Telecom USA as well as Ford Motor Company, where he sang "Ford Truck Man." He appeared at the *Total Nonstop Action Wrestling* pay-per-view show to play his controversial single "Courtesy of the Red, White and Blue." Later he entered the ring to wrestle Jeff Jarrett. He did an interview for *Playboy* magazine. He also played a USO show with rock gonzo guitar man Ted Nugent, a die-hard patriotic American son.

Keith appeared in the film *Broken Bridges,* where he played a country musician whose career is winding down. The movie also starred Kelly Preston, Burt Reynolds and Tess Harper. He opened I Love This Bar & Grill in Bricktown, Oklahoma City, Oklahoma. Later, a second bar was opened in Las Vegas. His concert rounds, including the Hookin' Up & Hangin' Out Tour, boasted opening acts Lindsey Haun, Miranda Lambert and Flynnville Train.

He has given the world a number of memorable songs. A partial list includes "Should've Been a Cowboy," "He Ain't Worth Missing," " A Little Less Talk and a Lot More Action," "Wish I Didn't Know Now," "Who's That Man," "You Ain't Much Fun," "Does That Blue Moon Ever Shine on You," "Me Too," "We Were in Love," "Dream Walkin'," "How Do You Like Me Now?!," "You Shouldn't Kiss Me Like This," "I'm Just Talkin' About Tonight," "I Wanna Talk About Me," "My List," "Who's Your Daddy?," "American Soldier," "Whiskey Girl," "As Good As I Once Was," "Big Blue Note," and "High Maintenance Woman." However, his most infamous tune is of course "Courtesy of the Red, White & Blue (The Angry American)." Many of the songs are New Traditionalist material, the style that he has continued to practice long after its period of popularity passed.

For most of his career he was a traditional country artist with the occasional element of pop in his songs. However, because of his tough stance, the adoption of a brasher sound, and his association with Willie Nelson, he was often cited as a latter day torch bearer for the Outlaw movement. Since Merle Haggard was his major influence, Keith can be very easily categorized with Johnny Cash, Kris Kristofferson and Waylon Jennings, among others.

Toby Keith is a solid American country artist. Aside from the controversy and his public feud with Natalie Maines of the Dixie Chicks, he has delivered a solid catalog of workingman songs that have had a major impact on today's music. His popularity as the spokesman for the red, white, and blue style of country music continues to reign strong.

DISCOGRAPHY:

Toby Keith, Mercury 54421.
Boomtown, Polygram 523407.
Christmas to Christmas, Polygram 527909.
Blue Moon, A&M 531192.
Dream Walkin', Mercury 534836.
How Do You Like Me Now?, DreamWorks 50209.
Pull My Chain, DreamWorks 450297.

Unleashed, DreamWorks 450254.
Shock'n Y'All, DreamWorks 450435.
Honkytonk University, DreamWorks Nashville 000430002.
White Trash with Money, Show Dog Nashville/Universal 000627002.
Love Me If You Can, Show Dog Nashville 0013.
Big Dog Daddy, Show Dog Nashville 005.
A Classic Christmas, Show Dog Nashville 15.
Greatest Hits, Vol. 1, Mercury 558962.
20th Century Masters — The Millennium Collection: The Best of Toby Keith, Universal 170351.
Greatest Hits, Vol. 2, DreamWorks Nashville 000232312.
Chronicles, Mercury 000482502.

Clint Black (1962–)

Mass Market Initiator

For the first sixty years of its existence country music existed in a specialized market. But when different elements were added to the traditional sound, the genre appealed to a new audience. But before the style could capitalize on this potential it needed someone to create a modern version of the mainstream. The mass market initiator arrived from Texas via New Jersey. His name was Clint Black.

Clint Black was born on February 4, 1962, in Long Branch, New Jersey, but was raised in a suburb of Houston, Texas. He started his musical career on harmonica at age thirteen, then switched to guitar two years later. While he honed his instrumental skills, he was also writing songs that reflected his tastes which ranged from mainstream country to progressive rock. His first live performance was as a member of his brother's group, the Full House Band. In 1979, he left school and found work in the construction industry and performed on the streets before graduating to coffee houses, bars and nightclubs.

In 1987, Black made enormous progress in his career when he met Hayden Nicholas, a guitarist and songwriter who boasted a proper home studio. The two collaborated on material and worked up a respectable demo that eventually found its way into the hands of Bill Ham, the manager of that lil' old band from Texas, ZZ Top. Ham was able to secure a recording contract with RCA Nashville, and Nicholas became bandleader, lead guitarist and chief songwriter for Black.

In 1989, Black's first single, "A Better Man," was released and became the first C&W debut single to top the charts in fourteen years. Overnight, Black leaped to the country music forefront topped with a performance at the Grand Ole Opry. He also watched his album, *Killin' Time*, go gold in less than six months and spawn three more number one singles: "Nobody's Home," "Walkin' Away," and the title track. The effort would spend three quarters of a year on the charts and sell two million copies, earning him the Country Music Association's Horizon Award for 1989, and Male Vocalist Award for 1990. As well, he captured the NSAI Songwriter/Artist of the Year Award.

In 1990, *Put Yourself in My Shoes*, his second release, boasted four Top Ten hits: "Where Are You Now," "Loving Blind," the number one singles "One More Payment" and the title track. The album would occupy the top position on the C&W charts, sell two million copies, make a respectable showing on the pop charts, but never received the same critical praise as its predecessor. That same year he even recorded a duet with legend Roy Rogers, "Hold On Partner." At this point in his career, Black was the undisputed number-one male country star; however, the winds of change were not blowing in his favor.

In 1991, he remained very active. He toured with the group Alabama, appeared on a number of television shows, and was inducted into the Grand Ole Opry. He married Lisa Hartman, a star on the television nighttime soap opera *Knots Landing*, which increased his star status, but put him under the microscope as celebrity marriages tend to do. Also around this time there was a new country music star of stellar magnitude named Garth Brooks who would outshine everyone on the circuit including Black.

Black started off 1992 entangled in a lawsuit with manager Bill Ham. The legal problems were finally resolved later in the year around the time that his third album, *The Hard Way*, was finally released. It raced to number two on the country music charts and also reached the pop Top Ten. "We Tell Ourselves" was number one that summer just in time for the start of his lengthy world tour.

His fourth studio album, *No Time to Kill*, was successful but wasn't as popular as his first three efforts. Nevertheless, the CD contained some highlights including the top single "When My Ship Comes In" and "A Bad Goodbye," a duet with Wynonna Judd which also became a hit. The record also boasted back-up from Kenny Loggins and Timothy B. Schmidt (of Eagles fame). At this point, Black could no longer claim to be the number one country male vocalist, and although his record sales were respectable, he seemed to have lost the shine of his powerful debut.

One Emotion, his fifth album, included "A Good Run of Bad Luck," a properly titled song considering the troubles he faced in the early part of the decade. In the 1990s, when country-pop became the new trend, he was seemingly forgotten but continued to forge on. Live performances remained his strong suit for the rest of the decade since his record sales plummeted.

In 1995, the seasonal offering *Looking for Christmas* appeared and proved an interesting collection of music in which Black broke Nashville rules by recording newly penned material instead of covers of old favorites. Highlights of the album included "The Kid," a strong ballad co-written with Merle Haggard. Other interesting songs were "The Finest Gift," "The Coolest Pair," and "The Birth of the King."

It would be two years before he released a new record, *Nothin' But the Taillights.* A decent effort, it was a far cry from his earlier releases that garnered much attention and won him awards. The title track was the best of the entire set. Other interesting songs included "Ode to Chet" and "The Shoes You're Wearing." It was in many ways a good buy only for the dedicated fans.

In 1999, he released *D'lectrified* which marked a major change in his music. The album included an eclectic selection of songs including "Bob Away My Blues" (a song written by Toy Caldwell of Marshall Tucker Band fame), Eric Idle's "Galaxy Song," Leon Russell's "Dixie Lullaby," and an updated version of the original Waylon Jennings song "Are You Sure Hank Done It This Way," as "Are You Sure Waylon Done It This Way." There was also original material including "Who I Used to Be," "Love She Can't Live Without," and an updated take on Black's own "No Time to Kill." Guests included Bruce Hornsby, Waylon Jennings, Steve Wariner and Black's wife Lisa Hartman-Black, duetting on the song "When I Said I Do."

It would be another six years before a collection of new material, *Spend My Time,* was released on the Equity label. It was more of an adult contemporary album than a country effort as it explored rock and pop influences such as singer-songwriters James Taylor and the Eagles. It was a disappointment for his longtime country music fans but proved an interesting new direction.

A year later, he emerged with *Drinkin' Songs and Other Logic,* which marked a return to a purer country sound. "Heartaches," "A Big One," "I Don't Want to Tell You," and the title track marked one of his best efforts in a decade. The songs were genuine and, except for a couple of odd inclusions, he appeared to be on the comeback trail. He continues to record and perform.

Clint Black is a country music enigma. He started with such great promise, but over the years his career waned in the wake of the efforts of other artists as well as his own mounting personal problems. Nevertheless, he remained a mainstay on the scene, concentrating on his live performances rather than recorded work to keep afloat.

Black boasts a country music voice. Yet, he was able to blend his Texas twang with the rock and roll he grew up listening to, combined with a defınite pop flavor. His ability to meld all of these influences into a cohesive and marketable product demonstrates the range of his vocal delivery. The familiarity and richness of his style has always been his major calling card.

Black is a New Traditionalist. He fused a mixture of influences — Merle Haggard, Bob Wills, George Jones, the Eagles, Gram Parsons, and the entire rock oriented pop singer-songwriter community of the 1970s — into one package. Along with Randy Travis and George Strait, he proved that country could expand its parameters to include rock and pop without losing its roots. Although his breakthrough style was greatly admired and copied in the late 1980s and early 1990s, others improved on what he had done, especially Garth Brooks.

Black was one of the first country artists to ignite the mass market popularity of country music in the early 1990s. Although the style had always been popular, after he broke ground, albums would become mega-sellers. Clint paved the way for such acts as Garth Brooks and the entire crop of female country pop singers including Shania Twain, Faith Hill and Martina McBride, among others.

Over the course of his long career he has worked with a number of individuals. A short list includes Steve Real, Dean Parks, Lenny Castro, Leland Sklar, Jim Horn, Billy Joel, Steve Wariner, Jerry Douglas, Reggie Young, Biff Watson, and Julian King. Of course his greatest partnership has been with Hayden Nicholas, a long lasting musical friendship that is a large part of the Clint Black story. His wife, the actress Lisa Hartman-Black, has also been an occasional duet partner.

Although he is best known as a country music artist, Black expanded his magnitude with appearances on the television shows *Wings, King of the Hill, Hope and Faith*, and *Hot Properties*. He further bolstered his appeal acting in the movies *Maverick, Still Holding On: The Legend of Cadillac Jack, Going Home,* and *Anger Management.* As well, he was a contestant on *Duets* in 2006 along with Randy Travis, Patti LaBelle, Smokey Robinson, and several others. He received a star on the Hollywood Walk of Fame as the result of the recognition for his contribution to the recording industry.

Black gave the world a number of memorable songs — originals and covers. A partial list includes "Nobody's Home," "Walkin' Away," "Where Are You Now," "Loving Blind," "One More Payment," "Hold On Partner," "We Tell Ourselves," "When My Ship Comes In," "A Bad October," "A Good Run of Bad Luck," "The Kid," "The Finest Gift," "The Coolest Pair," "The Birth of the King," "Ode to Chet," "The Shoes You're Wearing," "Bob Away My Blues," "Galaxy Song," "Dixie Lullaby," "Are You Sure Waylon Done It This Way," "Who I Used to Be," "Love She Can't Live Without," "No Time to Kill," and "When I Said I Do."

Clint Black is a country music performer who has had a rollercoaster career. Arguably, he played too many cards too soon, but he remained a prominent figure on the circuit. Whatever his shortcomings might be, he is credited as being the mass market initiator of the boom that brought the genre unprecedented success.

DISCOGRAPHY:

Killin' Time, RCA 9668.
Put Yourself in My Shoes, RCA 2372-2-R.
The Hard Way, RCA 66003-2-R
Clint Black, RCA 66151.
No Time to Kill, RCA 66239-2.
One Emotion, RCA 66419.
Looking for Christmas, RCA 66593.
Nothin' but the Taillights, RCA 67515.
D'Lectrified, RCA 67823.
Spend My Time, Equity Music Group 3001.
Christmas with You, Equity Music Group 3004.
Drinkin' Songs & Other Logic, Equity Music Group 3009.
Greatest Hits, RCA 66671.
Super Hits, RCA 67756.
Greatest Hits, Vol. 2, RCA 67005.
Super Hits [2003], RCA 67075.
Ultimate Clint Black, RCA 52551.
All American Country BMG Special Products 48808.
16 Greatest Hits, RCA Nashville/Legacy 78245.
All American Country, Collectables 8433.
The Collection [2 CD], Madacy Entertainment 52487.
The Collection [3 CD], Madacy 52411.
Killin' Time/Put Yourself in My Shoes, Hux 080.
The Love Songs, Equity Music Group 3016.

Travis Tritt (1963–)

A Particular Style

Throughout its rich history the state of Georgia has produced many gifted contributors to all styles of music. Blind Willie McTell, the Allman Brothers, James Brown, Amy Grant, Indigo Girls, Gladys Knight, Trisha Yearwood and Gid Tanner put the state on the musical map. In the 1990s, another artist from the Peach State made a major impact with his particular style. His name was Travis Tritt.

Travis Tritt was born in February 9, 1963, in Marietta, Georgia. He discovered music at an early age and learned how to play guitar. A few years later he began to write his own material with serious ambitions of becoming a successful recording artist. However, discouragement at home, the difficult choice between the itinerant life of a musician or a regular job and family responsibilities delayed his musical progress. But after two marriages and two divorces, he realized his true calling in life.

In 1982, he recorded a demo tape at a private studio that an executive at Warner Brothers owned. When the marketable potential of Tritt's songs shined through, he was given positive attention. After a few years of working the bar circuit, he developed his distinctive sound, blending honky tonk with southern rock.

In 1989, he was finally ready to launch his professional career. Warner Brothers signed him and released his debut effort, *Country Club*, which appeared the following spring. The title track hit the Top Ten, and his next two singles, "Help Me Hold On" and "I'm Gonna Be Somebody," reached number one and two, respectively. The hard-paced number "Put Some Drive in Your Country" stalled in the Top Five because of its strong rock and roll content, a non-favorite on country music radio.

Tritt had a hard time cracking Nashville's inner circle because he didn't fit the image of the new male singers that were turning country music on its ear. He had too much of a rock and roll edge to his music and too wild a stage show to appeal to the purer tastes that ran through Music City U.S.A.

In an effort to improve his image within industry circles, he signed with artist manager Ken Kragen, who had shaped the very successful careers of Lionel Richie, Trisha Yearwood and Kenny Rogers. The veteran manager worked his magic, and it enabled Tritt to hit multi-platinum territory with his second album, *It's All About to Change*. Three singles, "Drift Off to Dream," "Here's a Quarter (Call Someone Who Cares)," and "Anymore," reached number three, two and one on the charts, respectively.

By this time Tritt had established himself as one of the major country artists. He distanced himself from the other male hunks by not wearing a hat and infusing his music with southern rock elements. He enhanced this reputation with the release of his third album, *T-R-O-U-B-L-E*, in 1992 that yielded the number one hit "Can I Trust You With My Heart," and eventually the CD went gold. That same year he became a member of the Grand Ole Opry.

A year later, the album *Ten Feet Tall & Bulletproof* spawned the number one single "Foolish Pride," and eventually the collection went platinum. It also raced up the pop charts and peaked at number twenty, proving that his appeal went beyond the confines of country music. His live appearances were still drawing well as he toured on a regular basis.

In 1995, the compilation *Greatest Hits — From the Beginning* was released. A year later, he returned with the studio effort *Restless Kind*. Under the direction of producer Don Was, Tritt delivered a gritty collection of songs in the honky tonk, rockabilly and traditional vein during a time when country-pop artists were exploding onto the scene. It yielded two Top Ten hits, "More Than You'll Ever Know" and "Where Corn Don't Grow." Other highlights included "She Going Home with Me," "Helping Me Get Over You," and "Still in Love with You."

His concerts were a classic example of roughed-up country, which explored 1970s southern rock and contemporary Nashville sounds. Easily one of the loudest outfits on the country circuit, Tritt's band boasted a rock and roll edge that reminded many of Lynyrd Skynyrd and Molly Hatchet. It was this spirit that dominated his next recording, *No More Looking Over My Shoulder*. The singles "If I Lost You," the title cut, and "Start the Car" anchored the record.

He continued to refine his sound, a mixture of blues, southern rock, and honky tonk that dominated the next album, *Down the Road I Go*. He switched record labels for this recording, moving to Columbia Records. The album yielded the number one hit "Best of Intentions" and a couple of number two hits, "It's a Great Day to Be Alive" and "Love of a Woman." The song "Modern Day Bonnie and Clyde" scraped the bottom of the charts. But, more importantly, the effort provided fans with an alternative to the pop-drenched material flowing from Nashville.

His next recording, *Strong Enough*, his second on Columbia, contained more of a traditional country sound and a little less southern rock. It yielded some interesting tunes in "You Can't Count Me Out Yet," "If You're Gonna Straighten Up (Brother Now's the Time)," "Time to Get Crazy," "I Can't Seem to Get Over You," "County Ain't Country," "Strong Enough to Be Your Man," "Can't Tell Me Nothin'," and "You Really Wouldn't Want Me That Way."

He continued to deliver his version of Outlaw music with the release of *My Honky Tonk History*. Highlights included "Too Far to Turn Around," "The Girl's Gone Wild," "I See Me," "Small Doses," "Circus Leaving Town," "Monkey Around," and "What Say You," a contribution from folk-rocker John Mellencamp. The set contained power-driving country rock, tearjerker ballads and barroom stompers. While many country artists pursued crossover appeal, Tritt was happy to continue down his own path.

His next effort, *The Storm*, was the first on an independent label and once again featured a mixture of ballads, country soul, and gritty, funky blues that never strayed far from his honky tonk roots. It included "You Never Take Me Dancing," Hank Williams, Jr.'s "The Pressure Is On," "(I Wanna) Feel Too Much," "Doesn't the Good Outweigh the Bad," "What If Love Hangs On," "Something Stronger Than Me," "High Time for Getting" and a cover of Kenny Wayne Shepherd's "Somehow, Someday, Someway." The young blues-rock guitarist guested on the album as did Charlie Daniels with his trademark fiddle. Tritt continues to record and perform.

Travis Tritt is a country music rock. Throughout his entire career he was determined to make music on his own terms and didn't care how he was categorized. Although hailed as a New Traditionalist when he first broke in, his music took on a wider range of styles that included love ballads and fiery foot stompers. His individual sound has earned him a special place in modern country annals.

Tritt has a country-rock voice that is tailor-made for the path he has chosen. Although he is more than capable of belting out a ballad with pure tenderness, his calling card has always been the southern rock/honky tonk tunes. He can growl and moan with the best of them and could have easily been the lead singer of any of the southern rock acts including Lynyrd Skynyrd, Molly Hatchet, .38 Special, the Marshall Tucker Band, or the Allman Brothers.

He is a fine instrumentalist with a penchant for loud, screaming guitars that crank out hard driving bluesy, gritty country rock. His use of amplifiers, bass guitars, drums, and the occasional B-3 Hammond organ is more akin to rock than country. However, he always balanced his sound with more traditional country instruments like the Dobro, fiddle, and banjo.

Tritt began as a New Traditionalist, but when the trend faded, he had already shed the style for that of the genuine country-rock. In many ways, he could be classified as an alternative country artist with his penchant for southern rock. Yet, he has never distanced himself from his honky tonk roots despite exploring many different musical avenues. No matter what category he is placed into, he has always created music on his own terms.

Because of his ability to play in different styles, he has collaborated with a variety of artists. A partial list includes Marty Stuart, Patti LaBelle, Ray Charles, Ricky Skaggs, George Jones, Hank Williams, Jr., Waylon Jennings, Johnny Cash, Lorrie Morgan, Vince Gill, Buddy Guy, David Lee Roth, Gary Rossington, Kenny Rogers, Charlie Daniels and Kenny Wayne Shepherd. The names range across country, blues, soul, jazz, pop, hard rock and bluegrass.

He has given the world a number of great songs including "Country Club," "Help Me Hold On," "I'm Gonna Be Somebody," "Drift Off to Dream," "Here's a Quarter (Call Someone Who Cares)," "Anymore," "The Whiskey Ain't Workin'," "Nothing Short of Dying," "This One's Gonna Hurt You (For a Long, Long Time)," "Can I Trust You with My Heart," "Lord Have Mercy on the Working Man," "Foolish Pride," "Tell Me I Was Dreaming," "Sometimes She Forgets," "More Than You'll Ever Know," "Where Corn Don't Grow," "Best of Intentions," "It's a Great Day to Be Alive," "Love of a Woman" and "Modern Day Bonnie and Clyde." The variety of styles found throughout his extensive catalog is incredible.

His backup band constantly featured excellent musicians who were kindred spirits interested in creating the same kind of music he wanted to. A partial list includes Reggie Young, Billy Joe Walker, Jr., Steve Turner, Jimmy Joe Ruggiere, Hargus "Pig" Robbins, Mark O'Connor, Paul Franklin, Stuart Duncan, Larry Byrom, Gregg Brown, Mike Brignardello, Richard Bennett, Sam Bacco, Dana McVicker, and Matt Rollings.

The Travis Tritt story is that of a long, interesting career. His southern fried country-rock welded to honky tonk roots formed the basis of his exciting brand of music. He expanded the parameters of the New Traditionalist style without altering its simple format. In an industry where each artist boasts their distinct voice, he has delighted with his particular style.

DISCOGRAPHY:

Country Club, Warner Bros. 2-26094.
All About to Change, Warner Bros. 2-26589.
T-R-O-U-B-L-E, Warner Bros. 2-45048.
A Travis Tritt Christmas — Loving Time of the Year, Warner Bros. 2-45029.
Ten Feet Tall and Bulletproof, Warner Bros. 45603.
The Restless Kind, Warner Bros. 46304.
No More Looking Over My Shoulder, Warner Bros. 47097.
Down the Road I Go, Columbia 62165.
Strong Enough, Columbia 86660.
My Honky Tonk History, Columbia 92084.
The Storm, Category 5, 500103.
Greatest Hits: From the Beginning, Warner Bros. 46001.
Super Hits, Warner Bros. 47666.
The Lovin' Side, Rhino 78296.
The Rockin' Side, Rhino 78297.
Essentials, Warner Strategic 76167.
The Very Best of Travis Tritt, Rhino 74817.
Live in Concert, Big Band Concert 77405.

PART TWO

Alternative Country

The mainstream recordings that flow from the Nashville studios have always been the core of country music; however, not all performers embraced the traditional methods. The nonconformists, mavericks and outsiders were often shunned by the purists, yet their rebellious stance allowed them the freedom to deliver something different to the buying public as they created their own vision of the genre.

Alternative country was born from the Outlaw and progressive movements. When Willie Nelson turned his back on Nashville in the early 1970s he became the nominal head of the new music. Others like Merle Haggard, Johnny Cash, Waylon Jennings, and Billy Joe Shaver joined the cause and gained a foothold in the industry. Gram Parsons had a unique country sound he called American Cosmic music.

Throughout the 1980s, aging musicians like Cash, Nelson, Haggard, Jennings and Kris Kristofferson carried on what they had started a decade before. In the 1970s, Gram Parsons had died of a drug overdose; however, his protégée Emmylou Harris continued to expound his philosophy. But, as the New Traditionalists asserted themselves and dominated radio airplay, the outsider country movement faded into the background.

When Garth Brooks began his ascent to the top of the charts with his mixture of shiny new country, '70s singer-songwriter sensibility, rock and roll antics and pop feel, many embraced him as the messiah of the modern country movement. However, some demanded a choice from the mainstream pop stylings and as a result an underground movement gained new life.

The alternative movement spread throughout the country. Uncle Tupelo, a band out of Illinois, released *No Depression*, a mixture of punk rock songs and country flavored acoustic ballads. On the West Coast, the group X, punk legends with a taste for honky tonk, recorded a pure redneck album under the name the Knitters. Rank and File, and Lone Justice practiced "cowpunk" as well. The Blasters and Big Sandy were integral to the rockabilly revival scene. Jason and the Scorchers' debut album *Lost and Found* discovered an entire audience that craved electrified twang. Souled American, a Chicago band, mixed country and folk to create something fresh. The Blood Oranges featured a sound that was part punk rock and part country-inspired ballads with generous doses of bluegrass. Go To Blazes played hard rock and roll with country and blues overtones. Freakwater, an acoustic group, was the foremost exponent of old-time mountain folk ballads. Lambchop played lush country in a very pop oriented Nashville tradition. The movement even took off overseas where the punk outfit the Mekons shifted to American roots music. The lead singer, John Langford, eventually fronted a countrified outfit called the Waco Brothers.

Alternative country is a vibrant style that challenges mainstream Nashville. The different take on country has blossomed to include many related sub-genres such as progressive country, country-rock, contemporary country, singer-songwriter, roots-rock, country-folk, Outlaw country, alternative country-rock, contemporary folk, Neo-Traditionalist country, rockabilly revival, contemporary singer/songwriter and neo-traditional folk.

No matter the sub-genre, the basic style of all alternative artists is based on fast rhythms, rough-edged guitar licks and stark lyrics. This philosophy has allowed many to create their own brand proving that country music consists of more than what Music City U.S.A. has to offer.

This section contains some of the most controversial country personalities that have ever appeared on the scene. But their contributions to the contemporary scene are crucial, since they offer fans a clearly different choice from the mainstream. The following artists are covered in this section:

• Jimmie Dale Gilmore is another Texas rebel who desired to play the music on his terms. He blended his traditional country roots with elements of rock, blues and folk.
• Emmylou Harris is that rare artist who was able to reach the mainstream while delivering an eclectic body of work. After Parsons died, she assumed the role of torch bearer of Cosmic American Music and continues to this day to carry it proudly.
• Joe Ely, another Lone Star State renegade, played the music that he heard in his head and cut his own niche in alternative circles.
• Hank Williams, Jr., is more than just the son of his famous father Hank Williams, Sr. He established his own universe with tough, gritty honky tonk that was far removed from the mainstream.
• Steve Earle is a different breed of country artist and was once the poster boy for the alternative style.
• Lyle Lovett, an extremely talented artist, delivered a series of fine country albums. But the Texan's eclectic tastes have stretched the parameters beyond what anyone else has done.
• Dwight Yoakam blended traditional honky tonk with Buck Owens's Bak-

ersfield sound into his own musical vision. He never played by Nashville's rules.

- Mary Chapin Carpenter emerged from the small movement of folk-influenced country singer-songwriters of the late 1980s. Despite her anti–Nashville stance she found commercial success.
- Béla Fleck is a cosmic world fiddler whose eclectic taste makes him an extreme alternative country artist.
- k.d. lang was a controversial artist from the start, but there was no denying her talent. Sadly, she seemed to abandon country for a more pop flavor.

Jimmie Dale Gilmore (1945–)

Austin Outlaw

In the 1970s, Willie Nelson, fed up with the production techniques that were standard practice in Nashville, turned his back on the industry and returned to his Texas roots. He settled in Austin, where he decided to make music on his own terms and ignited his own brand of Outlaw country. Since then the capital of the Lone Star State has produced a number of important country musicians including the man known as the Austin Outlaw. His name is Jimmie Dale Gilmore.

Jimmie Dale Gilmore was born on May 6, 1945, in Tulia, Texas, into a musical family; his father played lead guitar in a small band. In order to overcome the boredom of growing up in a small town, the young Gilmore turned to music. Before he hit his teens the family moved to Lubbock, with a more prominent musical history as the birth place of Buddy Holly. It was here that Waylon Jennings, Terry Allen, Butch Hancock and Joe Ely started their careers. The latter two would figure importantly in Gilmore's future direction.

He spent the rest of his childhood in Lubbock and there he met his future singing partner, Butch Hancock. They formed a musical friendship that would last throughout their respective careers. Later, Gilmore met Allen, who suggested the idea of Gilmore writing original material. It was an important step in the development of Jimmie Dale's career.

He honed his writing and singing skills and made other friends in the music business including Joe Ely, who would follow a similar career path. It was the latter who turned Gilmore onto the folk and country blend of Townes Van Zandt, another crucial catalyst in Gilmore's maturation as an artist.

Gilmore and Ely formed the T. Nickel House band and with the later addition of Hancock they became the Flatlanders. Among a distinguished list of personnel that graced the group the list includes Steve Wesson and Tony Pearson. In 1972, the trio released a work recorded in Nashville that became a collector's item because of its limited availability. Many years later it would be re-released as *More a Legend Than a Band*.

The band welded a myriad of influences including acoustic folk, string-band, and country blues to create an interesting sound. The song "Dallas," which Gilmore wrote, would become a classic later in his career. At the time it was released as a single it created little interest and, subsequently, despite the great promise they held, the band split up.

Gilmore moved to Denver, and by this time music had become a mere hobby, but he was spurred on by his friend Ely, who had landed a recording contract and used some of Jimmie Dale's songs on his debut album. In 1980, Gilmore moved back to Austin and started to play clubs, focusing once again on a musical career. Finally, in 1988, he released his first solo record, *Fair and Square*.

Fair and Square was an interesting collection of songs, but it didn't represent the future path he would explore and make his own. His debut was more of a honky tonk effort that featured some of his basic trademarks including his old-timey, tenor vocals. Of note, Butch Hancock, Joe Ely, Townes Van Zandt and David Halley all contributed material.

His sophomore effort, the self-titled *Jimmie Dale Gilmore*, featured more of his own material and relied less on outside songs. Most importantly, many of the tunes were played in a straightforward honky tonk style that energized Gilmore's career and coincided with Austin's resurgence as an important musical center. There was a strong traditional flavor to the work, and it provided a glimpse of what lied ahead.

In 1990, the Flatlanders' original recording was re-released. Long a collector's item, it only enhanced Gilmore's current rise in popularity as did the *Two Roads* album, a duet with his pal Hancock. Their CD was the result of a live recording of their tour through Australia. But the best was yet to come with his third album.

After Awhile, the first release on his new label, featured more of a singer-songwriter than the honky tonk cowboy found on his two previous efforts. It indicated his new maturity as an artist. Highlights of the album included "Tonight I Think I'm Gonna Go Downtown," "Treat Me Like a Saturday Night," and "Blue Moon Waltz." A subtle work that finally showcased Gilmore's extensive talents, it catapulted him to the forefront of the alternative country scene and proved that he was ready to make music on his own terms.

By this time he was also performing in high spirits and was received very well. There was something special about a night of his music that many fans enjoyed. They, in turn, spread the message. The momentum was building as he managed to place himself in a very unique category above his contemporaries.

The trend continued on *Spinning Around the Sun*, a mix of contemporary and traditional country-flavored songs that featured a much more exuberant instrumental effort. The sound was capped off by Gilmore's unique voice, which gave the album a strong balance and pushed it to favorable critical acclaim. By this time he had firmly established himself as an alternative artist in the same category as Joe Ely, Butch Hancock and Dwight Yoakam.

In 1996, *Braver Newer World* was released and proved to be another strong effort to add to his catalog. Aside from his solid recording career, he was also a favorite touring attraction who sometimes featured guest appearances by Ely and Hancock in his shows. Although they had not played together in a group in some time, the excitement of seeing all three appear as a unit on stage was a sure thrill.

In 1998, the trio finally recorded a new Flatlanders track for the soundtrack to the film *The Horse Whisperer*. Although Gilmore's solo career was rewarding, the allure of working with Hancock and Ely was too strong to resist. By the time Jimmie Dale's solo album *One Endless Night* surfaced in 2000, the trio was touring again periodically and finally cut another album thirty years after the original. *Now Again* was so well received that another, *Wheels of Fortune*, soon followed. A concert tape of the group from their earliest days was released as *Live '72*.

In 2005, Jimmie Dale continued his solo career with *Come On Back*, an album of classic honky tonk and folk songs. The work was dedicated to his recently departed father. Joe Ely played on some of the cuts and served as producer. Gilmore continues to record and perform.

Jimmie Dale Gilmore is a country music songster. He has added an interesting chapter to the genre with his unique voice and different approach in creating his own sound. Although he will never be confused with any of the mainstream artists, he has followed his own path outside the traditional confines of Nashville.

Gilmore possesses a very interesting voice. There is a warmth to it, a friendly element that is folksy, inviting and instantly recognizable. His warbling tenor has constantly assured him a special place in the hearts of not only country fans, but music lovers from across the spectrum. The down-home nature of his songs is one of his most endearing qualities as a singer.

Gilmore is an alternative country artist. He has managed to blend his traditional sound with folk, blues and rock styles to create his own special musical universe. Although he can be placed in the same category as Joe Ely, Steve Earle, Dwight Yoakam, Mary Chapin Carpenter, k.d. lang, Béla

Fleck, and Lyle Lovett, like those mentioned above he possesses an individual sound.

Gilmore infuses his lyrical content with both his philosophical interests as well as his easy-going nature. A partial list of his songs includes "Dallas," "Tonight I Think I'm Gonna Go Downtown," "Treat Me Like a Saturday Night," "Blue Moon Waltz," "My Mind's Got a Mind of Its Own," "Gotta Travel On," "Guadalupe," "Just a Wave, Not the Water," "Red Chevrolet," "Deep Eddy Blues," "Beautiful Rose," "Midnight Train," "Chase the Wind," "Another Colorado," "I'm Gonna Love You," "Thinking About You," "Braver Newer World," "Borderland," "Sally," and "Outside the Lines." The wealth of his song collection runs the entire spectrum from his Zen cowboy tunes to more blended material.

His varied song material is a reflection of his many influences. He listened to his father's band often as well as to Lukas Day. These were the two prime musicians who made an important impact on him as youth. Later, he turned to the Texas rock and rollers Roy Orbison and Buddy Holly. In the 1960s, the Beatles and Bob Dylan infused a sense of folk-rock music in him. He would in turn have a profound effect on various musicians including his son Colin, who is a singer-songwriter based in Austin.

One of his outside projects included playing a small part in the movie *The Big Lebowski*. Gilmore's song "Braver Newer World" was featured in the film *Kicking and Screaming*. Although his acting ability is not as first rate as his musical skills, the opportunity to break away and perform in a different venue exposed him to a new audience.

The Jimmie Dale Gilmore story depicts the ability of a very talented individual to meld traditional country with his personal vision to create a special musical universe. The uniqueness of his catalog ensures him a place in country music history as the Austin Outlaw.

DISCOGRAPHY:

Fair and Square, Hightone 8011.
Jimmie Dale Gilmore, Hightone 8018.
After Awhile, Elektra/Nonesuch 61448.
Spinning Around the Sun, Elektra 61592-2.
Braver Newer World, Elektra 61836.
One Endless Night, Rounder 613173.
Come On Back, Rounder 13193.
Don't Look for a Headache, Hightone 8166.

Jimmie Dale Gilmore & the Flatlanders:
One More Road, Charly 30189.
More a Legend Than a Band, Rounder 34.
Unplugged, Sun 7011.

All American Music, Plantation 20.
Complete Plantation Recordings, Varese Sarabande 066561.
Now Again, New West 6040.
Wheel of Fortune, New West 6049.
Live '72, New West 6052.

Emmylou Harris (1947–)

Cosmic American Female

In the 1970s, progressive country or redneck rock became more than just a passing fad. New Riders of the Purple Sage, the Flying Burrito Brothers, Jerry Jeff Walker, Michael Murphey, Doug Sahm, and Asleep at the Wheel were all practitioners. There was another, Gram Parsons, who developed his own brand of advanced country. When he died, his protégée, a young girl from Alabama, took up the cause of his Cosmic American Music. Her name was Emmylou Harris.

Emmylou Harris was born on April 2, 1947, in Birmingham, Alabama, into a military family. She spent part of her youth in North Carolina, then moved to Woodbridge, Virginia, and finished high school there. She attended the University of North Carolina on a drama scholarship, and it was at this point that she began to study music seriously. Her main influences were the folk singers Bob Dylan and Joan Baez, and she found a partner in Mike Williams. They played at various coffee houses before she eventually quit school and moved to New York to become a folk singer, only to find out that the boom was over as psychedelic rock and roll was taking over.

She remained on the Greenwich Village club circuit and played at Gerdes Folk City, among other venues. She made friends with Jerry Jeff Walker, David Bromberg, and Paul Siebel. She married Tom Slocum, a fellow songwriter, in 1969, and a year later released her first album, *Gliding Bird*. On what should have been a joyous occasion, she found herself in a mess. Her marriage fell apart, she was pregnant, and her record label went bankrupt.

She craved a change in her life and moved to Nashville to raise her infant daughter on her own. Her marriage to Slocum ended in divorce and after some hard, discouraging, dues-paying months, she moved in with her parents on a farm outside of Washington, D.C., with her little girl.

She re-ignited her musical career, forming a trio with locals Gerry Mule and Tom Guidera and performing at local coffee houses and other small venues. In 1971, various members of the Flying Burrito Brothers, a country-rock act that had just lost their leader Gram Parsons, caught the trio's act. Chris

Hillman, who had taken over the lead vocal chores, was floored by Harris's vocal power and suggested she replace him when he left to join Manassas with Stephen Stills. Instead, she ended up with Parsons, who was searching for a female to counterbalance his solo act.

Parsons, who was in his Cosmic American Music phase, an offshoot of progressive music that fused country and rock and roll, welcomed someone with Harris's talent to the fold. She sang harmony on his debut album, *G.P.,* toured with him and then stuck around to add her distinctive vocal talents to this follow-up *Grievous Angel* album. The union ended on September 19, 1973, when Parsons was found dead in California of a drug overdose.

Harris, who had returned to Washington to fetch her daughter and belongings with full intentions of settling down in the Golden State, remained in the capital with her parents. She reunited with Tom Guidera to form the Angel Band, and the group landed a recording contract with Reprise. Meanwhile, when not performing with her new group, she returned to Los Angeles where she laid down tracks for a solo album that would eventually be called *Pieces of the Sky.*

Pieces of the Sky began a new phase in her career as the critically acclaimed album put her on the national music map. The work contained covers that ranged from Merle Haggard to the Beatles, plus a single, "If I Could Only Win Your Love," which became a Top Ten hit. "Light of the Stable," a Christmas single, featured backup from Dolly Parton, Linda Ronstadt and Neil Young. Brian Ahern produced the record and would become Harris's husband.

Her sophomore album, *Elite Hotel,* featured her backup group the Hot Band for the first time. It included legendary sidemen James Burton and Glen D. Hardin as well as Rodney Crowell, an as yet unknown rhythm guitarist and vocalist. The record was another smash and contained "Together Again," a Buck Owens tune, as well as "Sweet Dreams," a Patsy Cline song; both covers topped the charts.

In 1977, Harris added Bob Dylan to her list of credits. Previously, she had done session work for Neil Young and Linda Ronstadt. She also appeared in the documentary *The Last Waltz,* the Band's farewell tribute concert. Later that year, *Luxury Liner,* her third solo album, soon followed and won her more recognition on the strength of the singles "Makin' Believe" and "(You Never Can Tell) C'est La Vie."

In 1978, she continued her hot streak with *Quarter Moon in a Ten Cent Town,* which included her third number one single, "Two More Bottles of Wine," as well as "To Daddy," which peaked at number three, and "Easy from Now On." It featured Crowell's last appearance in the Hot Band. He left soon after for a solo career. Ricky Skaggs was recruited as a replacement.

Although her albums had featured country-tinged songs from the beginning, she was moving more strongly toward that direction with each successive release. In 1979, *Blue Kentucky Girl* was her most country-flecked effort to date, and it included the title track, the number one hit "Beneath Still Waters," and "Save the Last Dance for Me."

Roses in the Snow, the follow-up, was a full blown acoustic bluegrass work that yielded the Top Twenty song "The Boxer." The same year, she performed a duet with Roy Orbison on "That Lovin' You Feelin' Again" (which hit the Top Ten), released a Christmas album, *Light of the Stable,* and quit touring to concentrate on her motherly duties.

While shw was on sabbatical, *Evangeline,* made up of songs that had been left off previous albums, was released and contained two notable singles, "Mr. Sandman" and "I Don't Have to Crawl." Skaggs left the Hot Band, and Barry Tashian, once the lead singer for the rock outfit the *Remains,* replaced him. John Ware, the drummer, would be the last original member to leave Harris's backup group.

Once she reformed the Hot Band, Harris returned to touring. She cut *Cimarron,* an album that featured a duet with Don Williams, "If I Needed You," which peaked at number three, as did "Born to Run." "Tennessee Rose" was also a Top Ten hit.

The next effort, *Last Date,* a live album, included the number one hit "(Lost His Love) On Our Last Date," the Top Five hit "I'm Movin' On," and "So Sad (To Watch Good Love Go Bad)." Her next effort, *White Shoes*, the last one with Ahern as producer (the marriage had fallen apart and the couple would eventually divorce), included a remake of Donna Summer's "On the Radio," Johnny Ace's "Pledging My Love," Sandy Denny's "Old-Fashioned Waltz," as well as "Drivin' Wheel" and "In My Dreams."

Harris relocated to Nashville after the divorce and united with old friend Paul Kennerley. She had sung backup on his *The Legend of Jesse James* album. The duo wrote the material found on *The Ballad of Sally Rose*; Sally Rose was a pseudonym that she often used on the road. The album was a commercial failure, but it kindled a love and Emmylou and Kennerley would eventually wed.

The album *Angel Band,* an acoustic collection of traditional country spirituals, was a gentle record, but was only released after the album *Thirteen.* In 1987, she went a different musical direction when she teamed up with Dolly Parton and Linda Ronstadt to record *Trio,* which generated the number one single "To Know Him Is to Love Him," the number three "Telling Me Lies," and the Top Ten hit "Those Memories of You."

In 1990, another collaboration album appeared called *Duets* and featured Harris singing with George Jones, Willie Nelson, and previously recorded material with her mentor, the late Gram Parsons. She dissolved the Hot Band and formed the Nash Ramblers, a band that included Sam Bush on fiddle, mandolin, and vocals; Roy Huskey, Jr., on bass and vocals; Larry Atamanuik on drums; Al Perkins on banjo, guitar, Dobro and vocals; and Jon Randall on guitar, mandolin and vocals. They recorded the live *At the Ryman*, a set performed at Nashville's Ryman Auditorium that won a Grammy.

It was also during this period that she served as the president of the Country Music Foundation, displaying a different kind of talent, especially strong leadership qualities. During her tenure the Ryman Auditorium underwent a multimillion dollar restoration to become a premium venue.

In 1993, she left Reprise Records and moved to Elektra. For her new label she recorded *Cowgirl's Prayer*, the last album with Paul Kennerley, since the couple split up soon afterward. One single drawn from the CD, "High-Powered Love," failed to chart. Harris, a constantly evolving artist, craved a new musical direction.

She teamed up with producer Daniel Lanois, who had worked with rock acts U2, Peter Gabriel and Bob Dylan. *Wrecking Ball*, released in 1995, was an ambitious effort that saw her stretching out as an artist with cover versions of Jimi Hendrix's "May This Be Love," Steve Earle's "Goodbye," Julie Miller's "All My Tears," Gillian Welch's "Orphan Girl," and Kate and Anna McGarrigle's "Going Back to Harlan." It also featured the services of Neil Young as singer and writer. The album introduced her to the alternative rock audience.

She appeared on Willie Nelson's *Teatro* album, and then she released the live *Spyboy* album, supported by her new band. It consisted of guitarist Buddy Miller, drummer Brady Blade and bassist-vacolist-percussionist Daryl Johnson. The updated version of her material included "Boulder to Birmingham."

In 1999, Harris, Parton and Ronstadt collaborated on *Trio 2*, which went gold and earned them a Grammy for Best Country Collaboration with Vocals. It included the Neil Young chestnut "After the Gold Rush," which became a very popular video. Later, Emmylou and Linda recorded a duet album and toured together.

In 2000, she released *Red Dirt Girl*, her first album of self-penned material in five years. The album included backup from Bruce Springsteen, Patty Scialfa, Jill Cuniff and Patty Griffin. It was more of an alternative rock/folk piece than country album, but still reached number five on the charts. It also earned her another Grammy for Best Contemporary Folk Album.

That same year she guested on Ryan Adams's solo debut *Heartbreaker*. She participated in the soundtrack for the Coen Brothers film *O Brother, Where Art Thou?* A documentary/concert movie *Down from the Mountain* featured some of the artists from the film. Later Harris, along with some of the others from the movie, hit the road for the Down from the Mountain tour, in 2002.

In 2003, she released *Stumble into Grace*, which contained a number of self-penned tunes. Although it didn't produce any smash hits, it did inspire her to go on the road again. A year later, she was on tour with the Sweet Harmony Traveling Revue that included Gillian Welch, David Rawlings, Buddy Miller and Patty Griffin.

In 2005, she toured with Elvis Costello and collaborated on the duet "The Scarlet Tide," which was included in the movie soundtrack for *Cold Mountain*. That summer, *The Very Best of Emmylou Harris: Heartaches and Highways* was released on the Rhino label. She would also collaborate with pal Neil Young as guest vocalist on his CD *Prairie Wind*. Harris also appeared in the documentary-concert film *Neil Young: Heart of Gold*.

At this point in her career it seemed that she had abandoned her solo material in order to work with some of her idols and favorite singers. She recorded *All the Roadrunning* with Mark Knopfler of Dire Straits fame, and the two toured Europe and the U.S. together. It brought her back to the attention of music fans as the CD reached the Top Twenty in both England and America. Harris also contributed a performance of a Joni Mitchell song, "The Magdaleine Laundries," to the album *A Tribute to Joni Mitchell*. She continues to record and perform.

Emmylou Harris is a daring country personality. She has continued the artistic path her mentor Gram Parsons established — specifically that of the Cosmic American Music trail. Only someone with her talent, guts and determination could have created the iconoclastic body of work that she has with such heart, vision and vitality.

Her unmistakable, powerful, crystalline voice and her precise phrasing are the foundations of her style. It has enabled her to create a catalog that has had a profound impact on contemporary music. Her versatile vocal delivery has allowed her to excel in country, blues, rock, folk, and rock. She has performed as a solo artist, in various groups, duets and as part of special projects including movie soundtracks.

She has added her vocal muscles to the recordings of countless artists. A list of her recording partners includes: Neil Young, Roy Acuff, Ryan Adams, John Anderson, Lynn Anderson, Tom Astor, Matraca Berg, Glen Campbell, Johnny Cash, Tracy Chapman, Vic Chesnutt, Guy Clark, Bruce Cockburn, Sheryl Crow, Mary Chapin Carpenter, Iris DeMent, the Louvin Brothers, Rodney Crowell, Bob Dylan, Steve Earle, Vince Gill, Patty Griffin, George Jones, the Judds, Alison Krauss, Clint Black, Leo Kottke, Marty Stuart, Patty Loveless, Gillian Welch, Delbert McClinton, Midnight Oil, Dolly Parton, Bill Monroe, Willie Nelson, John Prine, Pure Prairie League, Linda Ronstadt, John Scofield, Gary Stewart, Pam Tillis, Townes Van Zandt, Keith Whitley, Don Williams, Lucinda Williams, Tammy Wynette, and Trisha Yearwood. She has always added a personal spark to every recording that she has participated in.

She has always been an active member of various causes. Along with Sarah McLachlan and others, she performed in 1997 and again in 1998 in the Lilith Fair touring shows, promoting feminism in music. She is an advocator of animal rights and a prominent member of PETA. She has also been the annual organizer of the Concerts for a Landmine Free World. The proceeds of the event have gone to the Vietnam Veterans of America Foundation in order to assist victims of conflicts around the world. Mary Chapin Carpenter, Nanci Griffith, Steve Earle, Joan Baez, and Bruce Cockburn have joined Harris on the road.

She has won a Grammy for Album of the Year, Best Female Country Vocal Performance, for Best Country Performance by a Duo or Group with Vocal, Best Contemporary Folk Album in 1995 for *Wrecking Ball* and again in 2000 for *Red Dirt Girl*. As well, she has won a Grammy for Best Country Collaboration. One of the greatest honors bestowed upon her is a fifth place ranking of the Forty Greatest Women in Country Music.

She has given the world a number of great songs. A list of her Top Ten hits includes "Together Again," "If Only I Could Win Your Love," "One of These Days," "Sweet Dreams," "(You Never Can Tell) C'est La Vie," "Makin' Believe," "To Daddy," "Two More Bottles of Wine," "Save the Last Dance for Me," "Play Together Again," "Blue Kentucky Girl," "Beneath Still Waters," "Wayfaring Stranger," "That Lovin' You Feeling Again," "If I Needed You," "Tennessee Rose," "Born to Run," "(Lost His Love) On Our Last Date," "I'm Movin' On," "In My Dreams," "Pledging My Love," "Telling Me Lies," "To Know Him Is to Love Him," "Those Memories of You," "Wildflowers," and "Heartbreak Hill." Whether as a solo artist or as a member of a duo or trio, she has added something to the session.

Emmylou Harris is a special talent who has influenced a number of artists including LeAnn Rimes, Reba McEntire, Angela Easterling, Angela Desveaux, Lavender Diamond, Wild Sweet Orange, No Speed Limit, Anne Davis, Faith Hill, Trisha Yearwood, Ashley Monroe, Mindy Smith, Po' Girl, Tift Merritt, Kathleen Edwards, Chitlin' Fools, Misty River, the Pierces, Nancy Atlas, Joanie Keller, K. C. Groves, Danielle Peck, Carrie Underwood, Patty Loveless, Miranda Lambert, Sara Evans, Taylor Swift, Catherine Britt, Megan Reilly, Susanna Van Tassel, Joy Lynn White, Valerie Smith, Vince Gill, Kathy Chiavola, Laura Cantrell, Kathie Baillie, Lucy Kaplansky, Patricia Conroy, Barry & the Remains, Iris DeMent, the Deighton Family, Marsha Thornton, and Rodney Crowell. Her drive, work ethic, creative energy, daring nature and determination are all admirable traits that every singer needs in order to survive the competitive music business.

The Emmylou Harris story consists of a career that stretches over five decades. She has created a tremendous body of work that any artist would be proud of and has championed many important causes. She has also continued the vision of her mentor, Gram Parsons, by traveling the Cosmic American Music highway with pride and distinction.

Discography:

Gliding Bid, Emus 12052.
Elite Hotel, Reprise 2236.
Pieces of the Sky, Reprise 2213.
Luxury Liner, Reprise 2998.
Quarter Moon in a Ten Cent Town, Reprise 3141.
Blue Kentucky Girl, Reprise 2-3318.
Light of the Stable, Reprise 2-3484.
Roses in the Snow, Reprise 2-3422.
Cimarron, Reprise 3603.
Evangeline, Reprise BSX-3508.
Last Date, Reprise 9237404.
White Shoes, Reprise 2-23961.
The Ballad of Sally rose, Reprise 2-25205.
Thirteen, Reprise 9253521.
Angel Band, Reprise 2-25585.
Bluebird, Reprise 9237761.
Brand New Dance, Reprise 2-23609.
At the Ryman, Reprise 2-26664.
Cowgirl's Prayer, Elektra 61541.
Wrecking Ball, Elektra 61854.
Spyboy, Eminent 25001.
Red Dirt Girl, Elektra 79616.
Nobody's Darling but Mine, Catfish 226.
Stumble into Grace, Nonesuch 79805.
Profile: The Best of Emmylou Harris, Reprise 2-3258.
Her Best Songs, K-Tel 1058.
Profile, Vol. 2: The Best of Emmylou Harris, Reprise 25161.
Duets, Reprise 2-25791.
Songs of the West, Warner Western 45725.
Nashville, Sundown 74.
Portraits, Warner Archives 45308.
Singin' with Emmylou, Vol. 1, Raven 93.
Love Hurts, Neon 35408.
Anthology: The Warner/Reprise Years, Rhino 76705.
3 for 1 Box Set, WEA International 48073.
Producer's Cut, Rhino 78174.
Singin' with Emmylou, Vol. 2, Raven 164.
Nashville Duets, Music Avenue 250024.
The Very Best of Emmylou Harris: Heartaches & Highways, Rhino 73123.
Rarities Box, Rhino 8122747442.
I've Always Needed You, Music Avenue 250110.
Artist's Choice: Emmylou Harris, Hear Music 7656.

Joe Ely (1947–)

Amarillo Honky Tonk

Texas is home to a myriad of musical styles including honky tonk, C & W, rockabilly, blues, western swing, Tex-Mex, jazz, folk, rock and gospel. Every artist who emerged from the Lone Star State absorbed the different influences to incorporate into their individual sound. One musician learned the lessons well and developed his own Amarillo honky tonk. His name is Joe Ely.

Joe Ely was born on February 9, 1947, in Amarillo, Texas. He moved to Lubbock where he discovered music and by thirteen was playing in rock and roll bands. At sixteen, fed up with the confines of school, he quit and became an itinerant musician. In order to support himself throughout his wanderings, which took him from his native state to California, New York, Tennessee, New Mexico, Europe and back to Texas, he worked a series of low paying jobs including dishwasher, fruit picker, circus hand, and janitor. The experiences of his nomadic wanderings would provide the material for the cycle of songs that would enable him to become a recording artist.

Upon his return to Lubbock, he formed the Flatlanders with cohorts Jimmie Dale Gilmore and Butch Hancock. They recorded one album of old-timey country music that wasn't released until 1990; and, by then, Ely was an established solo artist. Unfortunately, the band didn't last long enough in order to build a strong following.

After more traveling, he returned once again to Lubbock and formed his own band that included guitarist Jesse Taylor, steel guitarist Lloyd Maines, bassist Gregg Wright and drummer Steve Keaton. The group toured the honky tonk Texas circuit and after some dues paying, discouraging time they signed to MCA Records. In 1977, they cut their first album. The source of most of the material was Ely's various travels.

Although the first self-titled album didn't garner much attention, it contained contributions from his friend Butch Hancock including "She Never Spoke Spanish to Me" and "If You Were a Bluebird," among others. It also featured the Jimmie Dale Gilmore song "Treat Me Like a Saturday Night." Released during the height of the Outlaw movement, the album was a collection that championed the roots of the genre.

His second album effort, *Honky Tonk Masquerade,* made everyone — fans and critics alike — stand up and take notice. The work featured the excellent accordion skills of Ponty Bone and was a genuine Texas collection of songs reflecting a mixture of stylistic influences. "Fingernails" was barrelhouse rock

& roll; "West Texas Waltz" a honky tonk dance tune; and the title track was a weepy ballad. Overnight, Ely became an important name in country music circles.

His next album, *Down on the Drag,* further expanded his country music persona to that of a tough-skinned but gentle-hearted singer-songwriter. However, despite this appealing image, traditional radio programmers played little of his music, which meant slow sales. Ely's style was more of an alternative sound, which appealed to the underground crowd.

But some of the musical community recognized a good thing when they heard it. Merle Haggard took him on a tour of Britain in 1979, but it was a stint as a support act for the punk rock group the Clash that truly opened doors for Ely. He toured with the band throughout the U.S. as well as England and gained a whole new fan base from a very different source.

In the mid–1980s, when his sales had not improved, MCA Records dropped him. But, Ely, ever the battling artist, managed to record with the independent label Hightone. In 1990, MCA had a change of heart and resigned him. The *Live at Liberty Lunch* effort, which placed him at a renowned Austin club, was released and managed to make it to the top hundred of the C&W charts.

The exciting *Love and Danger* further proved that he was a solid songwriter and performer. He had drawn on many Texas influences to create his own fresh and genuine sound. Robert Earl Keen and Dave Alvin contributed songs to the effort, indicating the respect that Ely commanded throughout the musical community.

His concerts were important events to his underground fan base but were largely ignored by the mainstream audience. However, his alternative sound attracted the attention of different sections of the music listening public, which boosted attendance at his performances. Arguably, he was as good as any of the traditional acts and better than most.

Letter to Laredo was a collection of ranchero-flavored story songs — a true Texas influence — that featured Tom Russell's ballad "Gallo del Cielo." The album also introduced to the band flamenco guitarist Teye who proved to be a very important addition. Even legendary rocker Bruce Springsteen's background vocals didn't help the CD gain significant attention.

Ely's next album was *Twistin' in the Wind,* and when sales proved disappointing, MCA dropped him a second time. But he rebounded as he participated in the Tex-Mex supergroup Los Super Seven (which also included Freddy Fender and some members of Los Lobos). With this outfit he shared a Grammy Award for Best Mexican-American Music Performance.

He reached back into his past when he reunited with Gilmore and Hancock to record "South Wind of Summer," the first new Flatlander song in a quarter of a century. The tune was included in the box office hit *The Horse*

Whisperer. The three decided to reform the band and toured together in 2000. That same year, Ely released a third live album, *Live @ Antone's,* recorded at the renowned Austin club.

He continued to release CDs as a solo artist: *Streets of Sin* and *Happy Songs from Rattlesnake Gulch.* The latter was the first to appear on his own label, Rock 'Em Records, with plans to reissue his previous work, enabling him to be free of the strict standards of the major record companies. In 2007, a book of his writings was published by the University of Texas Press, illustrating yet more diversity from this very talented artist. Ely continues to record and perform.

Joe Ely is a country music devotee. He has contributed much to the genre in the past thirty years as a songwriter, performer and keeper of the flame. Although not a mainstream artist, he has proved over time that the genre can often be more exciting when it contains various elements of different styles.

His simple, yet expressive delivery is injected into each song, whether an original or cover. There is nothing complicated about his vocals, but he has an interesting voice. Because of his chameleon-like musical personality he has been lumped together with such diverse artists as Bruce Springsteen, Dwight Yoakam, blues/folk artist Ramblin' Jack Eliott, the very talented Kris Kristofferson and others such as Doug Sahm, Lyle Lovett, the introspective folk musician/rocker John Mellancamp and hard rocker Bob Seger. The versatility of Ely is an important trademark of the contemporary country artist.

A list of those that influenced Ely brings to light his diversified sound. He mixed into his musical universe the crisp rock and roll lyrics of Chuck Berry, the basic honky tonk grit of George Jones, the experimental courage of Buck Owens, the rockabilly of Buddy Holly, the songwriting skills of the Beatles, the country-rock sound of Gram Parsons and the Flying Burrito Brothers, the rock and roll of the Rolling Stones, the songwriting prowess of Bob Dylan, and the country renegade attitude of Merle Haggard and Waylon Jennings.

Ely is a legendary live performer. His ability to deliver his personalized, high-energy brand of country to enthusiastic audiences has enabled him to claim a special place as a performer. His versatility on stage allowed him to appear with such diverse groups as the Clash, rock legend Bruce Springsteen, Los Super Seven and James McMurtry. He has also done acoustic tours with eclectic artists Lyle Lovett, John Hiatt and Guy Clark.

He is an architect of the alternative country music stable and has never strayed from this center. He has delivered his individual sound in an honest, sincere fashion, but with a definite toughness. Along with Lyle Lovett, Steve Earle, Jimmie Dale Gilmore, k.d. lang and others, he has worked outside the Nashville mainstream.

Joe Ely's is the story of a West Texas kid who took the music he heard as a youngster to heart and choose to make a living at it. Stardom, limousines, arena rock audiences and gold albums were never important to him. The Amarillo honky tonk artist is interested in the music.

DISCOGRAPHY:

Joe Ely, MCA 2808.
Honky Tonk Masquerade, 2333.
Down on the Drag, MCA 3080.
Live Shots, MCA 5262.
Musta Notta Gotta Lotta, MCA 5183.
Hi-Res, MCA 5480.
Lord of the Highway, Hightone HT-8008.
Dig All Night, Hightone 8515.
Milkshakes & Malts, Sunstorm 05.
Live at Liberty Lunch, MCA MCAC-10095.
Love & Danger, MCA MCAD 10584.
Letter to Loredo, MCA 11222.
Twistin' in the Wind, MCA 70031.
Live at Antone's, Rounder 613171.
Streets of Sin, Rounder 613181.
Settle for Love, Hightone 8172.
Happy Song from Rattlesnake Gulch, Rock 'Em 001.
No Bad Talk or Loud Talk 1977–'81, Edsel 418.
Time for Travelin': The Best of Joe Ely, VOl. 2, Edsel 486.
The Best of Joe Ely, MCA 151.
Joe Ely/Honky Tonk Masquerade, BGO 502.
From Lubbock to Laredo: Best of Joe Ely, MCA 170244.
20th Century Masters—The Millennium Collection: The Best of Joe Ely, MCA
   Nashville 000176302.
Silver City, Rock 'Em Records 002.

Hank Williams, Jr. (1949–)
Honky Tonk Genes

Country music is a family affair. The Carters, the Cashes, and the Stonemans are just a few of the families of famous musicians that have carved a name for themselves in the industry. However, the more famous the parent, the harder it is for the next generation to achieve a solid position in the market. One individual struggled for years to create his own sound while trying to escape the shadow of his honky tonk genes. His name is Hank Williams, Jr.

Hank Williams, Jr., was born on May 26, 1949, in Shreveport, Louisiana. The son of the man many consider to be the messiah of the modern country music movement, he barely knew his father before Hank Sr. died on a snowy, fateful night in January 1953. To even consider a musical career was an overwhelming challenge in the shadow of such a legend.

But Hank's mother pushed her son in the direction of the stage in order to claim his position as the rightful heir to his father's throne. It was difficult for a young boy to understand the obstacles that faced him, however he sang Hank Sr. songs and made an immediate impression. By age eleven, he had already performed on the Grand Ole Opry stage.

When he was fourteen, his voice had matured enough in order for him to record. MGM Records signed young Hank to a contract, and he recorded "Long Gone Lonesome Blues," one of his father's songs, which became a hit and made the Top Five. Hank Jr. also performed all of the material for the biopic *Your Cheatin' Heart,* a tribute to his father, and starred in the film *A Time to Sing.*

His next hit, "Standing in the Shadows," was a self-penned tune and an effort to emerge from his famous father's legacy and establish his own name. Like every other musical artist, he wanted to be accepted on his own terms, not for what one of his noted relatives had accomplished. This goal would take a tremendous amount of effort and time.

Although a honky tonk man, he explored different styles including rock and roll and even tried performing under a different name, Rockin' Randall, to get away from the expectations pressed upon him. He forged ahead and managed to cut a few hit singles, including "All for the Love of Sunshine," which went to number one on the country chart. Despite other songs like "Luke the Drifter, Jr.," his personal life began to unravel by the time he turned eighteen.

Drug and alcohol abuse led to a suicide attempt in 1974. He decided a change of scenery was necessary and relocated to Alabama, where he met southern rockers Charlie Daniels and Toy Caldwell of the Marshall Tucker Band. He recorded *Hank Williams Jr. and Friends*, a fusion of hardcore country and rock and roll. Although it didn't produce a slew of hits, he had begun to forge his own individual sound.

It seemed that he was destined to overcome major obstacles throughout his entire life. Just when it seemed that his career was headed in the right direction and he had overcome his substance abuse problems, he fell down the side of a mountain, suffering severe injuries. Although he survived, it would take several operations to repair his fractured skull and crushed face.

It was 1977 before he was able to resume his career, and he returned with *The New South*, an Outlaw country album produced by Waylon Jennings. Despite the comeback attempt, it would take some time for Hank to regain his lost momentum. He finished the decade with a trio of Top Ten hits including a remake of Bobby Fuller's "I Fought the Law," "Family Tradition," and "Whiskey Bent and Hell Bound." It was a foreshadowing of things to come.

From 1980 to 1988, he enjoyed a strong run of Top Ten hits. It started in 1981 with three number one singles: "Texas Women," "Dixie on My Mind" and "All My Rowdy Friends (Have Settled Down)." The record *All My Rowdy Friends (Have Settled Down)* began a streak of fifteen gold and platinum albums that would earn him back-to-back Country Music Association Entertainer of the Year Awards, in 1987, and again in 1988. His music appealed to the young, rowdy, beer-drinking crowd.

During this period, his concerts were energized affairs that were like wild parties and easily enabled him to crossover to the rock and roll crowd. His wide appeal to different audiences in turn fueled his record sales. The more records he sold, the more his devoted audience wanted to see him perform live.

However, his rock and roll attitude alienated many of the hardcore country purists in Nashville. But Williams continued to pursue a different direction from mainstream country artists, using modern techniques and the available media. He shot a music video to showcase the single "All My Rowdy Friends Are Coming Over Tonight," which featured George Jones, Waylon Jennings, Willie Nelson and George Thorogood. It was named Video of the Year by the CMA in 1985. Later, ABC changed the lyrics with Williams's permission as a theme song for *Monday Night Football* telecasts.

By the end of the 1980s, Hank was losing his audience as tastes shifted to a different style. He would score a few more hits, including "There's a Tear in My Beer," an electronic collaboration with his long-dead father. By the mid–1990s, he no longer made the charts with regularity but continued to be a popular concert draw.

He remained in the spotlight as the singer of the theme song for *Monday Night Football,* winning him four Emmy Awards from 1991 to 1994. He emerged at the end of the decade with the album *Stormy,* which earned critical praise. Although his record sales didn't match those in the 1980s, they were still respectable.

In 2004, he appeared on *CMT Outlaws.* His cameo spots in the music videos of Charlie Daniels, Kid Rock, and newcomer Gretchen Wilson kept his name fresh in the public's mind. He was also a cast member of the movie *Larry the Cable Guy.* In December 2005, a good thing came to an end when he opened for the last time on the regular telecast of *Monday Night Football* and appeared in two playoff games in January 2006.

Recently he has stayed in the news for his charity donations as much as his bad boy behavior. He made a generous donation to the hurricane relief efforts in Mississippi and visited the only survivor of the Sago Mine accident in West Virginia after learning that the rescued guy was a big fan. In April 2006, he was arrested for an alleged assault on a waitress in a Memphis hotel. He was released without bond, and the trial was pending as this book went to press. He continues to record and perform.

Hank Williams is a savvy country music artist. Early in his career he tried to emulate his father but quickly realized that particular path would never gain him fame. He reshaped his image to appeal to a large cross section of the country music fan base and achieved star status. Many audiences wholeheartedly accepted his patriotic stance on many issues.

There is a growl, a grit and a guttural edge to his voice. He sings lyrics with an honesty and sincerity, which is an endearing quality. His voice is far distanced from that of his legendary father, yet on some of the latter's songs he sounds a lot like his dad. Hank Jr.'s vocal talent is best suited to belting out the Outlaw country and rock and roll inflected songs that made him famous.

Hank Jr. has a penchant for loud, electric guitars that pushes his music like a tidal wave. Although not the greatest guitarist to ever pick a country tune, he has a compact style where he says more with less. There is a simplicity to his music rooted in traditional country and blues. The starkness of his sound is one of his strongest characteristics as a singer and musician.

The greatest influence on him was Hank Sr. Although his late, famous dad had a profound effect on his music, the son used the honky tonk his father established as a guiding force throughout his career. Unlike others who never escaped the shadow of the elder Williams, Hank Jr. managed to do so by following his own path.

In turn, Hank Jr. has influenced a number of artists. A partial list includes Cody McCarver, Luke Stricklin, Charlie Allen, Cowboy Buddha, Hank Williams III, Confederate Railroad, Kid Rock, Travis Tritt, and the Kentucky Headhunters. In truth, he has paved the way for all the offspring of famous country musicians to make it on their own. Although he paid some hard fought, discouraging dues, his later success proved it worthwhile.

He has given the world an interesting catalog of music to enjoy. A partial list includes "Standing in the Shadows," "All for the Love of Sunshine," "Luke the Drifter, Jr.," "Family Tradition," "Whiskey Bent and Hell Bound," "Texas Women," "Dixie on My Mind," "All My Rowdy Friends (Have Settled Down)," "All My Rowdy Friends Are Coming Over Tonight," and "There's a Tear in My Beer." His success as a creative and prolific writer has often been compared to that of his famous father, who penned a large number of classic tunes.

Once Hank Williams, Jr. escaped his father's shadow he created harddriving country with a rock and roll, bluesy edge. His ability to retool himself as a southern rocker and Outlaw appealed to a large portion of the country music sect. His style always contained a raw edge to it, but his lyrics reflected an American patriotic value that endeared him to audiences. Like all others outside the mainstream he created music on his own terms.

The Hank Williams, Jr., story is the tale of a young boy who grew up in the shadow of his famous father and yearned to escape from it. He was able to create his own distinct career through perseverance, hard work, and a strong individualism. He became a star but never lost his honky tonk genes.

DISCOGRAPHY:

Songs of Hank Williams, MGM SE-4213.
Sing Great Country Favorites, MGM SE 4251.
The Era of Hank Williams, Crown 5327.
Your Cheatin' Heart: Hank Williams' Life Story, MCA-1438.
Ballads of the Hills and Plains, MGM SE-4336.
Blues My Name, MGM SE-4344.
Country Shadows, MGM SE-4391.
My Own Way, MGM SE-4428.
My Songs, MGM SE-4527.
Time to Sing, MGM SE-4540.
Live at Cobo Hall, Detroit, MGM SE-4644.
Luke the Drifter, Jr., Polydor 831 576.
Luke the Drifter, Jr., Vol. 2, , MGM SE 4632.
Songs My Father Left Me, MGM SE-4621.
All for the Love of Sunshine, MGM SE-4750.
Great Hits of Johnny Cash, MGM SE-4675.
Hank Williams, Jr., MGM 119.
Luke the Drifter, Jr., Vol. 3, MGM SE-4673.
Removing the Shadow, MGM SE-4721.
Sunday Morning, MGM 4657.
11 Roses, PolyGram 33070.
I've Got a Right To Cry/They All Used to Belong to Me, MGM 4774.
Sweet Dreams, MGM SE 4798.
Finders Are Keepers, Curb 4-22945.
Send Me Some Lovin' and Whole Lotta Loving, MGM 4857.
After You/Pride's Not Hard to Swallow, MGM 4862.
Just Pickin', No Singin' MGM SE 4906.
Living Proof, MGM 4971.
The Last Love Song, MGM 4936.
Bocephus, MGM 4988.
Insight into Hank Williams, MGM M3HB 4975.
Hank Williams, Jr., & Friends, MCA Special Products Polydor 831 575.
Hank Williams, Jr., & Friends, MGM 5009.
One Night Stands, Warner Bros. 538.
The New South, Warner Bros. 539.
Whiskey Bent and Hell Bound, Elektra 6E-237.
Habits Old and New, Warner Bros. 2-278.
Rowdy, Warner Bros. 2-330.

The Pressure Is On, Warner Bros. 2-535.
High Notes, Warner Bros. E2-60100.
Man of Steel, Warner Bros. 2-23924.
Strong Stuff, Elektra 60223.
Major Moves, Warner Bros. 25088.
Five-O, Warner Bros. 25267-1.
Montana Cafe, Warner Bros. 1-25412.
Born to Boogie, Warner Bros. 2-25593.
Doctor's Song, Curb 4-28227.
Hank Live, Warner Bros. 25538.
Standing in the Shadows, Polydor 835132-1.
Wild Streak, Warner Bros. 25725.
Lone Wolf, Warner Bros. 26090.
Luke the Drifter, Jr., Vol. 2, Polygram 8311576.
Pure Hank, Warner Bros. 2-26536.
Maverick, Warners Bros. 26806.
Those Tear Jerking Songs, Spin 839147.
Out of Left Field, Warner Bros. 45225.
I'm Walkin', Pair 1164.
Tribute to My Father, Curb 77640.
It's All Over but the Crying, PolyGram 847 981.
New South, Vol. 2, Curb 77722.
Hog Wild, Curb 015.
A.K.A. Wham Bam Sam, Curb 77813.
Three Generations of Hank, Curb 77868.
Stormy, Curb 77953.
I'm One of You, Curb 78830.
Early in the Morning & Late at Night, Curb 4-27722.
What You Don't Know (Won't Hurt You), Curb 4-22945.
You Brought Me Down to Earth, Curb 4-27584.
The Best of Hank Williams, Jr., MGM SE-4513.
Hank Williams, Jr., Greatest Hits, MGM SE-4656.
Hank Williams, Jr., Greatest Hits, Vol. 2, MGM 4822.
Living Proof: The MGM Recordings 1963–1975, Mercury 517320.
14 Greatest Hits, Polydor 825091-1.
Family Tradition, Curb 77723.
Hank Williams, Jr.'s Greatest Hits, Warner Brothers 2-60193.
Greatest Hits, Vol. 2, Warner Bros. 25238.
The Early Years (1976–1978), Curb 25514.
Greatest Hits, Vol. 3, Warner Bros. 25834.
America (The Way I See It), Curb 77922.
Family Tradition/Whiskey Bent and Hell Bound, Warner Bros. 25141.
Greatest Hits, Vol. 1, PolyGram 811903.
The Best of Hank Williams, Jr., Curb D2-77418.
The Bocephus Box, Capricorn 45104.
The Best of Hank Williams, Jr., Vol. 1: Roots and Branches, Mercury 849575-2.
Classic Songs, Capitol 77611.
Greatest Hits, Vol. 1, Curb 77638.
Country Classics, Special Music 5030.

Sensational Country Hits, Special Music 5031.
Greatest Hits, Vol. 2, Curb D2-776339.
Original Classics Collection, Vol. 1. One Night Stands, Curb 77721.
American Legends: The Best of the Early Years, Polygram Special Markets 520315.
Gospel Favorites, Rebound 520306.
20 Hits Special Collection, Vol. 1, Curb 7770.
Hits, Polygram 534667.
Hank Williams, Jr., Sings Hank Williams, Sr., Rhino 75284.
Early Years, Vol. 1, Curb 77916.
Early Years, Vol. 2, Curb 77809.
The Complete Hank Williams Jr., Curb 77944.
The Bocephus Box, Curb 77940.
Essential, Polygram International 544282.
The Almeria Club Recordings, Curb 78725.
World of Hank Williams Jr., Universal International 552021.
20th Century Masters — The Millennium Collection: The Best of Hank Williams,
    Jr., Mercury 000173002.
That's How They Do It in Dixie: The Essential Collection, Curb 78881.
Back to Back: Gospel Favorites, Polymedia 520306.
Best of the Early Years, Polymedia 520315.
Classic Songs, Vol. 2, Curb 78854.
The Very Best of Hank Williams, Jr., Polydor 823202.

Steve Earle (1955–)

Alternative Troubadour

From Jimmie Rodgers to Hank Williams, Sr., to Patsy Cline, country has attracted its fair share of rebels throughout its long, colorful history. One of the main ingredients the three aforementioned artists shared was a desire to make music on their own terms. Another of these controversial musicians emerged in the late 1980s and went about creating his sound, becoming an alternative troubadour. His name was Steve Earle.

Steve Earle was born on January 17, 1955, in Fort Monroe, Virginia, but raised in San Antonio, Texas. He received his first guitar at eight and just a few short years later he had honed his skills enough to win a talent contest in school. A troubled youth with an uneasy relationship towards authority, he left the education system prior to high school. At sixteen, he traveled the state with his uncle Nick Fain and eventually settled down in Houston. It was here he met his first wife, as well as his most important musical contact in Townes Van Zandt.

Earle supported himself with odd jobs and then decided to move to

Nashville. He worked during the day and at night honed his songwriting skills and played bass in Guy Clark's backing band. Earle made his recording debut on Clark's 1975 album, *Old No. 1.* He worked around Music City in various venues and eventually found employment as a staff writer for Sunbury Dunar publishers.

Although his career in Nashville held much promise, he returned to Texas. It was in the Lone Star State that he assembled his band, the Dukes, and started to play local clubs. A restless musician, he moved back to Nashville and married a second time, but the union was short-lived. He took a third wife soon after who bore his first child. The third marriage seemed to be the magic potion because he straightened out enough to concentrate harder on his stagnant music career.

He honed his songwriting skills and was hired by publishers in Nashville. Different artists recorded his songs: Johnny Lee had a Top Twenty hit with "When You Fall in Love," Carl Perkins recorded "Mustang Wine" and Zella Lehr waxed a couple of Earle's tunes. The firm also owned an independent label, LSI, and signed him to a record contract. Finally, he had a chance to wax his own material.

In 1982, the EP *Pink & Black* was released to good reviews, and it featured a solid backup from the established version of the Dukes. Eventually, Epic Records stepped in with a recording contract and signed him. Although a major boost to his career at the time, the relationship between the record company and Earle turned sour quickly. The end result was one single, "Nothin' But You," and a batch of songs that sold poorly.

The controversy continued as both Epic and his publishers dropped him. Earle fired his manager but connected with a producer at MCA Records who signed Earle to the label. The move paid off dividends as the debut album, *Guitar Town*, became a solid hit. The mixture of country twang with a rock and roll edge launched him as a promising new artist. The title track became a Top Ten single, and "Goodbye's All We've Got Left" reached the Top Ten a few months later.

In an act of revenge, Epic Records released *Early Tracks* to gain some mileage out of Earle's newfound status. His second effort for MCA, *Exit O*, featured a Dukes lineup that consisted of Bucky Baxter on steel guitar, vocals; Reno Kling on bass guitar; Mike McAdam on six and twelve string electric guitar, vocals; Ken Moore on organ, synthesizer and vocals; and Harry Stinson on drums and vocals. There were also guest musicians including John Jarvis on piano, Emory Gordy, Jr., on mandolin, Richard Bennett on acoustic, electric guitar and bass, and K. Neaux Boudlin on accordion.

While his career gained momentum, his personal life was a mess. He married a fourth and a fifth time, and sank deeper into substance abuse. But it didn't stop him from releasing his third album, *Copperhead Road*, more of a rock-oriented album than country. The effort made it into the Top Ten, and it included a duet with the Irish punk group the Pogues, which signaled Earle's increasing popularity in Europe, where he frequently toured.

When the Uni label, a division of MCA Records, went bankrupt, it spelled the end of *Copperhead Road's* growing popularity just before the record reached gold status. Earle's drug addictions and live-on-the-edge style got him in trouble at a concert in Dallas where he assaulted a security guard. The various women in his life—past and present—were also giving him a hard enough time that he called his fifth album *The Hard Way*. It spawned one minor hit, "The Other Kind," and was totally ignored by the country market.

The first few years of the 1990s saw him hit rock bottom. The commercial failure of *The Hard Way* gave MCA fuel to release him but not before issuing a live album, *Shut Up and Die Like an Aviator*, in 1991. He fell off the edge again when he was arrested for heroin possession and served time in a rehab center.

He emerged in 1994 from the rehab center a new man. He signed to the Winter Harvest label and released an acoustic collection, *Train a Comin'*. It received favorable reviews and earned Earle a new contract with Warner Bros. Records. In a business where many artists are lucky to get one break, somehow the artist with a penchant for trouble possessed enough promise and charisma to acquire another opportunity when most observers had written him off.

In 1996, *I Feel Alright* was released, and it also garnered strong reviews. The theme throughout the entire work focused on his recent battle with drug abuse and brief stay in prison. "Hard Core Troubadour," "Hurtin' Me, Hurtin' You," "The Unrepentant," and "South Nashville Blues" were the highlights of the album. More importantly, he won back the country audience that he had alienated in the past few years.

In 1999, he appeared with *The Mountain,* a bluegrass effort recorded with the Del McCoury Band. Earle wrote all fourteen tracks on the album, including "Carrie Brown," "Connemara Breakdown," "Pilgrim," and the "Graveyard Shift," among others. Emmylou Harris and Iris DeMent (vocals), Jerry Douglas and Gene Wooten (Dobro), Sam Bush (mandolin) and Stuart Duncan (fiddle) guested on the album. The lineup was augmented by Marty Stuart, Gillian Welch and John Hartford.

In 2000, *Transcendental Blues* was released and continued the comeback that had started with *I Feel Alright*. There were rocking numbers ("Everyone's in Love with You" and "All My Life"), ballads ("The Boy Who Never Cried" and "Lonelier Than This"), and dance numbers ("The Galway Girl" and "Until the Day I Die"). The diversity of the music the album continued underlined Earle's stance and opposition to the glossy products coming out of Nashville.

The next album release, *Jerusalem,* contained the song "John Walker's Blues," a tribute to John Walker Lindh, the young American who had been discovered fighting for the despised Taliban. Once again, Earle became a controversial figure and defended his position on the many television and radio shows he appeared on. The tour for *Jerusalem* was documented in a concert film and live album entitled *Just an American Boy.*

His political and musical viewpoints continued to be mixed on his next album, *The Revolution Starts ... Now,* a biting commentary on the war in Iraq and the president's failings. He didn't seem bothered to be pegged as a political hot potato; in fact he reveled in the controversy.

In 2007, he released *Washington Square Serenade.* The record dealt with his new surroundings, New York City, in an alternative country format. Some of the highlights included "Tennessee Blues," "Down Here Below," "Come Home to Me," and "Way Down in the Hole." It even features a duet with his seventh wife, the singer-songwriter Allison Moorer, "Days Aren't Long Enough." He continues to record and perform.

Steve Earle is a country music rebel. In many circles he is not even considered country, but rather a roots rocker. From the very beginning, he made it clear that he was going to produce music on his own terms and was willing to suffer the consequences of such a hard-line stance. Through it all, he has managed to retain a loyal following, has released some interesting if controversial albums, and, most importantly, survived.

Earle has a double-edged voice. His dual ability has enabled him to record songs that have one foot in country music and the other in rock. His delivery hints at the many paths that he is capable of taking a song down. Because of his explosive vocal gifts he has the ability to record in any genre.

To understand any artist one must look at the various influences that have shaped their overall sound. The country portion of Earle's artistic fuel includes Hank Williams, Sr., and Waylon Jennings. The former was a superstar who sparked the modern era, while the latter was one of the main proponents of the Outlaw movement. The Flying Burrito Brothers are another act that had an impact on Earle. On the rock side, The Rolling Stones and Bob Dylan had the strongest effect on his music.

Despite his rollercoaster career, Earle has influenced a number of artists, including Michael Carpenter, Eddie Spaghetti, the Thompson Brothers, Kasey Chambers, Mary Gauthier, Rocky Votoloato, Tim Barry, the Pierces, Audrey Auld, Pie Eyed Pete and the Pogues. His musical abilities, his bad boy image, his adamant stance on many controversial issues are all part of the package that attracts others.

Earle has managed to give the world a number of interesting songs. A partial list includes "Guitar Town," "Copperhead Road," "The Devil's Right Hand," "Hillbilly Highway," "Six Days on the Road," "Honey Don't," "Hard

Core Troubadour," "Goodbye's All We Got Left," "Rich Man's War," "This Dirty Little Town," and "Snake Oil," to name a few. No matter what style the tune is recorded in, he has put his stamp on every cut making it his own.

Steve Earle has been classified as a New Traditionalist, a roots rocker, a country rocker, and countless other names. To categorize the man's music is to pigeonhole his efforts, which is an unfair assessment of his catalog. The best label for his body of work is alternative.

Like his music, his life outside the business has been controversial. He has championed the anti-death penalty cause and written songs to support his point of view, including "Billy Austin," "Over Yonder (Johnathan's Song)," and "Ellis Unit One," featured in the movie *Dead Man Walking.* He has also been a regular performer in the Concerts for a Landmine Free World as well as the Vietnam Veterans of America Foundation.

He has collaborated with Jason Ringenberg on the song "A Bible & a Gun." He worked with the Supersuckers on their song "Creepy Jackalope Eye." He has recorded duets with Lucinda Williams, Chris Hillman for a Gram Parsons tribute album, Siobhan Maher Kennedy, Emmylou Harris, Stacey Earle, and Sheryl Crow.

The Steve Earle story is that of a restless artist who has put together a spotty career, but the music he made was on his own terms. He has not shied away from stating his opinion or stepped aside from a controversial issue. In fact, he has embraced the difficult way his entire career and in the process became an alternative troubadour.

DISCOGRAPHY:

Guitar Town, MCA MCAC-5713.
Exit O, MCA 3379.
Copperhead Road, MCA 19213.
The Hard Way, MCA 6430.
Shut Up and Die Like an Aviator, MCA 10315.
BBC Radio 1 Live in Concert, ROIR 20.
Train a Comin', Warner Bros. 45355.
I Feel Alright, MCA 46201.
El Corazon, Warner Bros. 46789.
The Mountain, E-Squared 51064.
Transcendental Blues, Artemis 51044.
Together at the Bluebird Cafe, American Originals 4006.
Jerusalem, Artemis 751147.
Just an American Boy, Artemis 51256.
The Revolution Starts ... Now, E-Squared 51565.
Live From Austin, TX, New West 6064.
Live at Montreux 2005, Eagle 20029.
Early Tracks, Koch, 7903.
This Highway's Mine, Audio Book and Music 4178.

The Essential Steve Earle, MCA 10749.

Angry Young Man, Nectar Masters 532.

Fearless Heart, Universal Special Products 20912.

Ain't Ever Satisfied: The Steve Earle Collection, Hip-O 40006.

The Very Best of Steve Earle: Angry Young Man, Telstar Television 532.

The Devil's Right Hand: An Introduction to Steve Earle, Universal International 112333.

Sidetracks, Artemis 751128.

The Collection, Spectrum Music 544768.

20th Century Masters — The Millennium Collection: The Best of Steve Earle, MCA 113155.

Chronicles, MCA Nashville 5015.

The Definitive Collection 1983–1997, Hip-O 54214.

Dwight Yoakam (1956–)

Bakersfield Honky Tonk

The contemporary country artist has more than eighty years of tradition to draw upon — an advantage that the pioneers certainly never enjoyed. This luxury has afforded the new generation an opportunity to experiment with the fundamental sounds of honky tonk, bluegrass, western swing, country-pop, the Bakersfield sound and even old-timey. One musician took the simple strains of past styles and forged a proper identity with his Bakersfield honky tonk sound. His name was Dwight Yoakam.

Dwight Yoakam was born on October 23, 1956, in Pikeville, Kentucky. He learned how to play guitar at the age of six while listening to the traditional tunes of Hank Williams, Sr., Johnny Cash and Buck Owens — all major influences on his developing sound. He briefly attended Ohio State University, but dropped out to follow his heart and become a successful country recording artist.

Yoakam arrived in Nashville during the pop-oriented Urban Cowboy movement and quickly discovered there was no room for his Bakersfield honky tonk. He connected with guitarist Pete Anderson, who had grown up listening to the same artists as Yoakam and therefore shared a similar taste. After a few discouraging months in Music City U.S.A., the pair moved to Los Angeles.

They thrived in the City of Angels, where their music was accepted on a much larger scale than back in Nashville. Yoakam and Anderson played country night clubs, as well as nightclubs that were usually reserved for punk and post-punk bands like the Dead Kennedys, the Blasters, X, Los Lobos, and the Butthole Surfers. Yoakam and his stripped-down honky tonk style appealed to the cowpunks, the supportive fan base that turned out at his performances.

In 1984, his first recorded material, an EP titled *A Town South of Bakersfield,* was a disc that alternative stations played a lot. The constant airplay enabled him to sign a record deal with Reprise Records. The first full-length effort, released in 1986, was *Guitars, Cadillacs, Etc., Etc.,* which received rave reviews from both the rock and country camps. It became a staple of college radio stations across the nation, and the cover version of Johnny Horton's "Honky Tonk Man" was a Top Five country single. As well, "Guitars, Cadillacs" was another single that pushed the album into platinum territory.

In 1987, his sophomore effort, *Hillbilly Deluxe,* spawned four Top Ten hits: "Little Sister," "Little Ways," "Please, Please Baby," and "Always Late with Your Kisses." It proved that he wasn't some flash in the pan but a rising star with staying power. His mixture of traditional honky tonk and Bakersfield sound would influence a number of artists.

His third album, *Buenas Noches from a Lonely Room,* was a dedication to his country music hero Buck Owens. The album, another successful effort, included the single "Streets of Bakersfield," Yoakam's first number one, which featured a guest vocal appearance from Owens. The tune "I Sang Dixie" also topped the charts, and "I Got You" reached the Top Five.

Next a greatest hits album, *Just Lookin' for a Hit,* featured the single "Long White Cadillac," which made the Top Five. Although it was a solid collection, it fared poorer than his previous recordings. However, Yoakam remained a top live attraction with his solid material and rock and roll performances.

In 1990, he released *If There Was a Way.* The highlights included "Turn It On, Turn It Up, Turn Me Loose," "You're the One," "Nothing's Changed Here," "It Only Hurts When I Cry," "The Heart That You Own," and "Send a Message to My Heart," a duet with Patty Loveless. The CD eventually went platinum and returned him to previous levels.

Yoakam didn't release any new material for two years, and his next effort was *Dwight Live,* which captured him on stage. The disc was a treat for audiences who had missed out on seeing the singer live. The sale of his albums helped him sell concert tickets and by this time he toured on a regular basis to an enlarged fan base that just couldn't get enough of his Bakersfield honky tonk sound.

In 1993, *This Time* returned him to the top of the charts with three Top Five singles: "Ain't That Lonely Yet," "A Thousand Miles from Nowhere," and "Fast as You." The album went platinum. For the next two years he concentrated on the performance side of his career. While not on tour, he worked on the material that would be found on his sixth studio effort.

In 1995, *Gone* went gold but didn't produce any major hits. However, some of the more interesting songs included "Nothing," "Gone (That'll Be Me)," "Sorry You Asked?" and "Heart of Stone." At this point, he was one of the more visible country artists, thanks to his various film roles including a supporting role in the Oscar-winning movie *Slingblade*.

He forged on and, in 1997, he appeared with *Under the Covers,* a collection of songs that had been hits for other artists in rock and country. It received mixed reviews and did very little for his stagnant career. The songs "Claudette" and "Baby Don't Go," a duet with Sheryl Crow, were the highlights of a weak effort. During this period country-pop ruled the airwaves, and Yoakam was left behind.

He rebounded with *A Long Way Home*. It was a triumphant return to his hard country roots and won back the favor of fans and critics alike. It contained the Top Twenty hit "Things Change" and "These Arms." His audience expected Yoakam to deliver what he was best known for: Bakersfield honky tonk. Anything outside the box was usually ignored.

The compilation *Last Chance for a Thousand Years: Greatest Hits* comprised songs from the '90s and contained his biggest hit single of the past six years, a reworking of glam rock band Queen's "Crazy Little Thing Called Love." The song was used in a GAP clothing commercial and enabled him to reach the lower ranks of the pop charts.

In 2000, he released *dwightyoakamacoustic.net*, a stripped down, all-acoustic set of his catalog that fans truly embraced. The intimacy allowed the lone artist to connect directly with the audience and was a priceless experience. He was able to give every song a special treatment that revealed new dimensions in the music.

That same year he released the more traditional studio album, *Tomorrow Sounds Today*. It was a cohesive work that featured some of guitarist Pete Anderson's best work in years. The highlight of the album was "Place to Cry," which reinstated him as one of the prime exponents of the honky tonk revivalist movement. It even featured a duet with Buck Owens and a cover version of Cheap Trick's "I Want You to Want Me."

In 2003, *Population Me* was released and featured a number of solid singles including "Late, Great Golden State," "An Exception to the Rule," and "I'd Avoid Me Too." It featured a combination of some of his best songwriting and musical muscle in some time, winning over a new group of fans while retaining his long time supporters.

A year later, *Dwight's Used Records* appeared and consisted of an anthology of duets with Deanna Carter, Heather Myles, Ralph Stanley and the Nitty Gritty Dirt Band. Along with his guests, he tackled songs from the catalogs of Johnny Cash, Webb Pierce, John Prine ("Paradise"), and Merle Haggard ("Holding Things Together"). Yoakam also served as producer.

In 2005, a CD of new material, *Blame the Vain,* appeared. It contained the songs "Intentional Heartache," the title track, and "I Wanna Love Again." That same year another concert set, *Live from Austin, TX,* was released. He continues to record and perform.

Dwight Yoakam is an alternative country star. He has consistently placed songs at the top of the charts and has enjoyed a prolific recording career. His special brand of Bakersfield honky tonk was one of the most copied styles in the last fifteen years. He has also made a serious impact in the movies playing memorable characters, usually psychotic killers.

He has a unique style that is part rock and roll, honky tonk, and Bakersfield sound. There is a twang in his voice and guitar playing that links him to his heroes George Jones and Merle Haggard. Although he has recorded some of their songs, he has never tried to emulate them; instead he has borrowed traits from their vast talent pools to mesh with his own abilities.

Elvis Presley, George Jones, Johnny Horton, Merle Haggard and Lefty Frizzell were all important influences. But it was Buck Owens and his exciting Bakersfield style that had the most serious impact on Yoakam's career. The elder statesman, with his group the Buckaroos, defied Nashville standards to include drums, loud electric guitars and bass guitars in a groundbreaking sound. He was a rebel who made country music on his own terms and passed the secret down to his young admirer.

In turn, Yoakam has influenced a number of artists including the Earps, Shurman, the Ghost Rockets, the Souvenirs, Thompson Brothers, and Eddie Spaghetti, among others. But, as one of the artists who is credited with returning country back to its roots, he had an impact on a number of musicians who desired to play honky tonk as a distinct individual style.

He has made contributions in different facets of the entertainment world. He appeared in the film *Red Rock West* and provided the musical score for it. In 1994, he had a large role on the television show *Roswell.* He starred as a clown in the movie *Painted Hero.* But his best and strongest performance was in the movie *Slingblade,* where he played an abusive drunk. The movie would go on to win the Oscar for Best Picture. He later portrayed another bad guy in *The Newton Boys.* His role as a detective in *The Minus Man* was a solid performance. Another of his great roles was as a psychotic killer in the film *The Panic Room,* which starred Jodie Foster. He also wrote, directed, scored and starred in *South of Heaven, West of Hell.* He later acted the part of an assassin in the action thriller *Crank.*

He has delivered an exciting body of work. A partial list includes "Honky Tonk Man," "Guitars, Cadillacs, Etc, Etc," "It Won't Hurt," "Little Sister," "Little Ways," "Please, Please Baby," "The Streets of Bakersfield," "I Got You," "Long White Cadillac," "You're the One," "It Only Hurts When I Cry," "Ain't That Lonely Yet," "Fast as You," "Pocket of a Clown," "Sorry You Asked,"

"Heart of Stone," "Sitting Pretty," and "Blame the Vain." His catalog is a varied and interesting one featuring his abilities as songwriter, musician, cover artist and singer.

    The Dwight Yoakam story is that of a multi-talented artist who has made many contributions to country music. He has also made a profound impact as an actor, displaying a different dimension to his talent. But the Kentucky native will forever be known as the man who delighted many with his honky tonk Bakersfield sound.

DISCOGRAPHY:

Guitars, Cadillacs, Etc; Etc; Reprise 25372.
Hillbilly Deluxe, Reprise 2 — 25567.
Buenas Noches from a Lonely Room, Reprise 25749.
If There Was a Way, Reprise 2-26344.
This Time, Reprise 45241.
Dwight Live, Reprise 45907.
Gone, Reprise 46051.
Under the Covers, Reprise 46690.
Come on Christmas, Warner Bros. 46683.
A Long Way Home, Reprise 46918.
La Croix d'Amour, WEA International 45136.
dwightyoakamacoustic.net, Reprise 47714.
Tomorrow's Sounds Today, Warner Bros. 47827.
South of Heaven, West of Hell, Warner Bros. 48012.
Population Me, Audium 8176.
Blame the Vain, New West 6075.
Live from Austin, TX, New West 6082.
Just Lookin' for a Hit, Reprise 25989.
Last Chance for a Thousand Years, Greatest Hits from the 90s, Reprise 47389.
Reprise Please Baby: The Warner Bros. Years, Rhino 76100.
In Other's Words, Reprise 48342.
Dwight's Used Records, Koch 9805.
The Very Best of Dwight Yoakam, Rhino 78964.
The Very Best of Dwight Yoakam [Bonus Track], WEA International 787964.
The Essentials, WEA International 62489.
Country Classics, Flashback 73357.
Platinum Collection, WEA Warner 8122740472.
Dwight Yoakam [DVA], Legacy Entertainment 5021.

Lyle Lovett (1957–)

Eclectic Texan

In the modern era of country music many different avenues were explored. The simple, traditional style was welded with rock, pop, folk, blues, punk, and even classical in an effort to create crossover success. Although many of these experimenters were shunned by purists because they played outside the mainstream, the artists who dared to create something new boasted a dedicated audience. One of these individuals gave the alternative set a huge boost with his undeniable talent and mixed sound that earned him the title: the eclectic Texan. His name is Lyle Lovett.

Lyle Lovett was born on November 1, 1957, in Klein, Texas, a small town that was named for his Bavarian grandfather. Although Lyle would someday make a serious impact, he didn't embark on a musical career until he was in university at Texas A&M, where he began to write songs. Eventually he would perform these originals as well as covers at local folk festivals and clubs. He traveled to Europe, where he continued to hone his skills as a songwriter and singer.

He returned to the United States in the early 1980s with a definite plan: he wanted to be a successful recording artist. He played clubs throughout Texas that gained a role in the television-movie *Bill: On His Own*, which starred Mickey Rooney. Another break occured when Nanci Griffith recorded his song "If I Were the Woman You Wanted," which appeared on her *Once in a Very Blue Moon* album. The two collaborated some more as he guested on several of her albums including the 1985 release, *Last of the True Believers*.

A third break came his way when Guy Clark heard one of Lovett's demo tapes and sent it off to MCA Records. A year later, the company offered a recording contract that would launch the career of a very individual artist. Meanwhile, Lovett appeared in *Fast Folk Magazine*, vol. 2, no.8.

In 1986, his self-titled album was released and drew raves from the critics. It yielded five singles: "Farther Down the Line," the Top Ten hit "Cowboy Man," "God Will," "Why I Don't Know," and "Give Back My Heart," with all of them placing in the country Top Forty charts. The album was the blueprint of his musical style in that Lovett's sound was rooted in country, but it was not the only style he was capable of exploring.

His sophomore album, *Pontiac*, was released in 1987 and demonstrated his eclectic and creative abilities. He incorporated jazz, folk, and pop into a country framework that pushed the music outside mainstream boundaries. With his second album, he appealed to pop and rock audiences, enhancing his reputation; however, this may have come at the expense of his country following. The album reached gold status, but yielded only two singles to make the top of the pop charts, "She's No Lady" and "I Loved You Yesterday," while none hit the country charts.

He toured *Pontiac* with a very different type of backing group that was dubbed "His Large Band." It consisted of guitarists, a cellist, a pianist, horn players, and a gospel-trained back-up singer, Francine Reed. It was definitely a strange outfit to play country music, but his concerts were well-attended events because they offered something for everyone.

His third album, *Lyle Lovett and His Large Band,* once again featured a mixture of jazz, pop and rock influences to go along with his country base. It was a critical and commercial success, but featured only one top single "I Married Her Just Because She Looks Like You," which was a minor hit. He also cut an interesting version of Tammy Wynette's "Stand by Your Man."

He relocated to California and pursued different interests. He produced Walter Hyatt's *King Tears* album, sang on Leo Kottke's *Great Big Boy* and cut "Friend of the Devil," which was included in the Grateful Dead tribute album *Dedicated.* He also made his acting debut in the movie *The Player.* In 1992, he finally released his fourth album of new material, *Joshua Judges Ruth.* It was a gospel and R&B record that the pop fans embraced, but one that the country crowd totally ignored.

In 1993, he was catapulted to near superstar status with his marriage to actress Julia Roberts. Suddenly, the retiring Lovett, who was just happy making his music, was thrust into the spotlight and became fodder for the gossip magazines. He appeared in another Robert Altman film, *Short Cuts,* and released *I Love Everybody*, a collection of early material that did very little to enhance his career.

In 1995, the fairy tale marriage ended in divorce, and Lovett returned to his country roots with *The Road to Ensenada,* which won back his lost country fans. It was a strong effort that did well in pop circles, but it performed extremely well on the country charts. Highlights included "Private Conversation," "Who Loves You Better," "It Ought to Be Easier," "I Can't Love You Anymore," and "Christmas Morning." The styles ranged from western sing to country-rock, folk and honky tonk.

With the divorce to Roberts well behind him, he continued to build on his strong musical career. In 1998, he released *Step Inside This House,* a tribute to his favorite songwriters, including Townes Van Zandt, Guy Clark, Willis Alan Ramsey, Walter Hyatt, Michael Martin Murphey, Robert Earl Keen, Eric Taylor, Vince Bell, Craig Calvert, David Rodriguez, and Steve Fromholz. The progressive Texas country album was a two-disc set and another winner. Song highlights included "Lungs," "Teach Me About Love,"

"West Texas Highway," "Bears," "Rollin' By," and "Ballad of the Snow Leopard and the Tanqueray Cowboy."

In 1999, *Live in Texas* captured him in front of an audience. It was well received because for the first time the dual sides of his musical personality were revealed: the talented songwriter and exceptional performer. It also featured his vast and diverse catalog, with songs like "Penguins," "Nobody Knows Me," "Wild Women Don't Get the Blues," "Church," and "Closing Time."

He remained a very different artist — one who was well-known, yet someone that was an acquired taste. His talent was a well hidden secret as he often performed behind the scenes on projects like the mostly instrumental soundtrack for the Robert Altman film *Dr. T. & the Women*. His diverse talent allowed him to participate and excel in a variety of mediums.

In 2003, *My Baby Don't Tolerate*, his first effort of new material in seven years, was released. It was a strong set of songs that included "Cute as a Bug," "Nothing but a Good Ride," "San Antonio Girl," and "The Truck Song." Most importantly, it was a straightforward country album that displayed his talents as songwriter and singer.

In 2007, Lovett revisited familiar territory with his new release, *It's Not Big It's Large*. The eclectic collection of songs included "Here I Am," "South Texas Girl," "Up in Indiana," and "This Traveling Around," running the spectrum from progressive country to gospel to loose jazz and blues. He continues to record and perform.

Lyle Lovett is a country music chameleon. Throughout his career he has demonstrated a passion for a variety of styles and a talent to excel in each one. Although country music fans are most delighted when he writes and sings in a country vein, it is impossible to confine someone with his immense abilities.

He has an interesting voice that only hints at his Texas roots. More importantly, it has the range to project his eclectic musical tastes. In many ways, his vocal delivery is deceiving because it is in sharp contrast to his personal appearance. To many he is known for his physical features more so than his incredible talent.

He is an excellent songwriter. His subtle, dry humor, incredible range and vivid imagination are the cornerstones of his writing ability. The wide appeal of his material, the subject matter, the delicate, crisp lyrics are all part of the package. Although he is well-known as a performer, his true strength is in his prowess as a tunesmith. Of his many gifts, the ability to pen a contemporary tune no matter the style is Lovett's greatest attribute as an artist.

He has given the world a number of great recordings. A partial list includes "Farther Down the Line," "Cowboy Man," "God Will," "Why I Don't Know," "Give Back My Heart," "She's No Lady," "I Loved You Yesterday," "I Married Her Just Because She Looks Like You," "Private Conversation," "Who Loves You Better," "It Ought to Be Easier," "I Can't Love You Anymore," "Christmas Morning," "Lungs," "Teach Me About Love," "West Texas Highway," "Bears," "Rollin' By," "Ballad of the Snow Leopard and the Tanqueray Cowboy," "Penguins," "Nobody Knows Me," "Wild Women Don't Get the Blues," "Church," "Closing Time," "Cute as a Bug," "Nothing but a Good Ride," "San Antonio Girl," and "The Truck Song." Whether singing a self-penned tune or a cover, he has injected each one with his special talent.

Lovett's development can be traced to the many different singer-songwriters who influenced him. A partial list includes Townes Van Zandt, Jerry Jeff Walker, Jesse Winchester, Randy Newman, Bob Dylan, Guy Clark and James Taylor. All are highly respected songwriters who forged strong careers because of their ability to pen deep, introspective, yet catchy tunes.

In turn, Lovett has influenced a small group of immediate followers including Freedy Johnston, Jann Arden, the Rivermen, Our Religion, and J Band. But anyone writing a country song — especially the alternative artists such as Jimmie Dale Gilmore, Steve Earle, Joe Ely and Dwight Yoakam — admired Lyle's talent. However, few can boast his deft touch or understanding of subtleties.

Lovett is one of many Lone Star State singers who have made an important impact on the modern country music movement. Others include Tanya Tucker, Ronnie Dunn, Natalie Maines, George Strait, Jimmie Dale Gilmore, Joe Ely, and Miranda Lambert. Of all the aforementioned artists, Lyle is perhaps the most Texan because he has often injected that genuine Texas feel in many of his songs. He is another of the many great musicians that can claim an authentic Texas birth certificate.

He has won four Grammy Awards. In 1996, he earned one for Best Country Album for *The Road to Ensenada*; in 1994, Best Country Duo/Group with Vocal for "Blues For Dixie," with Asleep at the Wheel; Best Pop Vocal Collaboration for "Funny How Time Slips Away," with Al Green; and, in 1989, Best Country Male Vocal for *Lyle Lovett and His Large Band*.

The Lyle Lovett story is that of a modern country figure with an abundance of talent. His eclectic tastes have made him one of the most interesting and successful alternative artists. Despite the diversity of his music there is no denying the eclectic Texan's important and many contributions to the genre.

DISCOGRAPHY:

Lyle Lovett, Curb MCA 11964.
Pontiac, Curb 42028.
Lyle Lovett and His Large Band, Curb 42263.
Joshua Judges Ruth, Curb 10475.

I Love Everybody, Curb 10808.
The Road to Ensenada, Curb 11409.
Step Inside This House, MCA 11831.
Live in Texas, MCA 11964.
Dr. T & the Women, MCA 112381.
My Baby Don't Tolerate, Lost Highway/Curb 000116202.
It's Not Big It's Large, Lost Highway 000896602.
Anthology, Vol. 1: Cowboy Man, MCA 170234.
Smile, MCA 113184.

Mary Chapin Carpenter (1958–)

Country Folk Style

Modern country music includes various other musical styles welded to a fundamental sound to create something new and fresh. Although rock and roll and pop were the two main strains, in the late 1980s there was a small, dedicated group who incorporated a strong dose of folk music into their sound. The lone figure of the anti–Nashville participants to break thorough commercially was a young woman with a country-folk style. Her name is Mary Chapin Carpenter.

Mary Chapin Carpenter was born on February 21, 1958, in Princeton, New Jersey, into a musical family. Her mother was an aspiring folk singer during the 1960s boom, and when Mary Chapin developed an interest in music at an early age, she was given a guitar. She was able to study the guitar and other instruments as she lived a youth filled with travel including a two-year stint in Japan.

Carpenter continued to develop her skills, but it wasn't until she was sixteen, when her family moved to the Washington, D.C., area, that she began to study music seriously. Perhaps in an effort to make new friends in a strange environment, she became involved in the city's folk scene. A one-year sojourn in Europe was a positive experience where she collected more material for songs that would someday make her famous.

After graduating from Brown University with a degree in American Civilization, she put a tremendous effort into her musical career. By this time she had started to write her own songs, and she was given ample opportunity to perform them at various coffeehouses. She mixed her original compositions with pop covers that contained a tinge of country.

Although her main style at this point in time was folk, it was also very eclectic. There was some rock and roll, a little bit of blues, and country in her sound. In order to be able to play at a coffeehouse and not get booed off the stage, a performer had to be well rounded. She continued to play at different places in order to build up a fan base and work on new material.

It was at one of these venues where she met guitarist John Jennings, and the two started to perform together. They made a demo of their thin but solid catalog that caught the attention of executives at Columbia Records. By 1987, Carpenter had signed on to the label and released her debut album, *Hometown Girl*.

Although *Hometown Girl* didn't make her an overnight success, it did lay the cornerstone of her career and foreshadowed her future releases. Some of the highlights included "Family Hands," A Road Is Just a Road," "Just Because," and the Tom Waits song "Downtown Train." While the record didn't create an enormous amount of mainstream excitement, it did earn her a dedicated, knowledgeable cult following.

Her second effort, *State of the Heart,* enlarged that fan base and provided two Top Ten singles, "Never Had It So Good" and "Quittin' Time." Her songs were delicate pieces of folk-country with a definite feminist point of view. While Nashville-influenced radio refused to play her tunes, the more progressive and college stations made Carpenter a staple of their programming, and it was there that she developed an enthusiastic following.

Everything began to change with her third album, *Shooting Straight in the Dark*; she was gaining momentum. The single "Down at the Twist and Shout" peaked at number two, and the sales of the album doubled what her two previous efforts had done combined. She was on the verge of a major breakthrough.

The fourth album, *Come On, Come On,* pushed her career into the mainstream spotlight. It contained three major singles: the number one hit "He Thinks He'll Keep Her," the Top Five hit "I Feel Lucky," and "Passionate Kisses." It also marked a change of direction in her material; the previous work had been more folksy than country, but the latest offering resonated with a definite country twang.

By this time she had escaped the coffeehouse tours and was performing at much larger venues to welcoming audiences. She had managed to greatly expand the cult base that had sprouted with the release of her first two albums into a healthy following without alienating anyone. Her music was for a diverse audience instead of a specific or narrow one

Stones in the Road, her next album, reverted back to more of a folk sound but was still a million seller, containing the number one hit "Shut Up and Kiss Me," the Top Ten hit "Tender When I Want to Be," "House of Cards," and "Why Walk When You Can Fly?" Her career was in full bloom at this point as her country-folk material had found a definite niche within the record buying public.

In 1996, *Place in the World* was released. The single "Let Me into Your Heart" was the top charting song. Other highlights included "Keeping the Faith" and "I Want to Be Your Girlfriend." At this point in her career, Carpenter was at the height of her popularity. The CD was interesting for another reason because it would be her last studio offering for the next five years.

In 2001, she resurfaced with *Time* Sex* Love*,* which expressed themes related to middle-age. The thoughtful, deep lyrics were still present, but the musical style was more abstract than ever before. She continued to perform on stage, and the mixture of the age of her audiences reflected the past fans and the new ones.

In 2004, *Between Here and Gone,* her next album,was released and would peak at number five on the country charts. It yielded the single "What Would You Say To Me," which failed to chart. The days of her music being commercially driven seemed over, but the quality of her material was still strong. Her life perspective had changed and was reflected in the material she played.

Her next album offering, *The Calling,* was a political commentary that included "Houston," a song about Hurricane Katrina and its social aspects. There was also "On with the Song," dedicated to the Dixie Chicks and the damage suffered to their career after the discerning comments they made about the Iraq War and the president. Carpenter continues to record and perform.

Mary Chapin Carpenter is a country music troubadour. She has displayed a strong folk side to her music and is in many ways a balladeer, a poet, a minstrel. The depth and breadth of her sound is different than the mainstream and even other alternative artists in the country vein.

She has a contemporary voice. It has neither a specific country or folk timbre but instead enough range to allow her to sing in the style that has become her unmistakable identity. It is a pleasant vocal delivery with strong phrasing that is instantly recognizable separating her from similar artists in the country-folk vein.

In the 1980s, there was a small movement of country-based singers who injected a strong dose of folk in their sound. Many remained in obscurity never achieving a commercial breakthrough. A partial list includes Deana Carter, Kate Campbell, Maura O'Connell, Dar Williams, Lucinda Williams, Cheryl Wheeler, Iris DeMent, Nanci Griffith, Beth Nielsen Chapman, Carlene Carter, and Suzy Bogguss. Only Williams, DeMent, Griffith, Carter and Bogguss have achieved a slightly commercial sound. Carpenter possessed more talent, as well as a stronger marketing sense of songwriting and lyrical content than the rest of the pack.

Her anti–Nashville stance makes Carpenter one of the most obvious alternative choices for country music fans. Despite this point of view, she has won two Academy of Country Music Awards: the first, in 1989, as Top New

Female Vocalist; and, the second, in 1992, for Top Female Vocalist. The Country Music Association awarded her the Female Vocalist of the Year prize in 1992, and again in 1993. She has also won Grammy Awards for her Best Country Album (*Stones in the Road*) and for Best Female Country Vocal Performance from 1991 to 1994.

Carpenter has given the world a number of great songs. A partial list includes "Never Had It So Good," "Quittin' Time," "Down at the Twist and Shout," "I Feel Lucky," "Passionate Kisses," "How Do," "Something of a Dreamer," "You Win Again," "Right Now," "Going Out Tonight," "Not Too Much to Ask," "The Hard Way," "The Bug," "He Thinks He'll Keep Her," "I Take My Chances," "Shut Up and Kiss Me," "Tender When I Want to Be," and "Let Me Into Your Heart." All the aforementioned songs were Top Twenty Hits. However, because of her songwriting ability and lyrical depth, the various CDs are filled with great tunes that didn't make the charts.

The Mary Chapin Carpenter story is a country music success story. Her facility for lyrics, exciting choice of material, strong musical elements, ability to meld two distinct styles into one cohesive sound and anti–Nashville stance are all part of the package. She has created a catalog of songs on her own terms and with solid results. She has proven her country-folk style to be a winner.

Discography:

Hometown Girl, Columbia 40758.
State of the Heart, Columbia 44228.
Shooting Straight in the Dark, Columbia 46077.
Come On, Come On, Columbia 48881.
Stones in the Road, Columbia 64327.
A Place in the World, Columbia 67501.
Time* Sex * Love*, Columbia 85176.
Between Here and Gone, Columbia 86619.
The Calling, Zoe 011431111.
Party Doll and Other Favorites, Columbia 68751.
Shooting Straight in the Dark/Come On, Come On, Sony Mid-Price 4998692.
The Essential Mary Chapin Carpenter, Sony 90772.

Béla Fleck (1958–)
New Grass Revival

Bluegrass had an influence on a number of musicians who incorporated the basic elements of the style into their own sound. One of these artists has taken the genre in many different directions with his banjo. He is Béla Fleck.

Béla Fleck was born on July 10, 1958, in New York. He developed a love for the banjo watching the television series *The Beverly Hillbillies* and hearing the movie theme song "Dueling Banjos." As a teen he started to play the instrument while studying guitar and music theory at the New York High School of Music and Art. This was a special time in his evolving career because the instrument was not offered as an elective in school, so he was forced to pursue his passion for learning from outside sources.

Three teachers and the most important influences during this period were Erik Darling, Marc Horowitz, and Tony Trischka. Béla also joined his first band, Wicker's Creek, which was positive step in his career development. He took advantage of the fact that he lived in New York City, soaking up different musical experiences. For example, he attended a concert by the jazz-fusion band Return to Forever, which featured keyboardist Chick Corea and bassist Stanley Clarke. This exposure encouraged possible experimentation on the banjo with different jazz styles, including bebop and fusion, building a future foundation.

He relocated to Boston and joined the bluegrass band Tasty Licks. Led by Jack Tottle, the group dabbled in various styles including jazz that enabled Fleck to participate in two albums of that vein. He was also encouraged to record his first solo album, *Crossing the Tracks,* for Rounder Records. Some of the musical partners on this album included Sam Bush and Jerry Douglas, two names he would call on in the future. Another friend at the time was bassist Mark Schatz whom with he spent an entire summer playing in the streets of Beantown.

The two moved to Lexington, Kentucky, to form the group Spectrum, which also included Jimmy Gaudreau, Glen Lawson, and Jimmy Mattingly. During this period, Fleck and Schatz also traveled to California and Nashville to record the album *Natural Bridge*, with David Grisman, Mark O'Connor, Ricky Skaggs, Darol Anger and Mike Marshall. In 1981, when Spectrum disbanded, Fleck moved on to another bluegrass group called New Grass Revival.

New Grass Revival included old friend Sam Bush on mandolin, fiddle and vocals. It also featured Pat Flynn on guitar and John Cowan on bass and vocals. With Béla on banjo the foursome took bluegrass to its outer limits with an innovative approach that saw them blend traditional sounds with rock and other styles of country music. They recorded five albums together and toured endlessly exposing Béla to a wider circle of musicians and critics who liked what they heard. One of the songs they did was a Fleck composition, "Seven By Seven," recorded near the end of his stay with the outfit.

When not busy with his duties as part of New Grass Revival, Fleck continued his solo career and released *Drive*, in 1988. A different project during this period was an acoustic supergroup named Strength in Numbers that included longtime friends Sam Bush, Jerry Douglas, Edgar Meyer and Mark O'Connor. They recorded *The Telluride Sessions*, which broke new ground in acoustic circles and received rave reviews. The eclectic effort featured compositions influenced by classical music as well as traditional bluegrass elements.

Before leaving New Grass Revival, Fleck was planting the seeds to form his own group. The first member recruited was Howard Levy, a harmonica and keyboard player whom Béla met at the Winnipeg Folk Festival. The second member chosen for the new band was bass player Victor Lemonte Wooten, introduced by a friend. In 1990, the Flecktones were formed and included Roy "Future/Man" Wooten on the drumitar, a personal invention that was a combination drum and synthesizer shaped like a guitar and guaranteed to give the band a unique sound.

The group members boasted many different skills, but they made it work. They released their self-titled CD that featured a mix of jazz and bluegrass; it was nominated for a Grammy. It was in some ways a twist on Bob Wills' idea of combining big band swing with country tones. Instead, Fleck and his mates welded the much traveled banjo sound, a drumitar, a strong jazz identity, and computer technology into their own vision of country music.

Flight of the Cosmic Hippo was the band's second offering and the last to feature Howard Levy. He departed the scene, and the remaining members carried on as a trio until they added Jeff Coffin on saxophone, another unusual instrument in a country-based group. They toured relentlessly and gathered much attention from all circles because of their uniqueness, as well as their musicianship. By this point in time, Fleck was considered to be one of the premier banjo players in the world.

The group's future releases featured much experimentation and overdubs. Over the years different contributors added to the Flecktones' studio efforts. Their albums included talents as diverse as Chick Corea, Bruce Hornsby, Branford Marsalis, John Medeski, Amy Grant and Dave Matthews. Their albums have always been a new adventure in music listening as the band never let itself grow stale.

The performance side of their career was as successful as their recorded output. They shared the stage with a number of different acts, including blues/pop/folk slide guitarist queen Bonnie Raitt, rock legends the Grateful Dead, and roots outfit the Dave Matthews Band. The Flecktones also enjoyed much television exposure on programs such as *The Tonight Show* (during Johnny Carson's days as host), Arsenio Hall, Conan O'Brien, *Saturday Night Live* and the David Letterman show.

They continued to create music with much flair and experimentation. In 2003, Béla Fleck & the Flecktones released the landmark three-disc set *Little Worlds*. On his own, Béla also departed from his country-based roots to record *Perpetual Motion,* a album of classical music. It was a critically acclaimed effort that won a pair of Grammys, including Best Classical Crossover Album. Of note, Edgar Meyer, the bass player from the one-time super group Strength in Numbers, collaborated on the album.

It encouraged Fleck and Meyer to further experiment, and they formed a banjo/bass duo which toured across the country. They recorded some of their live events and released *Music for Two,* an interesting CD that also included input from Sascha Paladino, Fleck's brother, who made significant contributions during the tour. Later, Béla and Edgar also cowrote and performed a double concerto for banjo and bass with the Nashville Symphony, which debuted in November 2003. There seemed to be no limits to what the banjo player was willing to try.

The recipients of multiple Grammy Awards going back to 1998, Béla Fleck & the Flecktones picked up the Best Contemporary Jazz Performance, Instrumental Grammy in 2000 for *Outbound,* a typically wide-ranging project. Some of the guests included guitarist Adrian Belew, and singers Jon Anderson and Shawn Colvin. The album was built around Fleck's concept of weird banjo sounds.

The Flecktones continued to weld country, jazz, funk, world music and rock into a very interesting package. They commanded respect throughout the musical world with guest appearances from Bruce Hornsby and Branford Marsalis on the outfit's album *Three Flew Over the Cuckoo's Nest.* As well, Amy Grant and Dave Matthews sang on some of the cuts.

Fleck, as a solo artist, recorded exciting world music projects. A good example was *Tabula Rasa,* which included Chinese musicians Vishwa Mohan Bhatt and Jie-Bing Chen. He was never afraid to experiment with his ability on the banjo, and it is this attitude that has helped him create such widespread country-based music. He continues to record and perform.

Béla Fleck is a unique country artist. In the face of fads and trends, he has consistently followed his private course without much concern for current flavors. He has created music with flair, showmanship and courage. The foundation of his sound and fortitude has always been his excellent banjo playing.

He is considered the greatest exponent of the banjo in the world. This observation is based on a cross section of musicians from country, blues, rock, jazz, folk and classical corners. That such a wide array of perspectives would share the same opinion underlines his vast talent on the instrument that has made him famous.

Fleck can express any sound or style on the banjo. His ability on the instrument is on par with Jimi Hendrix on the guitar, Little Walter on harmonica, Art Blakey on drums, and Art Tatum on the piano. A world musician who has always understood how to make albums that reflected a global perspective, Béla has never failed to dazzle with his virtuoso technique.

His rapid-fire licks, ability to sway sounds like oceanic waves, his precise, sparse solo attacks and penchant to delve deeply into one style are all part of the musical package. His versatile abilities have enabled him to experiment in just about any genre and have afforded him the luxury of welding different elements into a cohesive sound that has always been his very own. In comparison to Fleck other banjo players sound one dimensional.

Fleck has approached the music industry much differently from the typical artist. He and his band never fly, but instead they prefer criss-crossing the hundreds of thousands of miles in the comfort of a bus. They also tour extensively, performing in whatever arena that will have them, including amphitheatres, auditoriums, amusement parks, zoos and even a farmer's market. A typical week might include a series of concerts in the Pacific Northwest, one with the Utah Symphony, then off to the Midwest in Wisconsin, Michigan, or Ohio and then, perhaps, on to West Virginia.

A Flecktones concert is a world musical experience. Fleck doesn't restrict himself to country and bluegrass music. His instrument is set in a jazz milieu with backing from bass, sax and electronic drums. The eclectic nature of the instruments allows the Flecktones to be a jam band, able to deliver long improvised versions of Fleck's classics as well as cover songs. Often, they are augmented by eager musicians willing to sit in with them, playing bassoon, tabla, oboe and even ukulele. An element of classical music is also thrown in the mixture to create something truly unique.

Although he is not a pure country musician, Fleck has underscored the point in every project he has participated in and in every concert he has delivered that versatility is the key to survival in the cutthroat music business. He has embraced wholeheartedly the idea that modern country encompasses many different elements. To truly understand this point one must only examine the Flecktones' four major CD releases.

Live Art is classic Flecktones at their best. Recorded over a four-year period in the 1990s, the twenty-song collection features jazz fused with bluegrass to create something called Blu-bop. There are slow blues in the tune "Flight of the Cosmic Hippo" and ballads such as "Sunset Road." The album also includes the standout "Early Reflection," which harkens to his first musical impression, "The Ballad of Jed Clampett." The fast-paced and perfectly played interlude of the song from the hit show demonstrates Fleck's ability to have fun.

The Big Band: Live at the Quick displays the group's penchant for experimentation. It includes the basic setup of banjo, bass, drums and winds, played in the styles of jazz bluegrass, classical, funk, gospel and Middle Eastern. Andy Narrell on steel drums, Paul McCondless on oboe and other wind instruments, Paul Hanson on bassoon, Kagar-ol Ondar on vocals and Sandip Burman on tabla augment the basic Flecktones lineup. Song highlights include "Amazing Grace," "Hoedown" (the Aaron Copland-penned classic), "Ovombo Summit" and "Earth Jam."

The tour de force *Little Worlds* features elements of Celtic, Middle Eastern, Hawaiian, jazz, blues, hip-hop, bluegrass and rock and roll. It also includes such diverse instruments as ukulele, theremin and uillean pipes. "Next and Snatchin'" was just one of the many great songs from the 3-CD set. The *Ten from Little Worlds* compilation was released as an alternative to the triple CD set, a clever marketing strategy.

With the album *Perpetual Motion*, Fleck proved that he can create any sound with the banjo. Strains of masters Bach and Beethoven were included as well as Debussy, Chopin and Tchaikovsky. His single-note picking style is supported by the marimba, violin, cello and guitar.

Béla Fleck is an alternative country musician. He has — along with Joe Ely, Jimmie Dale Gilmore, Steve Earle, k.d. lang, Lyle Lovett and Dwight Yoakam — given all music fans a listening choice. He and the Flecktones have proven that country music can be packaged in many different forms without losing its true identity. Despite their bizarre take on bluegrass, they have added another dimension to the style that only enhanced its richness and possibilities.

The Béla Fleck story is that of a different type of country musician. But his eight Grammys and his nominations in more categories than anyone else in the history of the award underline his diverse talent. Although his brand of bluegrass is far removed from the sounds of Bill Monroe, Lester Flatt, Earl Scruggs and Ralph Stanley, Fleck has proven with his new grass revival that country overtones can be welded with any other style and still sound like country music.

DISCOGRAPHY:

Tasty Licks, Rounder 0106.
Crossing the Tracks, Rounder 0121.
Opening Roll, Rounder 0136.
Fiddle Tunes for Banjo, Rounder 0124.
Natural Bridge, Rounder 0146.

Too Hot for Words, Rounder 0161.
The Dreadful Snakes, Rounder 0177.
Live in Japan, Spectrum Rounder 0184.
Double Time, Rounder 0181.
Deviation, Rounder 0196.
On the Boulevard, Sugar Hill Sh-3745.
Inroads, Rounder 0219.
60 Plus Series, Rounder 11158.
New Grass Revival, EMI America ST-17216.
Daybreak, Rounder 11518.
Hold to a Dream, Capitol CS-46962.
Drive, Rounder 0255.
Places, Rounder 11522.
Friday Night in America, Capitol C2-90739.
The Telluride Sessions, MCA MCA-6293.
Béla Fleck And The Flecktones, Warner Brothers, 2-26124.
Flight Of The Cosmic Hippo, Warner Brothers 2-26562.
Ufo Tofu, Warner Brothers 2-45016.
Solo Banjo Works, Rounder 0247.
Three Flew Over the Cuckoo's Next, Warner Brothers 45328-2.
The Bluegrass Sessions: Tales from the Acoustic Planet, Vol. 1, Warner Brothers
    45854.
Live Art, Warner Brothers 46427.
Tabula Rosa, Waterlily Acoustics 44.
Left of Cool, Warner Brothers 46896.
Tales from the Acoustic Planet, Vol. 2, The Bluegrass Sessions, Warner Brothers.
Greatest Hits of the 20th Century, Warner Brothers 47301.
Outbound/Ten from the Quick/Ten from the Worlds, Sony Jazz 5186852.
Music Instruction: Banjo, Homespun Tapes B-208.
Outbound, Columbia 62178.
Perpetual Motion, Sony 89610.
Live at the Quick, Columbia 86355.
Little Worlds, Columbia 86353.
Ten from Little Worlds, Columbia 90539.
Music for Two, Sony 92106.
The Hidden Land, Sony 96417.

k.d. lang (1961–)

Cowgirl Rebel

The alternative stable of country artists consists of very diverse individuals who have made music on their own terms. Often they have ventured out of the genre into the realm of pop, jazz, rock, folk and blues. One of these singers, who from the start was very serious in creating her own musical universe, left little doubt that she was a cowgirl rebel. Her name is k.d. lang.

k.d. lang was born Kathryn Dawn Lang, on November 2, 1961, in Edmonton, Alberta, but moved out to the small farming community of Consort and enjoyed a prairie childhood. She grew up listening to a variety of music; however, it wasn't until her college years that she decided to pursue a musical career. Her main inspiration was Patsy Cline, and the pivotal experience of playing her idol in a theatre production fueled her ambitions.

By 1983, lang had already formed a band named the re-clines and with the assistance of guitarist-co-songwriter Ben Mink recorded a first album, *Friday Dance Promenade*. Although not a stunning debut, it did gain some notice in alternative newspapers. The follow-up, *A Truly Western Experience,* released a year later catapulted her to national attention in Canada.

This national attention included a coveted Juno Award, Canada's answer to the Grammys. lang won the Most Promising Female Vocalist Award in 1985 and was without a doubt one of the most visible country artists on the scene. In 1986, the American label Sire Records signed her to a recording contract.

Her first album for her new company, *Angel with a Lariat,* was a pleasant success with its mixture of rockabilly, honky tonk and 1950s-styled ballads. It received solid reviews as well as much play on college radio and alternative country stations. However, mainstream Nashville had not yet accepted the brash, stylish singer who often dressed in androgynous attire.

While her recorded material gained her noted attention, it was her concert appearances that truly blazed a trail. She was an enigmatic performer, entertaining the crowd with something new and exciting. Every show was a test, an opportunity to push the envelope to see how far the crowd could be taken.

She finally broke through on a national level in the United States when she teamed up with rock legend Roy Orbison to cut a version of "Crying," which was featured in the movie *Hiding Out.* Released at the end of 1987, the song was a big hit and announced her appearance on the country charts. That she was able to blend her abilities with Orbison's four-octave range proved she could hold her own against anyone.

In 1988, *Shadowland,* her second Sire album, was released to enthusiastic reviews. A homage to her idol Patsy Cline, *Shadowland* received the help of Cline's producer, Owen Bradley. The single "I'm Down to My Last Cigarette" broke through the Top Forty. Interestingly, the album was a hit on both the mainstream country lists and the alternative underground, a feat rarely accomplished.

Also that year she performed "Turn Me Round'" at the closing ceremonies of the Winter Olympics in her native Alberta. She participated in the television special *Roy Orbison and Friends: A Black and White Night,* providing background vocals. Later, she sang "Jingle Bell Rock" on *Pee-Wee's Playhouse Christmas Special.*

Absolute Torch and Twang, her third release, earned her a Grammy Award for Best Female Country Vocal Performance. The single "Full Moon of Love" reached the charts and established her identity more deeply in media circles. lang, who has always been controversial with her stage attire, risky concert performances, and choice of material, drew further attention when she declared her distaste for eating meat in 1990. Her "Meat Stinks" campaign was a gutsy protest for someone who hailed from cattle country in Alberta.

lang pushed the envelope even further in a magazine interview when she declared that she was a lesbian. The Nashville industry has always been rigid in its acceptance of anyone outside the narrow margins of the mainstream. But k.d., who had never backed away from stating her opinion, gambled that her declaration would not hurt her career.

Her fourth album, *Ingénue,* was a turnaround, a new starting point in her recorded career, because it was an adult contemporary pop effort and had very little country taste to it. "Constant Craving" was a Top Forty hit and won her another Grammy for Best Female Pop Vocal Performance. The album would attain platinum status in American, Britain, and Australia and double platinum in her native Canada. However, she lost much of the country section of her fan base while gaining a new one.

lang's work outside the framework of her career provided more exposure. She contributed most of the material for the soundtrack to the movie *Even Cowgirls Get the Blues.* She performed the song "Surrender" for the James Bond film *Tomorrow Never Dies.* Earlier she had worked with composer David Arnold on the album *Shaken and Stirred: The David Arnold James Bond Project.*

She resumed her personal career with the release of *All You Can Eat,* a direct follow-up to the adult contemporary pop line she had pursued on *Ingénue.* The album was a hit but not as much as its predecessor and once again didn't contain a trace of her once strong country roots. It seemed she had abandoned her cowgirl image.

Drag, released in 1997, was a collection of songs about smoking and didn't do much for her career. In 2000, she returned wth a vengeance with *Invincible Summer.* The album's theme was about the romance of being in love. "Summerfling," "Extraordinary Thing," "Suddenly," and "It's Happening with You" carried the message that she was trying to put across.

A totally different project was a record made with Tony Bennett on his *Playin' with My Friends: Bennett Sings the Blues.* Later she earned a fourth Grammy for Best Traditional Pop Vocal Album for her collaboration with the famous crooner on *A Wonderful World.* They even toured together, a move that bolstered her career on a performance level because it linked her with the older generation who had trouble accepting some of her modern views.

It was her time spent with Bennett that would in turn inspire her next project, *Hymns of the 49th Parallel.* It was a collection of tunes by Canadian songwriters that she covered with determination, heart and pride. Her touching tribute allowed lang to give a bow to those that had paved the way for her career to blossom in her native country. One of her most worthwhile projects, the album gave Neil Young's "After the Gold Rush" a different treatment that emphasized its noteworthiness. The album also included solid versions of Leonard Cohen's "Hallelujah," Bruce Cockburn's "One Day I Walk," and Joni Mitchell's "A Case of You."

She continued to tackle projects outside of her main career. She contributed "Little Patch of Heaven" to the Walt Disney movie *Home on the Range.* In 2006, she performed her song "Constant Craving" at the Outgames in Montreal. Later that year she performed a duet with Madeleine Peyroux on the latter's album *Half the Perfect World,* with a Joni Mitchell tune "River." She also guested on Nellie McKay's *Pretty Little Head* and provided a version of The Beatles' "Golden Slumbers" for the movie *Happy Feet.*

In 2006, *Reintarnation,* a compilation of music from her Sire years, was released. In 2004, she had left the company to sign with Nonesuch Records, and recorded *Hymns of the 49th Parallel.* lang continues to record and perform.

k.d. lang is a country music contributor. When she is interested in recording songs in the alternative country music vein, there are none better. However, this eclectic artist has explored different musical paths, leaving her audience constantly craving her to return back to her roots.

lang has the voice of an angel. The crystalline quality of her vocal delivery has always been her trademark, whether working on her own projects or on those of other artists. Her technique consists of hitting a middle note and shading it with a dual murmur. That is her calling card as a singer. Few have been able to project such a subtle power.

The versatility of her voice and her incredible method have allowed her to work on numerous projects, including movies and the records of others. She has been involved in many special recordings, most notably those of Tony Bennett and Roy Orbison. Despite her controversial point of view on certain subjects, there is no denying her abundant talent.

She has also worked in television, playing the lead role in the 1991 drama film *Salmonberries.* lang co-starred with Ewan McGregor and Ashley Judd in *Eye of the Beholder.* lang has also made guest appearances on the television sitcoms *Dharma and Greg* and *Ellen.*

Of all the artists outside the mainstream, she stands out as a special case. The path she has followed is done not to be different but to be herself; that is the essence of an alternative singer. Her choice of song material, the projects that she has worked on, her candid interviews, and the activist stances on controversial issues are all part of the package. Her music is deliciously eclectic and genuine, mixed with satire as well as humor.

She has given the world an interesting collection of songs. A partial list includes "Lock, Stock and Teardrops," "I'm Down to My Last Cigarette," "Three Days," "Constant Craving," "Lifted by Love," "Just Keep Me Moving," "Sexuality," "If I Were You," "Theme from the Valley of the Dolls," "Summerfling," "Miss Chatelaine," "Full Moon of Love," "Skylar," "Crying," "Extraordinary Thing," "Suddenly," "After the Gold Rush," "Hallelujah," "One Day I Walk," "A Case of You," and "It's Happening with You." Whether attempting an original tune or a cover version, her incredible singing technique always rings true.

The k.d. lang story is that of a different kind of country artist. Despite following her own unique career path, she has won many awards, including the Order of Canada in 1996. The cowgirl rebel has always known how to entertain with her special musical abilities.

DISCOGRAPHY:

A Truly Western Experience, Burnstead 86.
Angel with a Lariat, Sire 25441.
Shadowland, Sire 25724.
Absolute Torch and Twang, Sire 25877.
Ingénue, Sire 26840.
All You Can Eat, Sire 46034.
Drag, Warner Bros., 46623.
Invincible Summer, Warner Bros., 47605.
Live by Request, Warner Bros., 48108.
Hymns of the 49th Parallel, Nonesuch 79847.
3 for 1, WEA International 30077.
Drag/Invincible Summer, WEA International 48127.
Ingénue/Shadowlands/Drag, Warner 9362485422.
Reintarnation, Sire/Rhino 73366.

PART THREE

Groups

Long before country music became a viable industry, there were gatherings of semiskilled individuals — relatives, neighbors and acquaintances — who filled the Appalachian air with the traditional songs of their ancestors. In the 1920s, when record companies realized that there was a strong market for the music of mountain folk, there were a number of groups formed overnight to take advantage of the opportunity. As well, many of the outfits that had been playing for years turned professional in order to record.

Throughout the history of the genre there have been hundreds of groups. Some of the most important ones include Roy Acuff and His Smoky Mountain Boys, the Sons of the Pioneers, Bill Monroe and His Bluegrass Boys, Bob Wills and His Texas Playboys, Hank Williams, Sr. and his Drifting Cowboys, Hank Thompson and His Brazos Valley Boys, and Buck Owens and His Buckaroos, among others.

In some ways, today's groups have very little in common with old-timey bands like Dr. Humphrey Bate and His Possum Hunters, Gid Tanner and His Skillet Lickers, the Binkley Brothers, the Dixie Clodhoppers, the Morrison Family, the Delmore Brothers, the McGee Brothers, Bird's Kentucky Corn Crackers, Dr. Smith's Champion Hoss Hair Pullers, Wilmer Watts and the Lonely Eagles, the West Virginia Snake Hunters, Fisher Hendley and His Aristocratic Pigs, Bumboat Billy and the Sparrows, Seven Foot Dilly and His Dill Pickles, Joe Foss and His Hungry Sand-Lappers, Mumford Bean and His Itawambians and Ephraim Woodie and the Henpecked Husbands. However, certain connections do exist.

Many of the past groups had a huge influence on the music of today's artists. In particular, Bill Monroe, Bob Wills and Hank Williams, Sr. would form a powerful triad with their bluegrass, western swing and honky tonk styles, respectively. A good number of the modern country performers stole a page from legends like George Jones, Merle Haggard, Kenny Rogers, Johnny Cash, Patsy Cline, Eddy Arnold, and a host of others.

The songs that the legends recorded have found their way in many of the recordings of the contemporary country stars. Ricky Skaggs and Alison

Krauss have delved into the Bill Monroe, Lester Flatt and Earl Scruggs discography with relish. Nearly everyone has recorded at least one Hank Williams, Sr., song. The Patsy Cline catalog has been raided on several occasions. The songbooks of the Carters, Johnny Cash, Bob Wills, Waylon Jennings and Merle Haggard have provided a myriad of artists with much cover material.

There are also crucial differences in every aspect. For instance, today's groups use more electric instruments on their recordings and in concert. The inclusion of drums is also a modern touch. In retrospect, the influence can be traced back to Buck Owens and his rocking Bakersfield sound. His rebellious perspective on how to make country music had an impact on countless solo artists and bands.

The recording techniques used on today's CDs are far more advanced than that of the ancient equipment utilized to record the pioneers. The eighty-year-old scratchy records of such acts as the Carter Family, Jimmie Rodgers, Vernon Dalhart, Uncle Dave Macon, Riley Puckett, Gid Tanner and His Skillet Lickers and the Stonemans pale in comparison to the sophisticated and clean aspects of the current technology. Fortunately, for all music fans, many of the songs of yesteryear have been digitally remastered.

There are more venues for today's groups. There are hundreds of festivals — large, open air affairs, boasting a multiple lineup playing to vast, enthusiastic crowds. Interestingly, some of these events are in honor of past legendary figures such as Bill Monroe, Hank Williams, Sr., Jimmie Rodgers, and others. Ironically, the contemporary country musicians who perform at these events do so to pay homage to their idols.

The contemporary groups have more visual opportunities. Videos are an important tool and push record sales as well as concert tickets. There are television channels that exclusively promote country music videos, including CMT, VH-1 Country, and GAC.

The current groups also represent the entire spectrum of country music styles. There are bluegrass, western swing, honky tonk, country-rock, country-folk, alternative, traditional, neo-traditional, contemporary, country-blues, bluegrass revival, western swing revival, and Urban Cowboy bands. There is something for every taste.

Some of the important groups today include the Oak Ridge Boys, Big & Rich, the Gatlins, Little Big Town, Heartland, Cole Deggs & the Lonesome, BlackHawk, Blue Country, BR5-49, the Flying Burrito Brothers, Blue Rodeo, Little Texas, Little Big Town, Montgomery Gentry, Nitty Gritty Dirt Band, Prairie Oyster, Pure Prairie League, the Remingtons, and Sawyer Brown. There are hundreds of groups in the United States as well as around the world who play some form of country music. The groups featured in this book represent a cross-section of styles and include the following acts:

- Asleep at the Wheel dedicated their career to continuing the sound of Bob Wills, the Father of western swing. They have done so with pride and distinction.
- Alabama was a country-rock act and one of the most successful artists in the 1980s. They would later be acknowledged as the artist of the decade.
- The Judds were a mother-daughter duo who shot to the top of the charts with their clear, precise harmonies. Only tragedy stopped them from becoming the most successful artists in the history of the genre.
- The Mavericks hailed from Florida with their interesting mixture of Cuban sounds, blues, folk and country.
- The Dixie Chicks are three women who carefully crafted a sterling career only to watch it fall apart. They rebuilt it with patience, sass and talent.
- Brooks & Dunn are an award-winning duo whose mainstream sound has endured current trends.
- Rascal Flatts is one of the newer groups that has managed to reach the top of the heap with their blended vocals and strong musical abilities.
- Sugarland is a relatively new outfit with a strong pedigree. In a short time, they have acquired a large fan base.

Asleep at the Wheel (1970–)
Bump, Bounce, Boogie

One of the most engaging individuals in the early days of country music was Bob Wills. He was the first to successfully meld the swing of jazz with the roots of traditional country music. In doing so, he spawned an entire style that continues to reverberate to this day. One of the latter-day groups that took up the Wills mantle did it with their bump, bounce and boogie style. Their name is Asleep at the Wheel.

The story of Asleep at the Wheel begins with frontman Ray Benson. He was born Ray Benson Siefer on March 16, 1951, in Philadelphia, Pennsylvania. He grew up listening to a variety of music that included Bob Wills, Hank Williams, Sr., Louis Jordan and different jazz giants. He picked up the guitar and honed his skills until he was able to perform in front of an audience. He played in a number of groups during his teenage years and eventually drifted to West Virginia.

In 1970, in Paw Paw, West Virginia, he formed Asleep at the Wheel with Reuben Gosfield (who would adopt the stage name Lucky Oceans), and Leroy Preston on rhythm guitar. Soon after they added a female singer, Chris

O'Connell, who was still a teenager when she joined the group. They played straight country music until they heard Merle Haggard's *A Tribute to the Best Damn Fiddle Player in the World,* his personal homage to Bob Wills. From this point on they dedicated their careers to upholding the precious western swing style.

Another major influence on the fledgling group was Commander Cody & His Lost Planet Airmen, an eclectic outfit who had their biggest hit with "Hot Rod Lincoln." Their approach to progressive country had a strong impact on Asleep at the Wheel. It was through contact with Commander Cody that the members of Asleep at the Wheel relocated to San Francisco. It was during this California period that piano player Floyd Domino was added. The group gigged all over town but played most often at Berkeley's Longbranch Saloon. When the brilliant Irish singer-songwriter Van Morrison praised them, it enabled Benson and his band to secure a recording contract.

Their debut album, *Comin' Right at Ya,* released in 1973, didn't catapult them to instant fame. However, they forged on and relocated to Austin, Texas, on the recommendation of Willie Nelson, who was then moving toward superstardom. Asleep at the Wheel found a home in the Texas state capital, and a switch to the Epic label was another good move. Their self-titled second work included a cover of Louis Jordan's "Choo Choo Ch'Boogie," which hit the country charts. Soon after, they added fiddler Lisa Silver and trumpeter Bobby Womack and signed to Capitol Records.

Texas Gold was their breakthrough album. It included "The Letter That Johnny Walker Read," which went to the Top Ten of the country charts. They gained further exposure with an appearance on an episode of the television show *Austin City Limits.* Despite the many personnel shifts (there would be over eighty of them during their career), they managed to release a string of strong albums, including *Wheelin' and Dealin', The Wheel* and *Collision Course.* An instrumental version of Count Basie's classic "One O'clock Jump" won them their first Grammy.

One must marvel at the many ups and downs that the group has endured throughout a long career. In 1980, they released *Framed,* hoping to continue their successful run of solid studio albums. However, founding member Lucky Oceans left the group, and Chris O'Connell took time off to start a family. Despite being on the road for a large part of the year, the band experienced financial problems and turned to soundtracks to stay afloat.

In 1985, they released their first collection of new material in five years, but it was ignored. Their first greatest hits collection, *Pasture Prime,* renewed interest in the group. Benson, the leader of the outfit, managed to get another record deal with Epic Records. By this point they had regrouped adding fiddler Larry Franklin, steel guitarist John Ely, pianist/accordionist Tim Alexander, saxophonist Mike Francis, bassist John Mitchell and drummer David Sanger. As well, O'Connell returned to the fold.

Asleep at the Wheel 10 was a major comeback album for the group. It featured the Top Twenty "House of Blue Lights," as well as "String of Pearls," which won them a Grammy for Best Country Instrumental. The link between the band and their hero Bob Wills was further strengthened with the guest appearance of fiddle legend Johnny Gimble. The momentum had shifted in their favor, and once again they were a viable outfit ready to invade the world with their western swing tunes.

The album *Western Standard Time* featured the single "Sugarfoot Rag," which won them another Grammy for Best Country Instrumental. Although *Keepin' Me Up Nights* was not as successful an album as its two predecessors, it still kept them going. However, personnel changes continued to plague the group, as Chris O'Connell left again. Benson retained the services of Francis and Sanger, then added fiddler Ricky Turpin, bassist Dave Miller, and steel guitarist/Dobroist Cindy Cashdollar.

In 1993, the group issued *A Tribute to the Music of Bob Wills and the Texas Playboys,* which featured many guests including Garth Brooks, Vince Gill, George Strait, Dolly Parton, Marty Stuart and Suzy Bogguss. It included the song "Red Wing," which won them another Grammy. They followed it up with the excellent *The Wheel Keeps on Rollin'.*

In 1999, they paid a second tribute to Bob Wills with the album *Ride with Bob.* It featured fiddler Jason Roberts, who came by his musical prowess honestly, being a relative of Johnny Gimble, as well as pianist/second fiddler Chris Booher. It won them multiple Grammy Awards and featured diverse guests like the Manhattan Transfer and the Squirrel Nut Zippers, as well as country mainstays Dwight Yoakam, the Dixie Chicks, Reba McEntire, Lyle Lovett, Mark Chesnutt, Clay Walker and Shawn Colvin.

The group has continued to churn out records in the past few years, including Christmas music and live material. All of their releases have been recorded in the western swing framework. They are one of the hardest working bands, and they play hundreds of concerts every year. They continue to record and perform.

Asleep at the Wheel are country music historians. Their dedication to western swing and its founder Bob Wills has allowed them to keep a tradition alive that would have otherwise disappeared. They preserved a style of music that constantly finds an audience, and because of this they have always been a working band.

Ray Benson has a big baritone voice that allows him to deliver western swing tunes with gusto. Although he has shared the lead vocalist job with a number of different people including Chris O'Connell and Elizabeth McQueen among others, he has always remained the focal point of the group.

His distinctive voice is an essential element in the band's overall makeup and helped defined their sound.

Although they have endured more than eighty personnel changes over the years, they managed to remain a strong, viable band. Like his idol Bob Wills, Benson changed lineups frequently to keep the music fresh. Today, the group consists of Benson on lead guitar and vocals, Jason Roberts on fiddle, David Sanger on drums, David Earl Miller on bass, John Whitby on piano, Elizabeth McQueen on acoustic guitar and vocals and Eddie Rivers on steel guitar and sax.

Asleep at the Wheel always maintained a high visibility. For example, they appeared in the movie *Roadie*, which also included Meat Loaf, Blondie and Art Carney. In 2005, they staged a play about the life and music of Bob Wills, entitled *A Ride with Bob Wills*. The play included fifteen of the master's best known songs as well as more than twenty-five actors and musicians. It was a very interesting project that kept the band's name fresh on the circuit.

They have given the world a number of great songs. A partial list includes "The Letter That Johnny Walker Read," "House of Blue Lights," "Miles and Miles of Texas," "Boogie Back to Texas," "Hot Rod Lincoln," "New San Antonio Rose," "Roly Poly," "Cherokee Maiden," "Right or Wrong," "Faded Love," "Take Me Back to Tulsa," and "Stay All Night," "Red Wings, "Choo Choo Ch'Boogie," "Across the Alley from the Alamo," "You're from Texas," "Jambalaya," "Cotton Eyed Joe," and "Texas Fiddle Man." Whether performing an original composition or a cover version, they have never failed to inject the song with their brand of country swing.

The story of Asleep at the Wheel is a long, colorful history. Despite some lean times they remain the keepers of the flame that Bob Wills lit. Although their first attempts to mix some strange original material with western swing standards proved an unsuccessful formula, they eventually developed their own bump, bounce and boogie sound to become near legends.

ASLEEP AT THE WHEEL PERSONNEL
(1970–PRESENT)

Guitar	*Steel Guitar*
Ray Benson	Lucky Oceans
Chris O'Connell	Wally Murphy
LeRoy Preston	John Ely
Lucky Oceans	Cindy Cashdollar
Larry Franklin	Jim Murphy
John Ely	Eddie Rivers

Guitar

Jason Roberts
Haydn Vitera
Jim Murphy
Elizabeth McQueen

Bass

Gene Dobkin
Tony Garnier
Tom Anastaslo
David Dawson
John Mitchell
David Miller

Drums

LeRoy Preston
Scott Hennige
Chris York
Richard Hormachea
David Sanger
Tommy Beavers

Saxophone

Link Davis, Jr.
Patrick (Taco) Ryan
Michael Francis
Jim Murphy
Eddie Rivers

Lead Vocals

Ray Benson
Chris O'Connell
Gene Dobkin
LeRoy Preston
Link Davis, Jr.
Maryanee Price
Larry Franklin
Tim Alexander
Chris Booher

Steel Guitar

Eddie Rivers
John Ely
Cindy Cashdollar

Fiddle

Richard Cassnova
Link Davis, Jr.
Danny Levin
Bill Mabry
Larry Franklin
Ricky Turpin
Jason Roberts
Chris Booher
Haydn Vitera

Piano

Floyd Domino
Faulkner Evans
Tim Alexander
Chris Booher
John Michael Whitby

Accordion

Link Davis, Jr.
Tim Alexander

Harmony Vocals

Tim Alexander
Larry Franklin
David Miller
Jason Roberts
John Michael Whitby
Haydn Vitera

Lead Vocals	*Harmony Vocals*
Jason Roberts	Elizabeth McQueen
Haydn Vitera	
Elizabeth McQueen	

Organ	*Mandolin*
Floyd Domino	Danny Levin
	Ricky Turpin
	Jason Roberts

Clarinet	*Violin*
Patrick (Taco) Ryan	Danny Levin
Michael Francis	

Cello	*Dobro*
Danny Levin	Cindy Cashdollar

DISCOGRAPHY:

Comin' Right at Ya, EMI LN-10296.
Asleep at the Wheel, Epic 33097.
Fathers & Sons, Epic 33782.
Texas Gold, Capitol 11441.
Wheelin' & Dealin', Capitol 11546.
The Wheel, Capitol 11620.
Collision Course, Capitol 11726.
Served Live, Capitol 11945.
Framed, MCA 5131.
Asleep at the Wheel [1985], MCA 31281.
10, Epic 40681.
Western Standard Time, Epic 44213.
Keepin' Me Up Nights, Arista AL-8550.
Route 66, Capitol 98925.
Tribute to the Music of Bob Willis & His Texas Playboys, Capitol 81470.
The Wheel Keeps on Rollin', Capitol 31280.
Back to the Future Now — Live at Arizona Charlie's, Sony 67981.
Merry Texas Christmas, Y'all, High Street 10355.
Ride with Bob, DreamWorks 50117.
Take Me Back to Tulsa, Evangeline 4059.
Wide Awake! Live in Oklahoma, Delta 4717576.
Live at Billy Bob's Texas, Smith Music Group 6023.
Remembers the Alamo, Shout! Factory 31133.
Live from Austin, TX, New West 6111.
Reinventing the Wheel, Mega Force 9566.
Santa Loves to Boogie, Mri 9564.
Live, Capitol 16306.
Pasture Prime, Stony Plain 1251.

Greatest Hits ... Live & Kickin', Arista 18698.
Swing Time, Columbia Special Products 22634.
The Best of Asleep at the Wheel, CEMA Special Markets 57000.
The Swinging Best of Asleep at the Wheel, Epic EK-53049.
Still Swingin', Liberty 30285.
Super Hits, Arista 18883.
Comin' Right at Ya/Texas Gold, Koch 8172.
23 Country Classics, EMI 99424.
The Very Best of Asleep at the Wheel Since 1970, Madacy 1001.
20th Century Masters — Millennium Collection: The Best of
Asleep at the Wheel, MCA 170211.
Collision Course/The Wheel, Evangeline Recorded Works Ltd. 8022.
Texas Gold/Wheelin' & Dealin', Evangeline Recorded Works Ltd. 8023.
Greatest Hits, Capitol 41791.
Very Best of Asleep at the Wheel, Bismeaux Productions 9495.
The Best of Asleep at the Wheel on the Road, Madacy Entertainment 52697.
Western Standard Time/Big Wheel, Acadia 8158.

Alabama (1977–2004)

Mountain Music

From the very beginning, groups have played an integral part in the development and popularity of country music. At the birth of the industry, the old-timey string bands Gid Tanner and His Skillet Lickers, the Carter Family, the Stonemans, and Dr. Humphrey Bate and His Possum Hunters were some of the first of the rural Southern musicians to record. Later, Roy Acuff and His Smoky Mountain Boys, the Sons of the Pioneers, Bill Monroe and His Blue Grass Boys, and Bob Wills and His Texas Playboys revved up the genre. In the 1980s, a band took up the cause of its predecessors to become the biggest-selling artists with their mountain music. Their name was Alabama.

The foundation of Alabama consisted of three cousins — Jeff Cook, born August 27, 1949, in Fort Payne, Alabama; Randy Owen, on December 13, 1949, in Fort Payne; and Teddy Gentry, on January 22, 1952, in Fort Payne. Owen and Gentry lived in the Lookout Mountain area and learned how to play guitar together singing in church as youngsters. Later, they pursued various musical paths, playing in different country, bluegrass and pop outfits. It was in high school that the trio united their talents. Cook, by then a fiddler, keyboardist, guitarist and vocalist, teamed up with Gentry and Owen.

In 1969, they formed Young Country and won a battle of the bands that raised a few eyebrows. But the group's fortunes were put on hold while Owen and Cook attended college. After graduation, they moved to Anniston, Alabama, with Teddy Gentry. It was during this period that they paid their dues, earnestly working menial jobs to keep things together while honing their individual skills into one cohesive, marketable sound.

In 1972, they changed their name to Wildcountry and added drummer Bennett Vartanian to become a quartet. Although drums were not a traditional country instrument, Buck Owens had used them to establish his Bakersfield sound and a few other groups had adopted the practice. The three cousins, plus their new percussionist, performed in a number of local bars in order to build up a fan base. More importantly, they started to write their own material. One of their first songs was "My Home's in Alabama," but before they could secure a recording contract the outfit suffered through different personnel changes. After a series of drummers came and went, Rick Scott accepted the chair, and with this important piece in place, they were ready to climb to the next level.

In 1977, the group changed their name to Alabama and signed to GRT Records. The single "I Wanna Be with You Tonight" placed in the charts, encouraging the young musicians. But when the company went bankrupt, they were forbidden to record any more music. It would be two years before they were able to record again after buying their way out of the contract. When Rick Scott left the band, they replaced him with Mark Herndon, a hard-hitting drummer with a rock and roll edge, who provided the group with an exciting dimension to their basic sound.

The group had learned an important lesson through their business dealings with the GRT label and decided to self-record their first effort. They also utilized the services of an independent record promoter to gain the disc much needed airplay. The single "I Wanna Come Over" brought them to the attention of distributor MDJ Records, who released the single. In 1980, the same label released the group's "My Home in Alabama," which brought the group greater recognition. They combined their recorded success with a classic performance at the Country Music New Faces concert that garnered them a contract with a major label, RCA Records.

The first RCA single, "Tennessee River," ignited a run of twenty-one number one hits that stretched until 1987, making them one of the most successful acts of the decade. The song was found on their *My Home's in Alabama* album, which also included the title track, as well as "Why Lady Why" and a blueprint of their developing sound that would catapult them to the top.

Their second album effort, *Feels So Right*, indicated a maturity. The entire work flowed with a consistency that would become their trademark. "Love in the First Degree," the title track, and "Old Flame" were all chart toppers, continuing the run of number one songs.

The momentum was building. *Mountain Music,* their third studio album, contained all of the trademarks that made them such a great band throughout the decade. The rough edges had been smoothed out, and they excelled as a genuine country-rock band. They had not followed in the steps of southern blues rockers Lynyrd Skynyrd or .38 Special. Instead, they took a soft rock-pop approach. The title track, "Take Me Down," and "Close Enough to Perfect" were all number one singles, with the latter peaking in the Top Twenty of the pop charts. They had managed to record a solid modern country music album.

Their tours also gained attention. With three solid records available, they had a fair amount of material to draw upon in concert. More importantly, they were able to play the songs the same way live the way they had been recorded. The effortless musicianship was one of the keys to their success.

By their fourth album release, *The Closer You Get ...,* they were well established in country music circles. The vocal harmonies, the down-home charm, the strong ballads were all part of the package. Some of the highlights included the number one singles "Lady Down on Love," "Dixieland Delight" and the title cut. At this point in their career, they were considered the best country band on the circuit.

The band's fifth studio album, *Roll On,* proved to be another winner and also exposed the band's one major weakness: they had settled into such a groove that their music sounded formulaic. The ease with which they reeled off their vocal harmonies, instrumentation, and arrangements made them sound robotic at times. However, the album did feature three hit singles, "Roll On (Eighteen Wheeler)," "When We Make Love," and "If You're Gonna Play in Texas (You Gotta Have a Fiddle in the Band)."

The next album, *Forty Hour Week,* demonstrated the group working on all cylinders. It contained four number one singles: "Forty Hour Week (For a Livin')," "(There's a) Fire in the Night," "There's No Way," and "Can't Keep a Good Man Down." It was a healthy mix of good old fashioned rockers Alabama-style and interesting ballads. It was a fan favorite. It also crossed into the pop Top Ten.

After *Alabama Christmas*—a collection of holiday tunes that included "Happy Holidays," "Tennessee Christmas," and "A Candle in the Window"—the group released their seventh full-length studio album, *The Touch,* which included the number one single "You've Got the Touch." However, it was a weak overall effort, indicating that the group was beginning to slow down.

While the New Traditionalists ruled country music radio, Alabama continued to roll along with their special sound. The next album, *Just Us,* included a return to form with the song "(I Wish It Could Always Be) '55" and the number one singles "Face to Face" and "Fallin' Again." Although it wasn't their strongest album, it did confirm that they were still the top group on the circuit.

The next album, *Live*, was solid but didn't totally capture the magic of one of their concerts. Their studio efforts were better examples of their touch. *Southern Star*, released in 1989, marked the end of a very successful decade for the band. It contained two number one singles, "Southern Star" and "Jukebox in My Mind."

In the 1990s, the group didn't enjoy the same success as it had the previous decade, but they still managed to record platinum albums and chart top singles. The dynamics of country music changed, focusing more on individual acts rather than country bands. They continued to record and perform to the legions of fans around the world.

They began the decade with *Pass It On Down,* another winning album with the number one singles "Forever's As Far As I'll Go" and "Down Home." They were still a force on the concert stage, delighting millions of fans with their incredible musicianship, vocal harmonies and cherished songs. As the most successful country recording group, they had blazed a trail for all others to follow.

The subsequent album, *American Pride*, was the work of veteran musicians. It was a well-crafted set of songs that included the number one hit "I'm in a Hurry (And Don't Know Why)," as well as the touching "Between the Two of Them." Many of the songs the band had recorded over the years featured small-town southern virtues and good old fashioned U.S. patriotism. One of the best examples of this was "Richard Petty's Fans," a tribute to one of the legends of the state of Alabama.

Although they were considered the old guard in country music circles, the band wasn't above using modern techniques, including video to enhance sales. They did so with the song "Still Goin' Strong," from their *Cheap Seats* album. It also included their last number one single, "Reckless."

They continued to record the rest of the decade, but they never quite captured the glory of the 1980s. In May 2002, the band announced its Farewell Tour, which took place across the U.S.A. during 2003 and 2004. Afterwards, they retired from touring.

Alabama was a country music supergroup. They enjoyed tremendous success throughout their careers and became the number one band in the 1980s. To this day they are still a recognizable name and now boast a fan base that includes a second generation. They mixed their strong country strain with doses of rock and pop that broadened their appeal.

Before Alabama came along and changed the rules, most country bands were relegated to a supporting role. But Alabama restored the public's taste for country bands. They were pioneers from a musical perspective as well as from a business standpoint, and many other acts followed their established blueprint. They created the right music for the right audience and broke ground for later performers to follow.

Their style is rooted in country, particularly the Bakersfield sound of Buck Owens, bluegrass and Nashville pop. The group proved that there was a very large market for a band that could combine its country sound with different strains. Their modern style supported a New Traditionalist approach, but also included a country-pop touch, as well as a hard edge.

Throughout their history, the trio of Owen, Cook, Gentry (with later the addition of Herndon) formed the foundation of the group. But others made important recording session contributions, including Jim Cotton, Paul Goldberg, Josh Leo, Harold Shedd and Kristin Wilkinson. The concept of a country band was one that Alabama embraced and they developed a formula that enabled them to become one of the most important and influential outfits in the history of the genre.

They had a special influence on a number of their contemporaries including Exile, Shenandoah, the Charlie Daniels Band, Sawyer Brown, Restless Heart, Pirates of the Mississippi, Juice Newton, George Strait, the Mavericks, the Dixie Chicks, Rascal Flatts, Sugarland, and Pure Prairie League, among others.

Although they wrote most of their own material, they also recorded the songs of others. Ronnie Rogers, Greg Fowler, Dave Loggins, John Jarrard, Roger Murrah, Mark Gray, J. P. Pennington, Jim Hurt, Tim DuBois, Rick Bowles, Bob Corbin, Josh Leo, Gary Baker, Jeff Steven, Dave Gibson and Frank J. Myers all contributed material to the group. Alabama's ability to take the efforts of others and put their undeniable stamp on each song underlines the depth and breadth of their talent. They had the ability to spin any material into gold and platinum.

Some of their best known songs include "Mountain Music," "Tennessee River," "Why Lady Why," "Love in the First Degree," "Dixieland Delight," "There's No Way," "She and I," "You've Got the Touch," "Song of the South," "High Cotton," "Southern Star," "I'm in a Hurry (And Don't Know Why)," and "Reckless." Many of their efforts are treasured country classics that other groups have recorded and performed. The Alabama catalog is one of the deepest in country music.

Alabama earned dozens of awards and were the best-selling group throughout the 1980s. In 1982, they won a Grammy for Best Country Performance By a Duo or Group with Vocal for "Mountain Music." In 1983, they earned another for the single "The Closer You Get." From 1981 to 1985 they were the Country Music Association's choice as Entertainer of the Year. Later they would be recognized as the CMA's Artists of the Decade for the 1980s. In 1999, the Recording Industry Association of America named them Country Group of the 20th Century. They collected more American Music

Awards than any other artists in history. Their AMAs included the Award of Merit. In 2004, they were inducted into the Vocal Group Hall of Fame.

Alabama also garnered many non-musical awards mainly due to their charity donations. These included the Bob Hope Humanitarian Award, Country Radio Broadcasters' Humanitarian Award, and the Minnie Pearl Humanitarian Award. They would also receive the B.M.I. President's Trophy for Public Service and (perhaps their proudest achievement) the Spirit of Alabama medal awarded by then Governor Bob Riley of Alabama. Later, because of their fervent support of the men and women in America's armed forces, which included hospital visits and special ceremonies, they were awarded the USO Rising Star Award and the Pentagon 9/11 Medallion.

Their charity work in the community also bolstered their reputation. From 1982 to 1997 they held the annual Alabama June Jam in Fort Payne. The proceeds were donated to various charities in the nearby area to help with worthy causes. They also gave their time to a number of fund-raising activities, with each group member pursuing a special interest of his own. On July 4, 1993, the group opened up a 2,000-seat theatre in Barefoot Landing, Myrtle Beach, South Carolina, commemorating where they began their career. The song "Dancin', Shaggin' on the Boulevard" paid tribute to local nightclubs of Myrtle Beach.

In 2005, Alabama was inducted into the Country Music Hall of Fame during the thirty-ninth annual Country Music Awards in New York. It was a deserved award for a group that remains a cherished musical act in the hearts of many fans — country and pop. They always knew how to write a catchy tune with enough elements of various styles to appeal to a great number of people. With their mountain music, they proved that country music bands could be a mighty force.

DISCOGRAPHY:

Feels So Right, RCA 5025.
Mountain Music, RCA 4229.
Stars, Sun 148.
The Closer You Get ..., RCA 4663.
Roll On, RCA 4939.
40 Hour Week, RCA 85339.
Alabama Christmas, RCA PDCI 7014.
The Touch, RCA5649-2-R.
Just Us, RCA 4695-2-R.
Live, RCA 6528-2-R.
Southern Star, RCA 8527-2-R.
Tennessee Christmas, RCA 5051-9-RS2.
Pass It on Down, RCA 2801-2-R.
American Pride, RCA 66440-2-R.

Cheap Seats, RCA 66296-2.
Gonna Have a Party ... Live, RCA 66149.
In Pictures, RCA 66525.
Christmas, Vol. 2, RCA 66927.
Dancin' on the Boulevard, RCA 67426.
Twentieth Century, RCA 67793.
Alabama for the Record, Medalist 22916.
When It All Goes South, RCA 69337.
Christmas, BMG Special Products 46451.
The Farewell Tour [live], RCA 54371.
Lady Down on Love, Sum Day 674.
Songs of Inspiration, RCA 532.
Songs of Inspiration II, RCA 706065.
Wild Country [Gold Vinyl], Plantation PP-44.
Greatest Hits, RCA 07863.
Greatest Hits, Vol. 2, RCA 61040.
With Jerry Lee Lewis and Willie Nelson, Quicksilver 1013.
The Country Side of Life , Pair 1329.
In the Beginning, RCA 59910.
Greatest Hits, Vol. 3, RCA 66410.
Super Hits, RCA 66484.
Born Country, BMG Special Products 44514.
Double Barrel Country: The Legends of Country Music, Madacy 5330.
The Essential Alabama [1998], BMG International 67621.
For the Record, RCA 67633.
18 Great Songs, Import 701397.
Premium, Medalist 12915.
Legendary, BMG International 94044.
In the Mood: The Love Songs, RCA 67052.
Platinum & Gold Collection, RCA 55160.
The Best of Alabama: Original Hits, Paradiso 786.
Ultimate Alabama: 20 #1 Hits, RCA Nashville 64196.
All American Country, BMG Records 44514.
The Essential Alabama [2005], RCA 68635.
Country Legends, Country Legends 76551.
Livin' Lovin' Rockin' Rollin': The 25th Anniversary Collection, RLG Legacy 71918.
Collections, Sony 8287675663.
Christmas Collection, Madacy 52274.
Wild Country [Direct Source], Direct Source 68492.
16 Biggest Hits, RCA 87634.
Pocket Songs: Alabama, Pocket Songs PS-126.

The Judds (1983–1991)
Rockin' in the Rhythm

The term *groups* covers full-fledged bands as well as duos. The history of country music is peppered with famous twosomes, including Roy Rogers and Dale Evans, Johnny Cash and June Carter Cash, Brooks & Dunn, Tammy Wynette and George Jones, and Loretta Lynn and Conway Twitty. In the 1980s, there was a mother-daughter act who became the most successful pair in the history of the genre with their rockin' in the rhythm sound. They were the Judds.

Naomi Judd was born Diana Ellen Judd on Jan 11, 1946, in Ashland, Kentucky. She grew up listening to country music and aspired to a singing career, but an early marriage and young family impeded these ambitions. On May 30, 1964, daughter Wynonna Judd (born Christina Ciminella) entered the world. When the marriage fell apart, Naomi moved her small family, which now also included a second daughter, Ashley, to Los Angeles, California.

They struggled as Naomi, a single mom, worked at a variety of jobs to provide for her two daughters. When a promising relationship turned sour, she returned to Kentucky in the mid–1970s. They lived a hand-to-mouth, anti-modern existence in a rural area of the state, and for entertainment they listened to the Grand Ole Opry and harmonized together. It was evident that even in her preteens Wynonna possessed a strong, beautiful voice.

The small family moved once again, this time to northern California, where Naomi decided to complete her schooling as a nurse in order to give her girls a better life. After graduation she sought work in the medical field; however, the elder Judd decided to practice nursing in Nashville where mother and daughter could give a musical career a chance.

In 1979, the mother and daughter duo that would someday take Music City U.S.A. by storm arrived in town as just two more singers with a big dream. Their sole outlet was performing on the *Ralph Emery Show*, one of the best television avenues for country artists looking for their big break in Nashville. Emery, a vital link to country music, always recognized talent when he heard it, and the Judds had it in abundance. Naomi had begun writing intelligent material, and Wynonna's voice had developed into a polished jewel.

While Naomi worked as a nurse and Wynonna completed her high school career, they continued to hone their skills. Eventually, the promising pair caught the attention of the Woody Bowles and Ken Stilts management team. A rough demo contained enough of the mother and daughter musical magic to attract the executives at RCA Records. Their simple audition — Naomi on guitar and the two rich voices blending perfectly together — landed them a contract.

In 1983, they released their first single, "Had a Dream (For the Heart)," which peaked in the Top Twenty. A short EP collection of their best work entitled *The Judds: Wynonna and Naomi* was issued and served as a precursor to the more ambitious full albums that would catapult them to the top of the country music world. A short, successful tour confirmed that they were ready for national stardom.

In 1984, "Mama He's Crazy" became their first number one and would start a streak of eight consecutive top hits. The song was found on their eponymous debut effort, *Wynonna & Naomi*, and although the material didn't amount to their strongest set, it established the vocal power and intricate beauty of the Judds. Their second number one single, "Why Not Me," won the Country Music Association Single of the Year. For the rest of the decade they were a top act on the circuit, and their albums consistently reached platinum status.

The duo's third effort, *Rockin' with the Rhythm,* was well received by fans and critics. Highlights included "Have Mercy" and the title track. Other highlights included "Tears for You," "Cry Myself to Sleep," and "Dream Chaser." At this point in their career they were considered two of the top females on the circuit, and their only real competition was rising star Reba McEntire.

The undeniable talent and range of their vocal abilities enabled them to cover any type of material, and this was evident on their *Heartland* set. "Don't Be Cruel," the Elvis nugget, kicked off the album, but the rest of the songs fell between roots rock and mainstream country. "Turn It Loose," "Cow Cow Boogie," and "I Know Where I'm Going" anchored the set.

Their concerts were sold-out affairs that only underlined the power of their vocals as individual singers and as harmonizers. Although their studio work was exceptional and featured a fair share of killer tracks, on stage they set the world on fire. They were a dynamic act who knew how to work an audience into a high-pitched frenzy; their concerts had become events.

The next album effort, *River of Time,* displayed a different dimension to their sound because it included the use of electric piano and Hammond B-3 organ. Also Carl Perkins, Mark Knopfler, and Roy Huskey, Jr., made guest appearances. Song highlights included "Cadillac Red," "Guardian Angel," "Water of Love," "Sleepless Nights," and "Do I Dare." There was a definite punch to their overall delivery that remained country despite stretching the parameters of the genre.

When they released *Love Can Build a Bridge,* the potent mother-daughter combo had no idea that it would be their last studio album. Although not their strongest effort, it contained many highlights including "Born to Be

Blue," "John Deere Tractor," a Lawrence Hammond remake, and "Rompin' Stompin' Bad News Blues," which demonstrated a fusion of country and R&B.

The 1990s promised to be another decade of successful high-rated tours and best-selling albums until Naomi contracted chronic, acute hepatitis, an incurable, life-threatening disease. She spent the first year of the decade too weak to perform. Eventually, the most successful duo in country music history were forced to break up, but not before they rewarded their fans with a final 124-date tour.

Although it was a gruelling endeavor, Naomi finished the tour and retired. Industry watchers wondered if Wynonna would carry on as a solo act, and the secret of her decision kept everyone guessing for all of 1991. But, prompted by her mother and managers, she forged on and released her first album. It demonstrated she could be successful on her own as the work went multi-platinum. Naomi published her autobiography, *Love Can Build a Bridge,* the title of their farewell tour.

Wynonna carried on and built a solid career. Her self-titled debut album contained three number one singles, "She Is His Only Need," "I Saw the Light," and "No One Else on Earth," pushing the effort to triple platinum status. In 1993, she would repeat her success with *Tell Me Why,* which went platinum on the strength of four Top Ten songs: "Tell Me Why," "A Bad Goodbye" (a duet with Clint Black), "Girls with Guitars," and "Rock Bottom."

In 1996, *Revelations,* her third solo album, went platinum in a few short months. Although it contained ballads like "Don't Look Back," "Love by Grace," and "My Angel Is Here," there were also up-tempo R&B numbers, including "Somebody to Love You." The record also featured her version of "Freebird," a tribute to the legendary southern band Lynyrd Skynyrd.

Wynonna is a versatile singer capable of belting out torchy country tear jerkers as well as an array of blues-based fiery tunes. Her next album, *The Other Side,* demonstrated the latter half of her musical personality. The album confounded country listeners but retained a certain segment of her fan base. Although it was successful in the opinion of certain critics, it was a disappointment to a portion of her followers.

Occasionally, mother and daughter reunited for special events, including the 1999 New Year's Eve concert. They performed their greatest hits and some of Wynonna's solo work, thrilling the audience, and although fans would have loved a full reunion, they had to settle for a new single, "Stuck in Love," which was available on the album *New Day Downing*.

New Day Downing was another eclectic effort that included southern gospel, soul, rock material and ballads. The song "Can't Nobody Love You (Like I Do)" made the Top Forty while the second single, "Going Nowhere," showed poorly. Her solo career seemed to be slipping away as she experimented with music outside of the mainstream that had made the Judds famous.

In 2000, mother and daughter released their New Year's concert as an album entitled *The Judds Reunion: Live.* Meanwhile, daughter Ashley embarked on an acting career and became an acclaimed actress, appearing in the major films *Heat, A Time to Kill* and *Double Jeopardy.*

Wynonna's next effort, *What the World Needs Now Is Love,* had very little to do with the famous Bacharach-David tune. Instead it was a diverse album delivered by a mature artist. Among the highlights were a duet with her mother, "Flies on the Butter (You Can't Go Home Again)," "I Want to Know What Love Is" (with Jeff Beck on guitar), and "Burning Love," the old Elvis chestnut.

Her Story: Scenes from a Lifetime was not an anthology, but a chronological race of her career performed live. Wynonna's A *Classic Christmas* was an album of songs that were delivered in an old-fashion style. She continues to record and perform.

The Judds were a country music phenomenon. They were one of the most successful duos in history and certainly the greatest mother-daughter combination. Although their time in the sun was limited due to Naomi's health, during their prime they racked up impressive record sales and number one singles with regularity.

The starting point was their vocal power. Wynonna possesses one of the finest voices in country music. Her big throaty sound rings clear and loud on many of their best songs. She also displayed an ability to sing any kind of material, including steamy R&B, driving rock and of course the gamut of the country spectrum from tender ballads to up-tempo pop-influenced numbers.

Her phrasing is always nearly perfect. Her ability to wring out every ounce of emotion from a song is remarkable and is one of the cornerstones of her fame. The grit, the sweetness, the effortless ability to swing from one extreme to another in just a couple of notes are all important trademarks of her vocal prowess.

Naomi was able to constantly wrap her ringing harmonies around Wynonna's impressive lead vocals. Her talent in soaring, floating and lilting in counterpoint to her daughter's commanding style formed the basis of their marketable sound. The ability to complement one another turned simple words and melodies into classics.

They gave the world a number of great songs. A partial list includes "Had a Dream (For the Heart)," "Mama He's Crazy," "Why Not Me," "Have Mercy," "Tears for You," "Cry Myself to Sleep," "Dream Chaser," "Turn It Loose," "Cow Cow Boogie," "I Know Where I'm Going," "Cadillac Red," "Guardian Angel," "Water of Love," "Sleepless Nights," "Do I Dare," "Born to Be Blue," "John Deere Tractor," and "Rompin' Stompin' Bad News Blues." If Naomi had not contracted hepatitis, the duo would boast twice the catalog. However, despite this stroke of misfortune, the mother-daughter combo still provided listeners with a bounty of big hits.

Although Wynonna's solo career has been a solid one, the downfall of one of the most beloved groups in country music history robbed the genre of one of its most important acts. They were solid practitioners of mainstream country and championed the style with excellent taste, fantastic flair and undeniable power. Since going solo, the younger Judd has displayed an eclectic touch, exploring many different musical avenues.

The Naomi and Wynonna Judd story is a heartwarming tale of a mother and daughter who paid their dues and found fame. The most tragic aspect was the breakup because of ill health when they were at their full expressive powers. Despite this setback, they proved that they could rock in the rhythm with the best of them.

DISCOGRAPHY:

Wynonna and Naomi, RCA 8402.
Why Not Me, RCA 11520.
Rockin' with the Rhythm, MCA 11519.
Heartland, MCA 11516.
River of Time, MCA 11518.
Love Can Build a Bridge, MCA 11517.
The Judds Reunion: Live, MCA 170134.
The Greatest Hits, RCA 8318-2-R.
Classic Gold, RCA Special Products 1063.
The Judds Collection 1983–1990, RCA 66045.
Collector's Series, RCA 52278.
Talk About Love, RCA 66150.
This Country's Rockin, RCA 66162.
Live Studios Sessions, RCA 66434.
Christmas with the Judds & Alabama, RCA 66433.
The Number One Hits, RCA 66489.
In Concert, RCA 66681.
The Essential Judds, RCA 66680.
The Judds Collection, Curb 024.
Spiritual Reflections, Curb 77842.
Greatest Hits Vol. 2, RCA 11515.
Christmas Time with the Judds, RCA 6422-2-R.
Christmas Time with the Judds, Curb 78827.
#1 Hits, Curb 77965.
Reflections RCA 66431.

Wynonna Judd:
Wynonna, Curb/MCA 10529.
Tell Me Why, Curb/MCA 10822.

Revelations, MCA 11090.
The Other Side, MCA 53061.
New Day Dawning, MCA 170103.
What the World Needs Now Is Love, Curb 137.
Her Story: Scenes from a Lifetime, Curb 198.
A Classic Christmas, Curb 224.

The Mavericks (1989–)
Music for All Occasions

In the beginning, all country music groups played old-timey style. Band members were almost exclusively from the South and shared many common bonds. However, the outfits of today command a wide range of styles and hail from all over the planet. Because of this they have created an eclectic brand of country. One of these bands found success with their music for all occasions. They are the Mavericks.

Long before the Mavericks were formed in 1989 in Miami, Florida (not known as a strong country music center), they followed individual trails. Raul Malo was born on August 7, 1965, in Miami, of Cuban parentage. He picked up the bass in his teens and played in various bands throughout high school where he met Robert Reynolds, a friendship that he would call on later. Malo's first recording was with the Basics on the single "Paperheart," which was included on a promotional album. His eclectic taste in music included country artists such as Hank Williams, Sr., Johnny Cash, and Patsy Cline, as well as Cuban music, pop flavorings and a tinge of jazz.

Robert Reynolds was born on April 30, 1962, in Kansas City, Missouri. He picked up the bass at an early age and developed his skills until he was ready to pursue a musical direction. He also listened to Roy Orbison, Elvis Presley and country artists like Cash, Cline and Hank Williams, Sr.

When the two decided to form a band, Reynolds persuaded his friend Paul Deakin to join the group. The talented drummer had spent most of his time performing in progressive rock bands, and the idea of a country based sound with a rock and roll edge sounded intriguing. The threesome decided on the name, the Mavericks.

The trio had an interesting strategic plan: they elected to play in rock clubs avoiding country venues in order to work out their own material. To play in traditional country bars meant they would have been forced to play cover songs. Their strategy would pay off handsomely a couple of years down the road.

They released their independent album in the fall of 1990 that enabled the audience they had built up with their extensive touring of rock clubs to be able to purchase the band's music. More importantly, the record which was a big hit in Florida also caught the attention of the Nashville record companies. The trio went to Music City U.S.A. to perform in a showcase where many executives were present. In the end, they decided to sign with MCA Records.

Before they entered the studio to record their first full-length work, they added lead guitarist David Lee Holt, who boasted credentials with Joe Ely, Rosie Flores and Carlene Carter. The seasoned veteran added the extra punch they were looking for and would be a vital addition for their tours and recording sessions. With all the pieces now in place, they proceeded to work on their first album.

The *From Hell to Paradise* effort forced many of the critics to stand up and take notice, but it didn't sell well and was a disappointment. Only the cover of Hank Williams, Sr.'s "Hey, Good Lookin'" dented the charts. The collection of mostly Malo original songs was good, but the band needed to adjust their formula if they were to make any serious inroads on a commercial level.

What a Crying Shame, released in 1994, turned their fortunes around as it shot to the top of the charts with the title track cracking the Top Forty. They were gaining momentum as this work demonstrated a more focused and sharpened attack. The personnel change that brought Nick Kane into the group to replace guitarist David Lee Holt only strengthened their stance.

By the spring of 1995, *What a Crying Shame* had gone platinum on the strength of a slew of hit singles, including "O What a Thrill" and "There Goes My Heart," among others. The touring side of their career had exploded as the rabid fans came out in droves to enjoy the entertaining music in a live setting.

The band released *Music for All Occasions,* which once again received favorable critical acclaim as well as the usual number of hit singles. The highlights included "All You Ever Do Is Bring Me Down" (which featured Flaco Jimenez), the title track and "To Be with You." The album would eventually go gold and set the precedent for their most ambitious effort to date.

Trampoline displayed a working band that was not afraid to experiment, since it featured more of a pop and Latin texture than country-rock. The mainstream audience turned away from the record but the single "Dance the Night Away" scored big in the United Kingdom. Despite their success on MCA the group tired of the label and took a long rest. In the interim, Malo and Reynolds both pursued different solo projects.

Malo released a solo album recorded with the Latino group Los Super Seven. Meanwhile Reynolds played on the sessions of the pop band Swag. Sadly, one of the most exciting groups on the circuit had ceased to make their special brand of music. Fans hoped that Malo and Reynolds would reunite since neither were that successful pursuing their individual paths.

In 2003, the group reformed with guitarist Eddie Perez replacing Kane. They recorded a self-titled set that included the single "Air That I Breathe," which scraped the bottom of the charts. In 2004, a CD and DVD recorded in Austin, Texas, as part of their tour was released. The group continues to record and perform.

The Mavericks are a country music sensation. Their blend of Latin rhythms, pop, rock and traditional sounds is a far cry from the music of Gid Tanner and His Skillet Lickers or Dr. Humphrey Bate and His Possum Hunters, but it still works on many different levels. With their eclectic style they have added a very different dimension to the contemporary scene.

Malo, Reynolds and Deakin are the cornerstones of the group. Raul Malo, the lead singer, has a convincing voice that is pure country but with enough range to cover any style. On more rocking numbers like "In Them Old Cotton Fields Back Home" and "Dance the Night Away," he rolls along with relative ease. Reynolds is always steady on bass and provides solid background vocals. Deakin is the other half of the rhythm duo and his rock background is essential to the group's overall dynamics.

They have won several awards, including Vocal Group of the Year at the CMA show in 1995, and again in 1996. They would later win a Grammy for Best Country Performance by a Duo or Group with Vocal. The importance of the honors underlined the fact that they were being recognized for their very interesting take on country music, which they created with such flair.

The Mavericks are an alternative county music group. They melded a traditional sound with Latin flavors, pop and rock. It proved to be a successful formula, and the group enjoyed a number of hits including "Blue Moon," "Dance the Night Away," "Oh What a Thrill," "What a Crying Shame," "All You Ever Do Is Bring Me Down," "To Be with You," and "All That Heaven Will Allow." Their spiced up catalog makes for a very enjoyable listen.

The Mavericks are an essential part of the alternative scene. They encompass the theme that modern country is a combination of traditional welded to different elements. In their case, the various styles include Latin, jazz, blues and rock. Their ability to create a cohesive sound out of so many influences is a tribute to their talent.

The story of the Mavericks is an interesting tale of a group of musicians with a different vision of how country could sound. Despite the fact they took a sabbatical for a couple of years it didn't hurt their popularity because fans were waiting for their return. They are a fun, entertaining band who can with their multiple abilities and creativity provide music for all occasions.

THE MAVERICKS
(1989–)

Lead Vocals	*Lead Guitar*
Raul Malo	Eddie Perez (2003–)
	Ben Peeler (1990–1991)
	David Lee Holt (1991–1994)
	Nick Kane (1994–2003)

Bass	*Drums*
Robert Reynolds	Paul Deakin

DISCOGRAPHY:

Mavericks, Hip-O 40113.
From Hell to Paradise, MCA 10475.
What a Crying Shame, MCA 10961.
Music for All Occasions, MCA 11257.
Trampoline, MCA 70018.
It's Now! It's Live!, MCA 70026 and Sanctuary 84647.
Live in Austin, Texas, Sanctuary 84715.
Super Colossal Smash Hits of the 90's: The Best of the Mavericks, MCA 170112.
Super Colossal Smash Hits of the 90's: The Best of the Mavericks [Re-Release],
  Mercury 170120.
Music for All Occasions/Trampoline, MCA 1701632.
O What a Thrill: An Introduction to the Mavericks, MCA 1940.
20th Century Masters — The Millennium Collection: The Best of the Mavericks,
  MCA 170229.
Collection, Spectrum 170329
The Definitive Collection, MCA Nashville 000250102.
Collection, Spectrum Music 98332.
Gold, MCA Nashville 06361.

Dixie Chicks (1989–)

Little Cowgirls

Throughout the history of country music many females have made very important contributions. From the very beginning, they made their presence felt in groups (Carter Family), as duos (Lulu Belle and Scotty) and as solo acts (Patsy Montana). Although most of the women singers have been solitary figures, in the late 1990s a trio emerged that would shake the industry with their little cowgirls sound. They are the Dixie Chicks.

The story of the Dixie Chicks begins with the Erwin sisters, Martie, born on October 12, 1969, in York, Pennsylvania, and Emily, born August 16, 1972, in Pittsfield, Massachusetts. The two were raised in Texas, where they absorbed the myriad musical styles of the Lone Star State. Martie learned how to play the fiddle and honed her skills quickly, while Emily became a guitarist. The two practiced together and eventually formed a group that consisted of singers Laura Lynch and Robin Lynn Macy, both born in 1956.

The four graduated from the same high school in Addison, Texas, a suburb of Dallas and based their initial sound on bluegrass. In 1989, Martie finished third at the National Fiddle Championships, giving the group solid credibility and enabling them to record an album. The effort, *Thank Heavens for Dale Evans,* was waxed on an independent label and included instrumentals but didn't receive a lot of attention.

They continued to build their career by winning the best band prize at the Telluride Bluegrass Festival and opening for such major acts as Garth Brooks, Reba McEntire and George Strait. Their songs were rarely on radio playlists, but the four of them forged on determined to make it in the music business. The camaraderie and support that the individual members gave each other enabled them to endure the lean years.

After a Christmas release, *Little Ol' Cowgirl* appeared in 1992. Lloyd Maines, a steel guitar legend, played on both of the records, giving the group a more contemporary country sound. Meanwhile, the four talented singers continued to tour, concentrating on events in the Texas and Nashville areas, creating a solid name for themselves. Despite critical approval, they enjoyed sparse commercial success. To make matters worse, original member Macy left in 1992 to pursue a different musical path.

The three remaining members carried on and released a third album in 1993, *Shouldn't a Told You That,* with Lynch handling all of the lead vocals chores. The effort boasted a much stronger bluegrass sound. Despite playing at President Clinton's inauguration as well as on the nationally televised CBS *Sunday Morning* show, commercial success continued to elude them.

There were more changes. Natalie Maines — born on October 14, 1974, in Lubbock, Texas, the daughter of producer and steel guitarist session player Lloyd Maines — assumed lead vocal duties replacing Laura Lynch. They also switched to Monument Records, and now the group lineup was set. Martie Erwin, who had married and changed her name to Sidel, played the fiddle, mandolin and sang. (She would later divorce and remarry.) Emily played guitar, Dobro and banjo and shared vocal duties. Although Natalie Maines played guitar in concert, it was her solid, punchy vocal style that proved her value to the group and gave listeners a strong identity.

In 1997, they released the single "I Can Love You Better," which made it to the country music charts. In 1998, the album *Wide Open Spaces* appeared and yielded three number one singles: "There's Your Trouble," "Wide Open Spaces" and "You Were Mine." The effort would sell over twelve million copies in an era of monster-selling country records, establishing the Dixie Chicks as a top group.

In 1999, they opened for Tim McGraw, and this time their performance was not ignored. They proved their mettle and revved up the audience every night with their high energy style. By now they had honed their act into a smooth running machine that was a combination of music, power, sass and looks.

In 1999, they released *Fly,* an appropriate album name because the disc soared over the competition. It yielded two number one songs, "Cowboy Take Me Away" and "Without You," plus seven other hits that pushed the album to diamond status (that is, sales of ten million or more). It is a rare feat to have two albums in a row hit that mark. On the ensuing Fly Tour, they were headliners and worked the big arenas in front of their ever growing legions of fans.

The three ladies had found the winning combination. They wrote most of their own material, mixed bluegrass with mainstream country and appealed to a large cross section of the public. They projected a visual image on stage that encompassed an entire spectrum of emotions. In the era of girl-power music, they fit right in and assumed a leadership role.

With any major act there is controversy. The girls flaunted their independence, a strong feminist stance that irked some people. Their lyrics were also a source of debate as some of their songs were removed from playlists for their suggestive content. The Dixie Chicks never apologized for their boldness because they were romantic, adventurous women with fiery Texas spirits and a take-it-or-leave-it attitude.

Controversy continued to follow them. They performed "I Believe in Love" on the *America: A Tribute to Heroes* telethon in response to the 9/11 attacks. They also became involved in a dispute with their label over royalties and accounting procedures, a matter that was settled in court in a tangled web of lawsuits and countersuits.

In 2002, they released *Home,* produced by Lloyd Maines. The album marked a change of direction for the group because of the outside material and absence of drums. Their new sound was dominated by more driving bluegrass and tender ballads. The lyrical content of some songs, especially "Long Time Gone," attacked contemporary radio, but nevertheless the song became a number one hit on both the country and pop charts. Other hits included a cover of Fleetwood Mac's "Landslide" and Patty Griffin's "Top of the World," which sparked the name for the subsequent tour. Although it didn't sell like the last two CDs, *Home* won three Grammy Awards in 2003 for Best Country Performance by a Duo or Group with Vocal, Best Country Instrumental Performance, and Best County Album.

The Dixie Chicks were one of the most visible and popular acts on the circuit. Always controversial and living on the edge, they fell from favor on March 10, 2003, when Natalie Maines made disparaging comments about President Bush on the eve of the Iraq War.

The fallout that ensued cost the group millions of dollars and much built up momentum. They were blacklisted on many stations, and fans protested outside of their concerts, while inside the concert halls things weren't much better as they were often booed. The Dixie Chicks had become a political football.

Natalie Maines would later apologize for her statements, but the damage was irreversible. Perhaps, because the comment was made while she was on foreign soil (they were touring England at the time), criticism of the head of state on the eve before the country was about to go to war sparked the intense hatred. The career of one of the finest groups on the country circuit seemed in severe jeopardy.

Many country performers criticized them in an effort to enhance their own careers. In an attempt to stem the negative result, the group launched a publicity campaign aimed at solidifying their point of view. They appeared on television, took out full-blown ads in major magazines, and even had the support of Bruce Springsteen and Madonna.

The fallout would continue for some time. All endorsements were cancelled, and the American Red Cross refused a USO offer to perform. They toured on the Vote for Change tour, backing presidential hopeful John Kerry, a move that backfired, since he lost the election. The hatred directed at them brought concerns for their safety.

But they persevered. The rebound began at the 2006 Toronto International Film Festival with an award-winning documentary entitled *Dixie Chicks: Shut Up and Sing*. The documentary followed the girls from the three years that began on that fateful night in March 2003 up to 2006. A second effort, the song "I Hope," appeared on the *Shelter from the Storm: A Concert for the Gulf Coast* telethon, with all proceeds donated to benefit hurricane relief. A third part of the comeback was the song "Not Ready to Make Nice," a cheeky single that fared poorly as did its cousin "Everybody Knows." However, the accompanying video won back some fans.

The new album, *Taking the Long Way*, released in 2006, was more rock-oriented than country-oriented. The Dixie Chicks continued to struggle to escape the dark cloud that remained over them, the momentum was beginning to swing back into their favor. Although the single "The Incident" received minimal airplay, the album debuted number one on the pop and country charts.

Taking the Long Way eventually went gold, making the Dixie Chicks the first female group in chart history to have three albums debut at number one. In Europe, the album fared better as the singles "Not Ready to Make Nice" and "Everybody Knows" finished in a higher position. The comeback begun almost two years earlier was now gaining momentum as those once in favor of the war were changing their point of view.

The Accidents & Accusations Tour created controversy when some shows were moved to smaller locations for lack of ticket sales, while some performances were cancelled outright. In the end, arguably, the Dixie Chicks won. *Taking the Long Way* won four Grammy Awards for Album of the Year, Record of the Year and Best Country Performance by Duo or Group ("Not Ready to Make Nice"), and Best Country Album. The growing hatred of the Iraq War was credited with spearheading their memorable night at the ceremonies. They continue to record and perform.

The Dixie Chicks are country music rebels. They represent the fiery spirit of the genre that has been a trademark since the pioneers of country music first recorded, and is one that continues to this day. Their songs, lyrical content, stage show, off the cuff comments, defiance, and talent are all part of the package. They are one of the most genuine acts on the contemporary scene.

The intricate interplay of the group members as a trio is the foundation of their sound. Their skill in blending the various nuances of their multiple abilities has enabled them to catapult over their competition. There are hundreds of country music acts on the circuit, but there is only one Dixie Chicks.

Maines gives the group a tough yet tender lead vocalist with the goods to deliver live and on record. Her voice is instantly recognizable and is derived from the many female stars in the genre's history. Yet there is a definite contemporary sound in her vocal delivery with a pop punch that separates her from the rest of the female country contingent.

Emily Erwin (Robison) is a versatile performer who provides the group with a strong musical prowess. She plays banjo, Dobro, acoustic guitar, electric guitar, papoose, accordion, and sitar, and also provides background vocals. Her ability to give the band someone with a sure touch on a variety of instruments only empowers the entire outfit.

Martie Erwin (Maguire) is a first-rate fiddler and gives the group added musical muscle. Her playing and singing are counterpoint to Emily's efforts. Martie's musicianship was clearly established years ago when she placed third in the National Fiddle Championships. The elder sibling also displayed her talent at Southeastern University in Georgetown, where she occupied a chair in the school's orchestra.

The blending of the three members into one cohesive unit includes the right mixture of elements to create the enthralling sound that is the Dixie

Chicks. They fit together so well that they are able to present a united and smooth sound, often making it feel like they are one musician instead of three. The camaraderie and meshing of talents is a cornerstone of their success.

They have given the world a number of interesting, thoughtful and fervent songs. A short list includes "I Can Love You Better," "There's Your Trouble," "Wide Open Spaces," "You Were Mine," "Cowboy Take Me Away," "Without You," "I Believe in Love," "Long Time Gone," "Landslide," "Top of the World," "I Hope," "Not Ready to Make Nice," and "Everybody Knows." Each song is a carefully crafted tune that displays their individual talent and the ability of the entire group.

They have won numerous prizes including three American Music Awards and one Billboard Award, as well as a number of CMA top prizes including four consecutive Vocal Group of the Year Awards from 1998 to 2002, the Entertainer of the Year Award in 2000 and three separate Music Video of the Year Awards. They have also won multiple Grammys and MTV Rock the Vote's Patrick Lippert Award for the protection of freedom of speech.

Originally their music was built on bluegrass, but it shifted into a more contemporary style that could be best classified as contemporary country. It contains a pop strain as well as a tinge of rock. Their ability to experiment with different elements without sacrificing their base sound is a tribute to their immense talent.

Although not from Texas, they have often demonstrated the spirited Lone Star State attitude in many of their songs and especially in their comments. Their comment about President Bush in reference to his birthright started all the controversy. The Dixie Chicks have taken their place alongside other country music acts from the vast, musically rich state.

The story of the Dixie Chicks is one of many elements. After all of the controversy, the hit singles, the death threats, the triumphant comeback and everything in between, the Dixie Chicks remain a potent musical act. Their resurrection from the depths of the heap is an amazing feat and something very few could ever achieve. The fire, passion, and musicianship ensures that the little cowgirls will continue to deliver their winning brand of country music.

DISCOGRAPHY:

Little Ol' Cowgirl, Crystal Clear 9250.
Thank Heavens for Dale Evans, Crystal Clear Sound 9103.
Shouldn't a Told You That, Crystal Clear 9369.
Wide Open Spaces, Monument 68195.
Fly, Monument 69678.
Home, Sony 86840.
Top of the World Tour: Live, Columbia 5137932.

Taking the Long Way, Open Wide/Columbia 80739.
Collector's Box, Chrome Dreams 6004.
Combo, Sony 25626.
Wide Open Space/Fly, Sony 5205282.

Brooks & Dunn (1991–)

The Dynamic Duo

There have been many successful pairs throughout the history of country music. In the early 1990s, two southern boys, Brooks & Dunn, joined forces to become the dynamic duo.

Ronnie Dunn was born on June 1, 1953, in Coleman, Texas into a family of wanderers. The young Dunn would know thirteen schools in twelve years and learn the vagabond lifestyle inside out. His father was a pipe fitter, a man who roamed the country in search of work, while his mother was a religious woman. The juxtaposition of sin and salvation combined and confronted each other to make up the man that would he would turn out to be.

The choice between God, church and righteousness versus the Devil, beer joints and recklessness was a difficult one to make, but Dunn chose the latter after nearly becoming a Baptist minister. He left school and wandered for some time before landing in Tulsa, where he honed his skills on the bass. He found work quickly and developed into a genuine country singer.

Dunn became a valued studio musician and worked with the members of Eric Clapton and Bonnie Raitt's bands at Russell's, a notorious watering hole. It was a demo cut at the aforementioned establishment that enabled him to win the Marlboro Country Music Talent Search by playing hard-driving country. More importantly, he caught the attention of Arista Records executives.

Kix Brooks was born on May 12, 1955, in Shreveport, Louisiana. Compared to his future partner, Brooks had a quiet childhood surrounded by music. One of the biggest influences in his young life was Johnny Horton, who won numerous gold records for his many hits during the 1950s. Brooks made his debut at age twelve paired with Horton's daughter and continued to perform throughout his high school days. He also began to write songs but was a long way from a recording contract.

Because the audiences demanded a versatile performer, he was forced to learn a variety of musical styles that proved beneficial to his development as a musician. In the many bands he played in, he opened for acts like the Nitty

Gritty Dirt Band, Asleep at the Wheel and George Thorogood, among others. By the time he left Louisiana, Brooks was well schooled in country, blues, jazz and folk.

Brooks left the swamps of Louisiana to be a pipe fitter in Alaska before heading to the East Coast where he worked at ski resorts. He eventually drifted down to Nashville and wrote for the Tree Publishing company where he penned "Modern Day Romance," a number one smash for the Nitty Gritty Dirt Band. Eventually, he released a solo album that did little to enhance his tepid career.

The two men had traveled many miles and played in many beer joints before fate intervened. The matching of the pair was electric as they had been searching musically for one another all of their careers.

They performed and wrote songs together, learning how to mesh their individual styles in order to create a cohesive sound. By 1990, they had honed their skills and were ready to take the country music world by storm. The title track of their debut album, *Brand New Man,* was their first number one, and they repeated the feat with "My Next Broken Heart." Unlike many other artists at the time, the duo wrote all of their own material. Other highlights from their initial effort included "Still in Love with You," and the traditional-sounding "Cheating on the Blues."

It was with confidence that they entered the studio to record *Hard Workin' Man,* which yielded the number one hit "Boot Scootin' Boogie." Other highlights included the title track, "Rock My World (Little Country Girl)," and slower numbers such as "That Ain't No Way to Go" and "She Used to Be Mine." While their first album was earning triple platinum status, their second effort was topping the charts.

That same year they earned their first of eight consecutive Vocal Duo Awards from the CMA. After the streak was broken in 2000, they restarted the run in 2001 and stretched it to six years. The performance side of their careers was also booming as they toured constantly throughout the country. The successful CDs only increased the public's desire to see the two exciting musicians live on stage.

The duo's third effort, *Waitin' on Sundown,* was another massive hit that went triple platinum. Highlights of the record included "Little Miss Honky Tonk," "She's Not the Cheatin' Kind," and "You're Gonna Miss Me When I'm Gone." The range of material was representative of modern country including ballads, country-pop, and traditional-style numbers with a rock and roll edge.

In 1996, they released *Borderline* and enjoyed a major hit with "My Maria," one of the few songs that they didn't write themselves. At this point in their careers, the twosome worked a heavy tour schedule and were unable to devote as much time to recording as they would have liked to. The result was their weakest effort to date, but they remained the top duo on the circuit.

They rebounded with *If You See Her*. It was a masterful record celebrating the magic formula between Brooks & Dunn that had been evident from their first release. There were many highlights: "Your Love Don't Take a Backseat to Nothing," "If You See Him, If You See Her," "Husbands and Wives" (an original Roger Miller tune), "Way Gone," "Brand New Whiskey," and "Born and Raised in Black and White." The material was much stronger than on their previous effort.

When the duo were able to blend their voices and musical skills together, they produced a formidable record. However, when they were unable to do so, the result was a weak effort that sounded like two individual singers. Unfortunately, *Tight Rope* suffered from a lack of cohesiveness despite solid hits such as "Temptation #9" and "Texas and Norma Jean."

After missing out on winning duo of the year honors in 2000 (the award went to Montgomery Gentry), they started a new chapter. They also released *Steers and Stripes,* a diversified modern country album that featured pure, heavy ballads, some penetrating rock, and pop-tinged material. "The Long Goodbye," "My Heart Is Lost to You," "Unloved," and "See Jane Dance" anchored the album.

Like almost all country artists, they finally released a seasonal music collection, *It Won't Be Christmas Without You.* It was a solid set and enabled the pair to spend more time on their next release, the concept album *Red Dirt Road.* The entire work was a tribute to their roots and influences, including Bruce Springsteen and Keith Richards. They were able to reproduce the feeling of these songs on the road.

The duo's *Hillbilly Deluxe* album was a back-to-their-roots album after experimenting with elements of pop and rock in their neo-traditional style. From the opening track, "Play Something Country," to a cover of Nicolette Larson's "Building Bridges," which featured Sheryl Crow on backing vocals, the entire collection celebrated their country sensitivity. Other highlights included "Whiskey Do My Talkin'," "I May Never Get Over You," "Her West Was Wilder," and "She Likes to Get Out of Town."

The CD *Cowboy Town* followed a couple of years later. It was more of a rock and roll effort than mainstream honky tonk. Highlights included the title track, "Proud of the House We Built, "Tequila," "Drop in the Bucket," and "Ballad of Jerry Jeff Walker," which included guest vocals from the renowned singer. The rowdy rock numbers anchored the CD and made it sound like a true Brooks & Dunn effort. They continue to record and perform.

Brooks & Dunn are a perfect blend of country grit and tradition. As individual performers they had a difficult time making it in the music business, but when paired together it was magic. They were able to combine their special and unique talents into a cohesive sound from their very first record.

Ronnie Dunn possesses a soulful voice with a quiet intensity. He is a traditional country singer who could wrench every drop out of a ballad until it was wrung dry. His outstanding vocal delivery was fine on its own, but it needed a spark, an opposite sound to make it that much more powerful.

Kix Brooks provided the opposite to Dunn's musical personality. A high-energy showman with the ability to light the fuel under a song and turn up the heat, he was the perfect accompaniment to his partner. His power-packed delivery gave their songs an intensity, an extra dimension that Ronnie couldn't provide.

As songwriters they complement each other very well. A partial list of the tunes they have given to the world includes "Brand New Man," "My Next Broken Heart," "Neon Moon," "Lost and Found," "Hard Workin' Man," "We'll Burn That Bridge," "She Used to Be Mine," "Rock My World (Little Country Girl)," "That Ain't No Way to Go," "She's Not the Cheatin' Kind," "Little Miss Honky Tonk," "You're Gonna Miss Me When I'm Gone," "I Am That Man," "He's Got You," "How Long Gone," "Husbands and Wives," "Ain't Nothing 'Bout You," "The Long Goodbye," "Only in America," "Red Dirt Road," "It's Getting Better All the Time," and "Play Something Country." The song "Boot Scootin' Boogie" is a special case because it ignited the line-dance craze throughout the world.

Brooks & Dunn are the most successful country music duo in the history of the genre. They have won the Vocal Duo Award from the CMA every year from 1992 through 2007, with the exception of 2000. The numerous other honors they have received prove the value of the magical music the two created since they came together more than a dozen years ago.

While their studio work has done very well, their live show has only supplemented their appeal. They put on a high-energy concert that features the best attributes from each one and a blend of their talents. They have worked with a number of other acts on the road including Keith Urban, Montgomery Gentry, Gretchen Wilson, Big and Rich, and Sara Evans. In 2006, they opened for the Rolling Stones in Nebraska. A Brooks & Dunn concert is a total musical experience.

Both play guitar and sing on record and in concert. On tour, they have always enjoyed a strong backup band. The most recent members consist of Lou Toomey on guitar, Terry McBride on bass guitar, Dwain Rowe on keyboards and background vocals, Tony King on guitar and background vocals, Jimmy Stewart on fiddle, acoustic guitar and banjo, Gary Morse on steel guitar, lap steel guitar and Dobro, and Trey Gray on drums. There has also been a trio of female background singers including, at times, Kim Parent, Trez Gregory, and Julie Downs.

The award-winning duo have lent their strong talents to a number of other acts. They recorded a collaboration with Reba McEntire, "If You See Him/If You See Her." Dunn helped Lee Roy Parnell on his cover of Hank Williams's "Take These Chains From My Heart." He also contributed to Keith Urban's "Raise the Barn," as well as Ashley Monroe's "I Don't Want To." Because of their immense abilities Brooks & Dunn are sought out by many other artists in the music business.

The Brooks & Dunn story is an interesting chapter in country music. While both struggled for years trying to make it on their own, as soon as they were paired together it proved a musical renaissance for each of them. As the most successful two-artist act on the circuit they are indeed the dynamic duo.

DISCOGRAPHY:

Brand New Man, Arista 18658-2.
Hard Workin' Man, Arista 18716.
Waitin' on Sunshine, Arista 18765.
Borderline, Arista 18810.
If You See Her, Arista 18865.
Tight Rope, Arista 18895.
Steers and Stripes, Arista 67003.
It Won't Be Christmas Without You, Arista 67053.
Red Dirt Road, Arista 67070.
Hillbilly Deluxe, Arista 69946.
Cowboy Town, Arista 711163.
Greatest Hits, Arista 18852.
Super Hits, Arista 18882.
The Greatest Hits Collection, Vol. 2, BMG 63271.
Very Best of Brooks & Dunn, BMG International 65914.
Waitin' on Sundown/Hard Working Man/Brand New Man, Madacy 51676.
Collections, Sony BMG 82876820372.
The Collection: Hard Workin' Man/Brand New Man, Madacy 52486.
The Collection: Brooks & Dunn/Hard Workin' Man, Madacy 52630.
Forever Brooks and Dunn, Madacy Special MKTS 52862.
Neon Moon, Phantom 218112.
Scootin' Boogie, Phantom 218122.

Rascal Flatts (1999–)

Pleasant Harmonies

The old-timey bands of the 1920s were usually large outfits consisting of many different members. Although there are groups on the circuit today who can boast a multiple lineup, the most effective country bands seem to be those with a limited number of members. A good example is the group of Ohio singers known as Rascal Flatts.

The story of Rascal Flatts begins with Gary LeVox, born on July 10, 1970, in Columbus, Ohio. He developed a love of music from an early age, and while growing up was an eager participant in family jam sessions. His rich, multi-layered voice blended well with other members during these gatherings especially that of his second cousin Jay DeMarcus.

Jay DeMarcus was born Stanley Wayne DeMarcus, Jr. on April 26, 1971, in Columbus, Ohio. He also developed an early love of music and learned how to play guitar, bass, keyboards, and mandolin. The multi-instrumentalist honed his skills and even at a young age eyed a musical career.

Joe Don Rooney was born on September 13, 1975, in Baxter Springs, Kansas, but was raised in the tiny Oklahoma town of Picher, where he also developed a love of music. He learned how to play guitar and honed his skills in various groups while a teenager.

All three took different paths before uniting to become a trio. LeVox graduated from Ohio State University and found work at the Ohio Department of Mental Retardation and Developmental Disabilities. He had never given up his musical ambitions, and when DeMarcus suggested he come down to Nashville to join his band, Gary jumped at the chance to be reunited with his cousin.

DeMarcus had left Ohio in 1992 and found a spot in the Christian group East to West. They scored a record deal and released a self-titled album in 1993. However, the outfit fell apart, and Jay found work in Chely Wright's backup band, where he met Rooney. Once LeVox moved down to Music City U.S.A. it didn't take long for him and DeMarcus to form their own outfit. One night when the guitar player couldn't make a gig, DeMarcus asked bandmate Rooney to sit in. He did and the magic between the three was evident; Rascal Flatts was born.

DeMarcus and Rooney gave their notice to Wright quickly, and the three began exploring the musical possibilities that they could create as a trio. They landed a record deal with the Lyric Street label and began to write enough material for a full-length album. Some of the songs had already been written during their long journey as itinerant musicians. They honed the songs until they reflected a professional, mature polished sound.

Their self-titled debut demonstrated a strong country base with pop and R&B elements. It yielded a number of hits, including "Prayin' for Daylight" and "This Everyday Love." But the record was more than just a collection of songs; it was the culmination of the lives of three nice guys who struggled for many years before they connected together.

Sometimes when the initial effort of an artist is delivered and becomes a big hit, too much is expected of their follow-up. Rascal Flatts' sophomore album, *Melt*, not only solidified their talent but expanded on what they had to say on the first record. The CD's first track, "These Days," was a smash hit and propelled the CD to sell one million copies in less than two months. The ballads were top notch, and the rest of the songs ran together with frightening power.

In the age of MTV, the good-looking members of Rascal Flatts took full advantage to expand their fan base with a music video. The "I Melt" video created a firestorm of controversy for brief nudity, and many protesters wanted it banned from CMT and Great American County. The group's Joe Don Rooney and model Christina Auria starred in the mini-flick. Eventually, the band released an edited version that blurred sensitive areas deemed inappropriate. The clean-cut image of the three average guys in the band suffered slightly, but overall they gained many new fans for their boldness.

The success of the first two records enabled the band to secure better concert venues, and they didn't fail to take advantage of the opportunity, selling out shows all over the country. Their live act was one of the hottest tickets around, and they enlarged their fan base quite nicely with each successive appearance. They delivered a package of solid musicianship, flair and looks.

The group's third studio album, *Feels Like Today*, saw them shift closer to a pop center and leave their country base. Nevertheless, it was another solid effort that went multi-platinum with its fiery ballads, soulful harmonies, and first-rate material. The song "Bless the Broken Road" was the band's first number one. Other highlights included "Fast Cars and Freedom," "Skin (Sarabeth)" and "What Hurts the Most."

They expanded their appeal by appearing in different venues, including a live performance of "Bless the Broken Road" on the reality television show *American Idol* with contestant Carrie Underwood. They would later play the same song on the television sitcom *Yes, Dear*. They also played on the soundtrack for the Disney movie *Cars*, singing "Life Is a Highway." The various publicity outlets helped pushed sales of their next studio album, *Me and My Gang*.

Me and My Gang contained many highlights, including "What Hurts the Most," a number one single. The title track, "My Wish," and "Stand" were also chart toppers. The record would take the number one spot on Billboard 200 Pop charts and become country music's best-selling album since the release of Tim McGraw's *Live Like You Were Dying*. Rascal Flatts continue to record and perform.

Rascal Flatts are a country music success story. They have managed to mesh their various talents into one cohesive unit that appeals to a cross-section of listeners from mainstream country-pop to adult contemporary. The marketing strategy behind the group is phenomenal and is a reason why three nice, average guys have been able to make such a heavy impact in a short time.

Any discussion of the group must begin with their vocal abilities. Gary LeVox is a powerful lead singer who can work his way through any style, including up-tempo pop, country torch and tender ballad. DeMarcus and Rooney provide more than adequate backing support. Another and extremely important dimension to their total sound is their skill in blending all three voices into one cohesive package.

There is a definitive commercial pop element in their vocal delivery that has triggered their immense success. The easy-going, pleasant appeal and enjoyable accessibility of their music is another factor in their popularity. Their slim but interesting catalog is a testimony to the potent delivery of first-rate material.

Their instrumental technique is subtle. Although they will never set the world on fire with their skills, they are more than adequate. Their ability on guitar, bass, keyboard and mandolin are overshadowed by their vocal harmonies. Although some studio musicians have been used to round out their overall sound, the group is more than capable of creating a solid wall of music.

They have given the world a number of great songs. A partial list includes "Life Is a Highway," "Fast Cars and Freedom," "Skin (Sarabeth)," "My Wish," "These Days," "Mayberry," "I Melt," "What Hurts the Most," "Bless the Broken Road," "Stand," "Prayin' for Daylight," "This Everyday Love," "Feels Like Today," and "Me and My Gang." Despite their limited catalog they have already provided a wealth of music.

The group is firmly established as a country-pop act, and along with Shania Twain, Martina McBride, Faith Hill, Tim McGraw and Trisha Yearwood, they have embodied the spirit that was first established in Nashville in the 1960s. With their multi-faceted abilities, Rascal Flatts could easily play and excel in any style. However, they have found success with the current brand of country music and continue to explore its dimensions.

They are also a good example of how to build a career. Rascal Flatts have utilized videos extensively to drive their message and music to appeal to a wider audience. The band has also chosen only first-rate material on their studio recordings, including both originals and cover versions. They have made very few mistakes in their professional career.

Rascal Flatts have won numerous awards. They have been the CMA Vocal Group of the Year four consecutive times from 2003 through 2008. The ACM voted them Top Vocal Group on three different occasions. They have also won the ACM Song of the Year for "I'm Movin' On." "Life Is a Highway" has also won them a truckload of hardware and is a song that has defined their sound.

The Rascal Flatts story is a classic example of marketing savvy, professional choice and, most importantly, talent. The three average members have proven that nice guys don't always finish last. As long as they continue to entertain audiences with their pleasant harmonies they will remain on top of the charts and in the hearts of fans everywhere.

DISCOGRAPHY:

Rascal Flatts, Lyric Street 165011.
Melt, Lyric Street 165031.
Feels Like Today, Lyric Street 165049.
Me and My Gang, Lyric Street 165058.
Still Feels Good, Lyric Street 000038402.
Feels Like Today/Me and My Gang, EMI 507148.
Best of Ballads, Cut 53104.

Sugarland (2002–)

Premium Quality Tunes

The state of Georgia has always been a hotbed of musical styles including blues, gospel, country, pop and rock. Gid Tanner was a native and became one of the most successful acts during the 1920s and 1930s with his Skillet Lickers. Two generations later, another group from the Peach State made an impact with their premium quality tunes. They are Sugarland.

Sugarland was formed in 2002, but prior to this all three members had a long, colorful musical history. Kristen Hall was born in Georgia and developed an early interest in music. Her big break came in the late 1980s when she hooked up with the Indigo Girls in a studio in Atlanta. She later toured with the group as their guitar technician, during which occasionally she would perform one of her songs. In 1990, she released a solo album, *Real Life Stuff,* and continued to appear with the Indigo Girls but now as their opening act. A second effort, *Fact & Fiction,* was released to high critical praise. In 1994, *Be Careful What You Wish For* was an album of greater polish and accessibility. When Amanda Marshall included Hall's composition "Let It Rain," on her debut CD, which sold well, it only boosted Kristen's career. Later she would relocate to California, only to return to the Atlanta area.

Jennifer Nettles was born on September 12, 1974, in Douglas, Georgia. The music bug hit hard and early; she performed in school assemblies, church and regional theatre during her childhood. In college, she formed Soul Miner's

Daughter with Cory Jones. The acoustic duo would go on to release two albums, *The Sacred and Profane* and *Hallelujah,* made up of songs that the two wrote. In 1999, she formed the Jennifer Nettles Band, which recorded three studio and two live albums. The highlight of their concert performances was at Lilith Fair in 1999. She often crossed paths with Kristen Hall and Kristian Bush.

Kristian Bush was born March 14, 1970, in Knoxville, Tennessee. He learned how to play the guitar as well as the mandolin and honed his skills in a variety of groups while growing up. His journey led him to form the folk duo Billy Pilgrim with Andrew Hyra. They recorded a self-titled work, and a second album, *Bloom.* They were based in Atlanta and received help from Amy Ray of Indigo Girls, putting Kristian in the path of Kristen Hall. Later, they released *Time Machine* before each went their separate ways. By this time, Hall, Nettles and Bush had begun working together.

The trio had often performed at Eddie's Attic in Decatur, Georgia, before they decided to combine their talents. Initially, they released EPs of demos, which were available on the Internet as well as at their live shows. Their recording career took some time to blossom, but since they were all well-seasoned performers the live side of their career was already churning.

In 2004, the groundswell popularity of the trio caught the attention of Mercury Records, and the single "Baby Girl" b/w "Stand Back Up" was released. Soon after, *Twice the Speed of Life,* their first full-length work, appeared. It yielded five major hits: "Baby Girl," "Something More" (which peaked at number two), "Just Might (Make Me Believe)," "Down in Mississippi (Up to No Good)," and "Stand Back Up." The album would go double platinum.

In 2005, they performed on Country Music Television's *Crossroads* with rockers Bon Jovi. Nettles added her powerful vocals to the single "Who Says You Can't Go Home," which would go to number one on the country charts. They continued to tour to enthusiastic audiences alongside Brad Paisley.

The following year was another successful one, but also one of change. They toured with Brooks & Dunn, most celebrated country music duo in history. The trio performed "Something More" at the Grammy Awards; however, Sugarland lost out on being named Best New Artist. The band later played at the 2006 CMT Awards with bassist Annie Clements adding a punch to their intricate sound. The saddest news for fans was the departure of founder Kristen Hall, who decided that she had grown tired of touring. Bush and Nettles continued as a duo.

The twosome released their next album, *Enjoy the Ride,* which included the title track, their first number one, as well as "Settlin'," another chart topper. The latter became the theme song for the 2007 ACC Men's Basketball Tournament as well as the SEC Men's Basketball Tournament. Later in the year they performed "Stay" at the CMT Awards and "Everyday America" at the ACM Awards. They continue to record and perform.

Sugarland is a country music mainstay. They have risen quickly after their formation to occupy a top spot among all groups on the circuit. The meshing of the individual talents into one cohesive sound is a compliment to their various abilities. Whether as a trio or a duo, they have delivered a potent musical punch.

Nettles is the group's lead singer and boasts one of the best voices in country music today and is blessed with an impressive range. She possesses a gospel and soul tinge in her delivery that is rather unique in country music; it has allowed her to infuse the group's material with a distinct mark. Her talent has been recognized throughout the music community as she participated in many different projects outside of the group's fold.

Although her vocal delivery stands out, it is even that much more special when blended with the voices of her two bandmates. Although Bush spent most of his time in a folk medium, he has the ability to belt out a solid mainstream country tune. Hall was able to hold her own in the trio, and the loss of her contributions forced the other two to double their efforts.

They are all adept musicians, with Bush taking the nod as the most accomplished and versatile. Their mainstream studio sound works perfectly in a live setting since they have been able to duplicate on stage what they have done on CD. They bolstered their sound with various guests on their recorded work. Interestingly, despite the closeness of the trio, other musicians were able to sit in and fit well into the group dynamic.

Although they are unable to boast the longevity of modern groups such as the Oak Ridge Boys, Asleep at the Wheel and Alabama, Sugarland has covered much territory in their short existence. Their mainstream sound has captivated audiences, and they have proven very capable of capitalizing on every opportunity that has come their way. The group is a classic example of how rapidly a current artist can climb up the ladder of success.

In their short career together they have delivered a number of quality songs. A partial list includes "Baby Girl," "Stand Back Up," "Something More," "Just Might (Make Me Believe)," "Down in Mississippi (Up to No Good)," "Who Says You Can't Go Home," "Settlin'," "Stay," and "Everyday America." Of course, the catalog is even more extensive if one considers their solo work and the material recorded with other groups before the formation of Sugarland.

The group has performed at many festivals, and that experience is one of the key factors responsible for their quick success. As well, they have wisely utilized videos to enhance their reputation. They are media savvy, and that knowledge has allowed them to catapult ahead of outfits that have been around much longer than a mere five years.

The Sugarland story is a tale of three individual musicians who found each other to create something special. In a very short time, they have gained a tremendous amount of mainstream attention — much more than the trio did as individuals. Although Hall has left the group, the remaining two have proven they are still a force to be reckoned with. Despite the fact that the catalog of material featuring all three is rather slim, they have excited crowds with their premium quality tunes.

DISCOGRAPHY:

Twice the Speed of Life, Mercury 02532.
Enjoy the Ride, Mercury Nashville 07411.

PART FOUR

Country-Pop

The roots of country-pop stretch back to the rise of rock and roll in the 1950s. Until then, country music had been an isolated style restricted to a very narrow market. But rockabilly proved that traditional honky tonk when welded with other styles could produce mass appeal and crossover success.

The first phase of the sub-genre was called countrypolitan for its blending of rural sensibility and urban sophistication. Chet Atkins, the superpicker, was also the producer at RCA Records and desired to expand the parameters of country studio recordings in order to gain a wider appeal. He often took very simple and catchy country tunes and placed them in orchestral arrangements with an emphasis on the strings to create a smooth, polished style. Later, Owen Bradley, the producer at Decca Records, another mastermind, crafted a more lush environment for Patsy Cline, making her a superstar.

Countrypolitan eventually envolved into the Nashville Sound since most of the records were recorded in Music City, U.S.A. Jim Reeves and Eddy Arnold were two other singers who benefited from the marriage between the two distinctive genres. Although opposition gave birth to the Outlaw movement and the Bakersfield sound, country-pop was there to stay.

In the 1970s, the country-pop style gained even more widespread acceptance as producer Billy Sherrill carried on the work of Atkins and Bradley. George Jones, Tammy Wynette, Charlie Rich and Conway Twitty achieved regular crossover success. Acts such as folk singer John Denver and crooner Olivia Newton-John enjoyed tremendous success, with the former winning CMA Entertainer of the Year in 1975.

At the end of the decade, the Urban Cowboy craze was just another derivative of the country-pop style. It melded traditional sounds with a soft-rock approach that appealed to a more cosmopolitan crowd. Kenny Rogers, Dolly Parton, Barbara Mandrell and Crystal Gayle all enjoyed massive hits into the early 1980s.

By the middle of the 1980s the New Traditionalists ruled the airwaves with their return to the roots honky tonk style. However, the slick production techniques laid the groundwork for a new version of country-pop that blended with the elements of rock and roll: the driving beat, the big sound studio trappings, and the arena rock antics.

Garth Brooks arrived on the scene at the right time with the right product. He was a country artist but owed much of his sound to rock and roll and pop. He achieved the kind of success that not even Atkins and Bradley could have imagined. Soon a number of other artists — mainly females, including Martina McBride, Faith Hill, Shania Twain, Carrie Underwood — appeared on the scene and would dominate the charts.

Since then, many rock acts have crossed over into the country charts with pop-flavored material. Sheryl Crow, Los Lonely Boys, MercyMe, Kid Rock, Jimmy Buffett, Elton John, Uncle Kracker, John Mellencamp and Bret Michaels became practitioners of the style.

The debate between the supporters of country-pop and the purists rages on. There is no denying the fact that the country-pop of Brooks, Hill, Twain and Tim McGraw has brought in new fans and taken the genre into the record-selling stratosphere. On the other side, the purists argue that the crossover singers have taken their sound too far away from country roots.

Some of the country-pop artists not discussed in this book are John Denver, Big and Rich, Trace Adkins, Eddie Rabbitt, Olivia Newton-John, Billy Ray Cyrus, Lynn Anderson, Earl Thomas Conley, Mac Davis, Donna Fargo, Anne Murray, Juice Newton, Jerry Reed, Jeannie C. Riley, Linda Ronstadt, Matraca Berg and Pam Tillis. The artists who are included are a representative sampling of the modern country-pop movement from its 1960s stylings to the present sound:

- Tammy Wynette was one of the major artists in the 1960s and 1970s. She lived the life that she sang about with painful reality.
- Ronnie Milsap was a major contributor to the country-pop movement as a singer, musician, songwriter and producer.
- Dolly Parton is one of the true superstars of country music whose career dates back to the 1960s and stretches to the present. She had something to offer in every decade.
- Barbara Mandrell was part of the 1970s wave of country-pop artists whose career was nearly destroyed by a car accident.
- Crystal Gayle followed in her sister's (Loretta Lynn) footsteps and eventually moved out of her sibling's shadow.
- Tanya Tucker was a country-pop phenom who became a star before she was old enough to legally drive an automobile.
- Garth Brooks took country music into the stratosphere with his marketable ideas, his talent and his style.
- Trisha Yearwood is a country music jewel and one of the most popular performers. She is also married to Garth Brooks.
- Shania Twain is one of the most visible country-pop performers and also

one of the most successful. The Canadian songbird has made a large impact on the American and international markets.

- Martina McBride possesses a voice that can cover any type of material and make it sound new and fresh.
- Tim McGraw is the number one male country star now that Brooks is out of the business.
- Faith Hill is one of the most important modern country artists. She has successfully melded traditional country with pop elements to gain a wide fan base.

Tammy Wynette (1942–1998)
Stand by Your Man

Country music, like the blues, has several standard themes, including loneliness, love gone bad, and travel. The emotion poured into the lyrics, melodies and musicianship is responsible for the power, fire and popularity of each style. There have been many artists who sang with much pain and intensity because they lived the life they sang about. One of them is the female singer who will be forever linked to her signature song, "Stand By Your Man." Her name was Tammy Wynette.

Tammy Wynette was born Virginia Wynette Pugh on May 5, 1942, in Itawamba County, Mississippi. Her father was a musician, but he died when Wynette was just eight months old, and she was shipped to her grandparents' farm in Mississippi, while her mother moved to Birmingham, Alabama, to do military work. It was a rough childhood filled with hard labor and poverty. Little Virginia turned to music for comfort. She idolized Hank Williams, Sr., Skeeter Davis and Patsy Cline. The young girl taught herself a number of instruments that had once belonged to her father and often sang gospel tunes with family members.

After working as a waitress, receptionist, barmaid and factory worker, she decided on a career as a beautician and hairdresser. At seventeen, she married Euple Byrd, a union that produced three children and ended in divorce a short time later. To complicate matters, her third child suffered from spinal meningitis, which meant hefty medical bills that far exceeded what she made as a hairdresser. In order to make extra money, Wynette sang in clubs.

She caught her first big break in 1965, when she landed a regular spot on the *Country Boy Eddie Show*, a local television program that led to appearances on Porter Wagoner's syndicated show, which received much more exposure. The following year she made the move to Nashville, and after some hard, discouraging dues-paying months finally was signed to Epic Records.

Her first single, "Apartment #9," nearly cracked the country Top Forty. She rectified that situation with her next single, "Your Good Girl's Gonna Go Bad," which peaked at number three and introduced the world to Tammy Wynette, the stage name she had adopted. A duet with David Houston, "My Elusive Dreams," became her first number one in a string of Top Ten hits that would stretch for more than a decade. Her next single, "I Don't Wanna Play House," also reached the Top Ten.

In 1968, she reinforced her burgeoning career with three number one hits: "Take Me to Your World," "D-I-V-O-R-C-E," and the song that would become her signature, "Stand by Your Man." She performed at different venues, earning critical praise for her distinctive vocal delivery and electrifying performances. It was also around this time that she became involved with one of the great singers of country music, George Jones.

The year 1969 was another triumphant one. She placed two more songs — "Singing My Song" and "The Ways to Love a Man" — at the top of the charts. The album *Tammy Wynette's Greatest Hits* eventually went gold, making her the first female country artist to achieve this goal. Her rising career held great promise on the eve of a new decade.

She started off the 1970s with a number of her songs used in the soundtrack for the film *Five Easy Pieces*. She also continued to score top hits, including "Good Lovin' (Makes It Right)," "He Loves Me All the Way," and "Bedtime Story." But the biggest news of the decade was her relationship, marriage and divorce to Jones. She had remarried a second time but left her husband to wed George. The union produced a child, a number of great songs recorded together, and much heartache.

George Jones, known as the "Cadillac Voice of Country Music," had a severe drinking problem. It created a stormy relationship that provided fodder for the gossip magazines. However, the pair also recorded a number of hit songs including "Take Me," "The Ceremony," "Old Fashioned Singing," "Let's Build a World Together," "We're Gonna Hold On," "(We're Not) The Jet Set," "We Loved It Away," "God's Gonna Getcha for That," and "Golden Ring." In 1975, the marriage ended in divorce, although they continued to work together into the 1990s.

In 1976, she married Michael Tomlin, but the marriage was annulled a few weeks later. Despite the stress of her personal relationships, she continued to record top songs during the decade, including "My Man," "Kids Say the Darndest Things," "Another Lonely Song," "Woman to Woman," "You and Me," "I Still Believe in Fairytales," "Womanhood," "One of a Kind," and "No One Else in the World," among others.

Throughout the decade she was a country music queen. She challenged

Loretta Lynn, Dolly Parton, Lynn Anderson and Crystal Gayle for the title. In 1978, she married George Richey, which became her longest relationship lasting until her death in 1998. It was during her reign as a top female artist that she began to experience serious physical ailments including problems with her gall bladder and kidney, and nodules on her throat.

Although she would continue to score top singles and albums, it happened with less frequency. "Crying in the Rain," "Cowboys Don't Shoot Straight (Like They Used To)," "Another Chance," "A Good Night's Love," "Your Love," "Talkin' to Myself Again," and "Beneath a Painted Sky" were all hits, but none of them reached the number one spot. Her physical ills continued to plague her, and she was hospitalized numerous times, often after enduring major surgery. To combat the pain she became addicted to large doses of medication.

She attempted to bolster her career with a television role on a soap opera but made bigger headlines when she filed for bankruptcy in 1988. By the end of the decade the country music queen was regulated to has-been status by many cynics. But the spirit that she always possessed would enable her to reach the brass ring one more time.

Her comeback began in 1991 when she recorded a song with KLF, a British techno pop group, entitled "Justified and Ancient (Stand By the JAMs)." The song would go to number one on the pop charts in almost twenty different countries, and the accompanying video accelerated her return to form. Wynette capitalized on a remark made by future First Lady Hillary Clinton in reference to her signature song "Stand by Your Man." The comment was a publicity bonanza and freshened Tammy's name even more.

In 1993, she collaborated on an album with Dolly Parton and Loretta Lynn, two of her biggest rivals. Although it didn't spawn any top singles, the record did announce to the world that Wynette still possessed a strong voice. A year later she recorded *Without Walls,* a collection of duets with partners Wynonna Judd, Elton John, Lyle Lovett, Aaron Neville, Smokey Robinson and Sting, to name a few. The project showed the respect that she still commanded throughout the musical community.

In 1995, she recorded a duet album with George Jones. She also continued to suffer physical problems that kept her hospitalized on numerous occasions. After years of experiencing various ailments, she succumbed to cardiac arrhythmia on April 6, 1998. The vocalist many called the First Lady of Country Music was fifty-five years old.

Tammy Wynette was a genuine country singer. From the very first few notes of her very first single it was apparent that she was born to be a country vocalist. Her tone, her delivery, and her talent were all the necessary ingredients she needed to become a sensation on the country circuit. The controversy that surrounded her throughout her career is also part of the story.

Wynette's voice was tailor-made for country music. When she sang about heartbreak, it came from a woman who had known it firsthand. When she talked about hard financial times, once again her voice rang true with experience. The special timbre in her voice ensured that she would become famous before her death and remain a legend after her demise.

With her plain yet powerful vocal style she ushered in countrypolitan, a mixture of the Nashville Sound with an urban sophistication. It was this particular genre that she and partner George Jones specialized in and perfected to become for a time in the 1970s the king and queen of country music. During this period their only serious rivals were Loretta Lynn and Conway Twitty. The two couples flipped back and forth, winning awards during the decade.

Wynette enjoyed a great number of hit singles. A partial list includes "Apartment #9," "Your Good Girl's Gonna Go Bad," "My Elusive Dreams," "I Don't Wanna Play House," "Take Me to Your World," "D-I-V-O-R-C-E," "Stand by Your Man," "Singing My Song," "The Ways to Love a Man," and "Take Me," among others. No matter the material, she was always able to inject each song with her own personal style.

Wynette had a major influence on a number of female country singers. A short list includes Lynn Anderson, Barbara Mandrell, Reba McEntire, Lorrie Morgan, Sandy Posey, k.d. lang, Joanie Keller, Tammy Cochran, Clarice Rose, LeAnn Rimes, Patty Loveless, Faith Hill, Trisha Yearwood, Shania Twain, Crystal Gayle, the Dixie Chicks, and Tanya Tucker. In reality, anyone that came after she hit the charts took a page out of Tammy's book.

Although she worked with a number of artists, her closest partner was George Jones. The pair made great music together in the studio, and their performances were events, but domestic life was too unstable. The power of their relationship was underlined by the fact that after their divorce they could still spark the magic on vinyl and in concert.

The Tammy Wynette story is a tale of a classic country female singer. She enjoyed a tremendous amount of success, but her personal life always seemed one of turmoil. Even after her death, lawsuits continued to plague her name. Whatever difficulties she suffered during her career and private life, she remains a shining star in the country music universe.

DISCOGRAPHY:

Your Good Girl's Gonna Go Bad, Epic/Legacy 66998.
D-I-V-O-R-C-E, Epic BN-26392.
Stand by Your Man, Epic BN-26451.
Inspiration, Epic BN-26423.
Run, Angel, Run [Original Soundtrack], Epic BN-26474.
The Ways to Love a Man, Epic BN-26519.
Christmas with Tammy, Epic 3E-30343.

Tammy Wynette, Harmony 30096.
Tammy's Touch, Epic BN-26549.
First Lady, Epic 30213.
The World of Tammy Wynette, Epic 503 (2).
Five Easy Pieces [Original Soundtrack], Epic KE-30456.
It's Just a Matter of Time, Harmony 30914.
We Sure Can Love Each Other, Epic EQ-30658.
Bedtime Story, Epic KE 31285.
My Man, Epic KE 31717.
Kids Say the Darndest Things, Epic 31937.
The First Songs of the First Lady, Epic 30358.
Another Lonely Song, Epic 32745.
Woman to Woman, Epic 33246.
I Still Believe in Fairy Tales, Epic 33582.
'Til I Can Make It on My Own, Epic 34075.
You and Me, Epic 34289.
Let's Get Together, Epic 34694.
One of a Kind, Epic 35044.
From the Bottom of My Heart, Pair 1073.
Womanhood, Epic 35442.
Just Tammy, Epic 36013.
Only Lonely Sometimes, Epic 35485.
Encore: George Jones & Tammy Wynette, Epic 37344.
You Brought Me Back, Epic FE 37104.
Soft Touch, Epic FE 37980.
Even the Strong Get Lonely, Epic 38744.
Good Love & Heartbreak, Epic 38372.
Sometimes When We Touch, Epic PET-39971.
Higher Ground, Epic EK-40832.
Next to You, Epic EK-44498.
Heart Over Mind, Epic EK-46238.
Without Walls, Epic 52481.
Back to Back: George Jones and Tammy Wynette, Exelsior 7207.
'Til I Get it Right, Platinum Disc 17912.
Tammy Wynette Live, Country Legends 76654.
Matter of Time, Bear Family BT 13260.
Take Me to Your World/I Don't Want to Play House, Koch 7944.
Tammy's Greatest Hits, Epic BN-26486.
Tammy's Greatest Hits, Vol. 2, Epic 30733.
The Very Best of Tammy Wynette, Columbia P65-5856.
Greatest Hits, Vol. 3, Epic PET-33396.
Tammy, K-Tel 3350.
Greatest Hits, Vol. 4, Epic 35630.
Biggest Hits, Epic EK-38312.
20 Years of Hits, Epic E 240625.
Anniversary: 20 Years of Hits, Epic 450393 2.
Country Store Collection, Country Store CST 1.
Best Loved Hits, Epic EK-48588.
20 Greatest Hits, TeeVee 6002.

Tears of Fire: The 25th Anniversary Collection, Epic E3K-52741.
Always Gets It Right, Sony Special Products 16558.
Winners [1995], Sony Special Products 17737.
In Concert, Hallmark 30292.
Super Hits, Epic 67539.
The Best of Tammy Wynette, Sony 4840462.
In Concert Singing Her Songs, Country Stars 55440.
Together Again, K-Tel 4022.
The Best of Tammy Wynette, Prism 1115.
Greatest Hits: Live in Concert, Prism 237.
Inspirational Favorites, Ranwood 8273.
On Stage, Hallmark 30949.
Collector's Edition, Sony 69560.
Super Hits, Vol. 2, Sony 69557.
D-I-V-O-R-C-E/Your Good Girl's Go Gonna Bad, Epic 494898.
The Definitive Collection, Sony 494355.
16 Biggest Hits, Epic/Legacy 69437.
Best of Tammy, Music Digital 6187.
Live, Goldies 63237.
In Concert, Charly 1259.
Back 2 Back, Intercontinental 1207.
Tammy Wynette/Tanya Tucker Platinum Disc 1772.
I Love Country, Sony 4611272.
The Best of Tammy Wynette, Sony 4913102.
Welcome to My World, Hallmark 31276.
Tammy Wynette, Castle Pulse 445.
Legends in Concert, Epic/Legacy 87150.
Singing My Songs, 4AM 4045.
Hall of Fame 1998, King 3829.
Collection, Perforax 083.
Love Songs, Epic/Legacy 87150.
Some of the Best Live, Fabulous 161.
Without Walls/Your Good Girl's Gonna Go Bad, Epic 0072.
The Essential Tammy Wynette, Sony 90645.
Sing Their Greatest Hits, Gusto 387.
Queen of Country, Rajon 18.
Making Love/Heart Songs, Platinum Disc 3354.
Great Tammy Wynette, Rajon 27274.
The Best of Tammy Wynette, Pegasus 183.
Singing My Song, Musicrama 51981.
The Ways to Love a Man/Tammy's Touch, Raven 237.
Country Legends, Country Legends 76654.
Country's First Ladies, Musical Memories 33502.
Classic Hits, KRB Music 8304.
Favorites, KRB Music 8401.

Ronnie Milsap (1944–)
The Country-Pop Master

In the 1990s, a number of country-pop artists exploded onto the scene with their commercial appeal and slick production techniques. Although much of it sounded new and fresh, the genre had been around for a very long time. In the 1970s, when most of the country-pop divas of the past ten years weren't even born, a country pop master was establishing the parameters of the style. His name was Ronnie Milsap.

Ronnie Milsap was born on January 16, 1944, in Robbinsville, North Carolina. Born without sight, he showed his musical gifts at a young age and was encouraged to develop them. Within a year of seriously taking up music he had mastered the violin, piano, guitar and a number of other instruments. The blind prodigy astonished many veteran musicians with his dexterity and speed.

In his teens, he formed his first rock band, the Apparitions. Although he had the opportunity to become a lawyer, Milsap opted for a career in music. He found employment as a member of J. J. Cale's band in the early 1960s and learned much from Cale, a country/rock artist who would later write the songs "Cocaine" and "After Midnight," both of which Eric Clapton made famous.

In the mid–1960s, Milsap formed his own group, and they scored one hit, "Never Had It So Good." He then moved to Memphis, where he found plenty of work as a session ace working with Elvis Presley on the songs "Kentucky Rain" and "Don't Cry Daddy." When not in the studio, Milsap and his backing band were performing at local clubs. At this point in his career, he was also writing songs and had a hit with "Loving You Is a Natural Thing." He released his initial self-titled album, but his once promising career slowly ground to a halt.

Milsap craved a change of direction and moved to Nashville, where he landed a recording contract with RCA Victor Records. In 1973, his first single, "I Hate You," was a Top Ten hit. A year later, he scored three consecutive hits with "Pure Love," "Please Don't Tell Me How the Story Ends," and "(I'd Be) A Legend in My Time." This was a foreshadowing of future events as he would blossom into one of the most successful country artists with a fifteen-year string of Top Ten hits, including many number one songs.

In 1977, he continued his streak of top hits with "It Was Almost Like a Song," which gave him crossover appeal. Other top charting tunes included "Let My Love Be Your Pillow," "Let's Take the Long Way Around the World,"

and "Nobody Likes Sad Songs." At this point he was still very much recording material in a traditional country vein. But as the decade came to a close
he started to shift to a more pop-oriented sound.

By 1980, country music was caught up in the Urban Cowboy fad. As
well, traditional country artists, such as Dolly Parton, Barbara Mandrell and
Kenny Rogers, were superstars enjoying monster hits with their crossover
material. Milsap began the decade with the album *Milsap Magic*, which yielded
the top singles "Cowboys and Clowns," "Misery Loves Company," "My
Heart," and "Silent Night (After the Fight)." But he also scored on the pop
charts with "There's No Gettin' Over Me" and "Smoky Mountain Rain."

A couple of greatest hits packages were sandwiched between his previous release and his next album effort *Inside*; he proved that he still possessed
the magic touch. The songs "Any Day Now," "He Got You," and "I Wouldn't
Have Missed It for the World" were all number one hits, giving him a grand
total of nine consecutive top tunes. His reign continued with the next album
release.

Keyed Up contained two top songs, "Don't You Know How Much I Love
You" and "Show Her." However the streak would come to an end with the
Top Five song "Stranger in My House." While the New Traditionalists were
poised to take over the radio waves, Milsap cut through their sound with his
distinct country-pop material.

He returned to the top of the charts with the album *Lost in the Fifties
Tonight*. It yielded five number one songs, including the title track, "Happy,
Happy Birthday Baby," "How Do I Turn You On," "In Love," and "She Keeps
the Home Fires Burning." The master still maintained the magic touch and
proved that he had never lost it.

By 1987, with the New Traditionalists firmly entrenched as the number
one trend on the circuit, he continued to score with his pop-flavored sound.
Heart & Soul contained the number one hits "Snap Your Fingers" and "Where
Do the Nights Go." His last number one hit was "A Woman in Love," from
The Essential Ronnie Milsap collection.

Still, he continued to enjoy chart success with the Top Five songs "Houston Solution, "Stranger Things Have Happened," "Are You Lovin' Me Like
I'm Lovin' You," and "Turn the Radio On." "Since I Don't Have You" peaked
in the Top Ten. But by the early part of the 1990s his reign was over. Ironically, the country-pop that he helped to keep alive during the 1980s would
explode with the likes of superstars Garth Brooks, Shania Twain and Faith
Hill all selling incredibly large numbers of records.

As he continued to release albums, he toured constantly to enthusiastic
crowds who never tired of his hits. He would chart with "L.A. to the Moon"
and "True Believer," but they were a far cry from the number one songs he
had turned out with such regularity ten years before. In 2006, "Local Girls"

stalled at number fifty-four in the charts. He continues to perform and record sporadically.

Ronnie Milsap was a country music hit machine. For over a decade he regularly placed number one songs on the charts. He trails only Conway Twitty and George Strait on the all-time list as producers of top charted tunes. His easy style, excellent material and special delivery were the reasons why he enjoyed such wonderful success.

Ronnie Milsap has a voice that was tailor-made for the country-pop tunes that he crafted with such grace during his career. There is a familiar tone, a soothing element that takes the listener along through the journey of the particular song. He created a style that is instantly recognizable within the first two or three notes sung.

He recorded a number of gems. A partial list includes "It Was Almost Like a Song," "Smoky Mountain Rain," "No Gettin' Over Me," "Any Day Now," "A Woman in Love," "Please Don't Tell Me How the Story Ends," "Pure Love," "(I'd Be) a Legend in My Time," "Daydreams About Night Things," "What Goes On When the Sun Goes Down," "Let My Love Be Your Pillow," "Only One Love in My Life," "Nobody Likes Sad Songs," "Cowboys and Clowns," "Misery Loves Company," "My Heart," "Silent Night (After the Fight)," "Am I Losing You," "Any Day Now," "He Got You," "Where Do the Nights Go," "A Woman in Love," "How Do I Turn You On," and "Lost in the Fifties Tonight (In the Still of the Night)." His songs remain classic country tunes as a new generation discovers them.

Ronnie Milsap was a country-pop artist long before the genre became the dominant format in the 1990s. He paved the way for Garth Brooks, Shania Twain, Faith Hill, Trisha Yearwood, Tim McGraw, and Martina McBride. He also blazed a trail for many of the new breed performers, including LeAnn Rimes, Ashley Monroe, Taylor Swift, Sara Evans, Carrie Underwood, Catherine Britt and Miranda Lambert, among others.

He worked with a number of session musicians and singers, including Charlie McCoy, Reggie Young, Farrell Morris, Mike Leech, John Hughey, Bobby Emmons, Shane Keister, Bruce Dees, Tom Collins, Gene Chrisman, Kenny Rogers, Dolly Parton, Bobby Wood, Rob Galbraith, David Briggs, and Elvis Presley. A virtuoso, Milsap was adept at the violin, piano, guitar, mandolin and a number of various woodwinds. It is understandable why so many artists desired to utilize his bountiful skills.

The Ronnie Milsap story is one of genuine success. He overcame many obstacles, including blindness, to become one of the top artists in the genre. His string of consecutive number one hits is astonishing and one that few will ever challenge. He created the path that many others would follow as the country-pop master.

DISCOGRAPHY:

Ronnie Milsap, Warner 1934.
Pure Love, RCA 0500.
Where My Heart Is, RCA 0338.
A Legend in My Time, RCA 0846.
Night Things, RCA 1223.
A Rose by Any Other Name, Warner Brothers 2870.
It Was Almost Like a Song, RCA 5986.
Live, RCA 5978.
Only One Love in My Life, RCA 2780.
Images, RCA 3346.
There's No Getting' Over Me, RCA 4060.
Milsap, Magic, RCA 3563.
Out Where the Bright Lights Are Glowing, RCA 3932.
Inside, Buddah 99760.
Keyed Up, RCA 5993-2.
One More Try for Love, RCA 5016.
Lost in the Fifties Tonight, RCA 7194.
Christmas with Ronnie Milsap, RCA 5624-2.
Heart & Soul, RCA 7618-2.
Stranger Things Have Happened, RCA 9588-2.
Back to the Grindstone, RCA 2375-2.
Back on My Mind, Pair 1105.
True Believer, Liberty 80805.
Sings His Best for Capitol, Capitol 31839.
Christmas in Dixie, BMG Special 44536.
Branson City Limits [live], Unison 9009.
Wish You Were Here, Music Club 50125.
Believe It, Pair 1031.
Live [2002], Image 1775.
Just for a Thrill, Image 1778.
Country Class, Bear Family 19221.
Greatest Hits, RCA 8504-2.
The Essential Ronnie Milsap, RCA 66534.

Dolly Parton (1946–)

Smoky Mountain Voice

There have been many important female country singers throughout the annals of the genre's history that have made formidable contributions equal to that of their male counterparts. Maybelle Carter, Sara Carter, Patsy Cline, Kitty Wells, Dottie West, Loretta Lynn, Tammy Wynette and Barbara Mandrell have all made an impact. However, despite a long list of women singers in country music, none have equaled the total media impact of the Smoky Mountain Voice. Her name is Dolly Parton.

Dolly Parton was born January 19, 1946, in Sevierville, Tennessee, the fourth of twelve children. Her upbringing in the Locust Ridge region of Tennessee next to the Smoky Mountains was tough, and she was ridiculed for her attire. But she found solace in music because not only did it take her away from the reality of her financial situation, it was also clearly evident that Dolly had talent.

It was Parton's uncle, the Reverend Jake Owens, a fiddler and songwriter, who gave her a guitar when she was seven. Parton honed her skills and at ten was a regular on a local radio program, *The Cass Walker Farm and Home Hour*. She would stick with the show off and on for some six years. At twelve, she made her Grand Ole Opry debut, and while in her teens she cut her first single, "Puppy Love," released on the Goldband label.

A later single, "It's Sure Gonna Hurt," bombed and Mercury Records dropped her. Not to be denied, she continued to cut singles on various independent labels, but none of them brought her fame. After graduating from high school, Parton moved to Nashville where she met Carl Dean, whom she would later marry.

Her career in Nashville advanced much more slowly than she wanted it to, and even a collaboration with Bill Owens proved unsuccessful. However, by the mid–1960s Parton was starting to build some momentum. After signing with Monument Records, she recorded "Happy, Happy Birthday Baby," which nearly made the charts. The next two singles, "Put It Off Until Tomorrow" and "The Company You Keep," did a little better, setting the stage for "Dumb Blonde." It was only a minor hit but it enabled her to join the *Porter Wagoner Show*, a top syndicated television program.

Her years with Wagoner — 1967–1974 — were good ones. She was known as Miss Dolly on the show and replaced the immensely popular Norma Jean. It was a tough struggle at first, but she quickly warmed the hearts of the audience and became a staple. During this period she recorded many Top Ten singles, including "The Last Thing on My Mind," "Just Because I'm a Woman," "In the Good Ole Days (When Times Were Bad)," "Mule Skinner Blues (Blue Yodel No. 8)," "Joshua," "Coat of Many Colors," and "Jolene," which reached number one in early 1974.

After leaving Wagoner, Parton continued to enjoy success charting a number of singles, including "I Will Always Love You," "The Bargain Store," "Baby I'm Burning," "Two Doors Down," "You're the Only One," "Starting Over Again," and "Old Flames Can't Hold a Candle to You." In 1976, she had her own syndicated television show, and her career receive another boost when artists Rose Maddox, Kitty Wells, Olivia Newton-John, Emmylou Harris and Linda Ronstadt covered her songs.

But her popularity was solidified in 1977 with the release of "Here You Come Again," which became a crossover hit and made her a household name. The combination of her diverse song material, sex bomb image, appearance on the cover of many country and mainstream publications ensured her superstar status. After years of struggling, Dolly was ready to take center stage. She did not disappoint.

In the next few years she would build upon her momentum to achieve greater success. She had three consecutive number one hits: "Starting Over Again," "Old Flames Can't Hold a Candle to You," and "9 to 5." The latter song introduced Dolly the actress in the movie *9 to 5*, a feminist tale that co-starred Jane Fonda and Lily Tomlin.

Dolly appeared in a number of other films, including *The Best Little Whorehouse in Texas* with Burt Reynolds, *Rhinestone Cowboy* with Sylvester Stallone, *Steel Magnolias* with Julia Roberts and Shirley MacLaine, *Straight Talk* with James Woods and the movie adaptation of *The Beverly Hillbillies*. Perhaps not the most talented actress, she utilized every one of her skills to come across as a likeable, fun character in the roles she portrayed.

She also continued her run at the top of the charts with "But You Know I Love You," "I Will Always Love You," "Islands in the Stream," "Tennessee Homesick Blues," "Real Love," "Think About Love," "Why'd You Come in Here Lookin' Like That," "Yellow Roses" and "Rockin' Years." Her chart success only enhanced her popularity, which at this point was on an international level. In North America, she was one of the top entertainment figures.

Her ability to maintain such a hectic schedule proved to be overwhelming, and as the 1980s wore on her fame waned. Many of the songs during this period were heavily pop influenced, and her hard-core country music fans began to turn away. She also spent an increasing amount of time busy with other projects, including her theme park, Dollywood, that opened in 1985. As well, she suffered various health problems, and her image that had worked so well in the 1970s and early 1980s was considered wrong for the latter part of the decade.

She signed with Columbia Records and recorded the rootsy *Trio* album with Linda Ronstadt and Emmylou Harris. The record spawned three Top Ten hits, including "To Know Him Is to Love Him," "Telling Me Lies" and "Those Memories of You." Her solo album, *White Limozeen,* yielded "Why'd You Come in Here Lookin' Like That" and "Yellow Roses." During this period, she also hosted her own network television variety show, which had a short run lasting but one season.

In 1991, Parton had a number one single with Ricky Van Shelton, "Rockin' Years," then disappeared from the charts as country radio began to play the music of younger contemporary stars. However, she continued to appear in movies, and her concerts sold out. She also released an acclaimed album, *Honky Tonk Angels*, a collaboration with Tammy Wynette and Loretta Lynn. When Whitney Houston took Dolly's composition "I Will Always Love You" to number one, it helped Dolly remain in the limelight.

In 1994, she published her autobiography, *My Life and Other Unfinished Business*. Her album *Treasures*, released in 1996, was an effort of unusual covers of material ranging from Merle Haggard to Neil Young. In 1999, she released *Trio Two*, a second collaboration with Ronstadt and Harris. Since then *The Grass Is Blue, Little Sparrow* and *Halos and Horns* have been added to her extensive catalog. Dolly Parton continues to record and perform.

Dolly Parton is a country music icon. Although there have been many important female stars to grace the genre in the past forty years, none have been able to deliver the same total package. She is a household name, one of the most recognizable figures on the celebrity stage today. While her music career has declined since the mid–1980s, she remains one of the most original voices in the history of the genre.

Despite her multi-talented abilities in every media outlet, any discussion of her career begins with her voice. She is a powerful singer, a possessor of a soothing, comforting, down-home vocal style that has always been the cornerstone of her entertainment career. There is hint of a southern upbringing, a mountain life, combined with a polished cosmopolitan range that projects a complete package. From her major hits to her more obscure cuts, there is no mistaking the voice as anyone else's but Parton's.

If Parton had stuck to music and had never branched out into other areas, she would still be a superstar. But her ability and skill in conquering different media has allowed her to enjoy a much more varied career than the average female country singer. She has been one of the most photographed and interviewed women in the world during her long, successful run.

Parton has always been self-sufficient, a trait that is one of the genuine keys to her success. She has written many of her own hits and was never afraid to take a chance. Her vision and self-confidence as an artist always enabled her to push ahead into new, exciting territory. There has always been a part of the little girl who grew up poor in a family with twelve children in the Smoky Mountains in every endeavor she has ever undertaken.

Like many other important music lights, Parton has influenced a number of individuals. She was a leader among female figures, and her work is a good study for anyone interested in making it in the field of entertainment. She left a special mark on LeAnn Rimes, Trisha Yearwood, Faith Hill, Kelly Clarkson, Shania Twain, the Dixie Chicks, Alison Krauss, Iris DeMent, k.d. lang, Kathy Mattea, Lee Ann Womack, Lorrie Morgan, Martina McBride, Mary Chapin Carpenter, Nanci Griffith, Patty Loveless, Reba McEntire, Rosanne Cash, and countless others. Her influence has spilled over to pop music to include Britney Spears and Christina Aguilera among others.

Parton has given the world a treasure trove of songs, including "Happy, Happy Birthday Baby," "Put It Off Until Tomorrow," "The Company You Keep," "Dumb Blonde," "The Last Thing on My Mind," "Just Because I'm a Woman," "In the Good Ole Days (When Times Were Bad)," "Mule Skinner Blues (Blue Yodel No. 8)," "Joshua," "Coat of Many Colors," "Jolene," "I Will Always Love You," "The Bargain Store," "Here You Come Again," "Baby I'm Burning," "Two Doors Down," "You're the Only One," "Starting Over Again," "Old Flames Can't Hold a Candle to You," "Here You Come Again," "Starting Over Again," "9 to 5," "But You Know I Love You," "Islands in the Stream," "Tennessee Homesick Blues," "Real Love," "Think About Love," "Why'd You Come in Here Lookin' Like That," "Rockin' Years," "To Know Him Is to Love Him," "Telling Me Lies," "Those Memories of You," and "Yellow Roses." Her catalog is one of the fullest, most complete in the history of country music and deeper than any other female singer.

Dolly has won many awards during her long illustrious career, including Grammys, CMA awards and a variety of other honors. But her greatest moment in the limelight occurred in 2006 when she was honored at the Kennedy Center for her outstanding achievements. A number of individuals, including Alison Krauss, were on hand to honor one of the leading country female icons of all time.

The Dolly Parton story is one of perseverance, laughter and triumph. It is the tale of a little girl who grew up poor in a remote area, but with the values of family, love and God to guide her through life she succeeded over many obstacles. The sheer determination, talent and hard work of Dolly Parton, the Smoky Mountain Voice, enabled her to make a lasting impact on country music.

DISCOGRAPHY:

Dolly Parton Sings, RCA Victor 4762.
Hits Made Famous by Country Queens, Somerset SF-19700.
Hello, I'm Dolly, Monument SP-18085.
Dolly Parton Sings Country Oldies, Somerset 29400.
Dolly Parton and George Jones, Starday SP-429.
Just Because I'm a Woman, RCA SP-3949.
In the Good Old Days (When Times Were Bad), RCA SP-4099.
The Fairest of Them All, RCA 4288.
Just the Two of Us, RCA 4039.
My Blue Ridge Mountain Boy, RCA 4188.
As Long As I Love, Monument SP-18136.
A Real Live Dolly, RCA 4338.
Once More, RCA 4388.
Two of a Kind, RCA 4490.
Golden Streets of Glory, SP-4396.
Joshua, RCA 4507.

Coat of Many Colors, RCA 4603.
Touch Your Woman, RCA 4686.
The Right Combination/Burning the Midnight Oil, RCA 4628.
Together Always, RCA/Victor SP-4761.
My Favorite Songwriter, Porter Wagoner, RCA SP-4752.
Mine, RCA ACL-1-0307.
We Found It, RCA 4841.
My Tennessee Mountain Home, RCA 3178.
Bubbling Over, RCA 10286.
Jolene, RCA 10473.
Bargain Store, RCA 10950.
Dolly, RCA 1221.
Love Is Like a Butterfly, RCA 10712.
All I Can Do, RCA 1068.
Say Forever You'll Be Mine, RCA 1116.
New Harvest ... First Gathering, RCA 12188.
Here You Come Again, RCA 12544.
Heartbreaker, RCA 12797.
Great Balls of Fire, RCA 3361.
Dolly Dolly Dolly, RCA 13361.
Porter & Dolly, RCA 11700.
9 to 5 and Odd Jobs, RCA 4830.
Heartbreak Express, RCA 3076.
HBO Presents Dolly Parton, RCA Victor 812.
Burlap & Satin, RCA 6080.
The Great Pretender, RCA 84940.
Rhinestone [Original Soundtrack], RCA 85032.
Once Upon a Christmas, Camden, 74321890962.
Real Love, RCA 85414.
Rainbow, Columbia 42968.
White Limozeen, Columbia 44384.
Home for Christmas, Columbia 46796.
Eagle When She Flies, Columbia CT-46882.
Slow Dancing with the Moon, Columbia 53199.
Honky Tonk Angels, Columbia 53414.
Heartsongs: Live from Home, Columbia 66123.
Something Special, Columbia 67140.
Treasures, RCA 53041.
Hungry Again, MCA 70041.
The Grass Is Blue, Sugar Hill 3900.
Little Sparrow, Sugar Hill 3927.
Halos and Horns, Sugar Hill 3946.
For God and Country, Work Music Group 79756.
Live Well, Sugar Hill 3998.
Those Were the Days, Sugar Hill 4007.
World of Dolly Parton, Monument 31913.
The Best of Dolly Parton [1970], RCA Victor 4449.
The Best of Dolly Parton [1975], RCA 1117.
This Is Dolly Parton, RCA 0007.

The Dolly Parton Story, Embassy 31582.
The Hits of Dolly Parton, RCA 42192.
The Great Dolly Parton, Camden 1171.
Dolly Parton Collection, Pickwick 053.
You Are, RCA 5044.
Collection, Monument 22105.
Dolly Parton, Camden 1208.
The Very Best of Dolly Parton [2002], BMG 74321971332.
Greatest Hits, RCA 6058.
Queens of Country, Force 1001.
Collector's Series, RCA 6338-2-R.
Magic Moments with Dolly Parton, RCA 89620.
Portrait, Pair 1116.
Just the Way I Am, Pair 1009.
Think About Love, RCA 89871.
The Best There Is, Collectables 9426.
The World of Dolly Parton, Vol. 1, Monument 44361.
The World of Dolly Parton, Vol. 2, Monument 44362.
The Love Album, RCA 030725.
Greatest Hits, Vol. 1 [Import], RCA 040724.
The Love Album, Vol. 2, RCA 045521.
The Best of Dolly Parton, Vol. 3, RCA 5706-2-R.
Greatest Hits [Import], RCA 059627.
Little Things: 18 Great Country Songs, Country Stars 55419.
The RCA Years 1967–1986, RCA 66127.
The Collection [Germany] RCA 39872.
Collection, Castle CC5353.
Two of a Kind [Compilation], Pair 1335.
The Greatest Hits, Telstar 2739.
The Essential Dolly Parton, Vol. 1: I Will Always Love You, RCA 66533.
Anthology, Connoisseur Collect 165.
2gether on 1, RCA 94562.
I Will Always Love You and Other Greatest Hits, Sony 67582.
Super Hits [1996], RCA 66852.
Dolly Parton -Plus- Faye Tucker, Alshire 5351.
The Best of Dolly Parton [Import], Camden 74321476802.
The Ultimate Collection, RCA 443632.
The Essential Dolly Parton, Vol. 2, RCA 66933.
I Believe, BMG 44617.
The Encore Collection, BMG Special Products 44521.
Jolene: Greatest Hits, Simply the Best 5638.
Great, Goldies 63184.
The Best of Dolly Parton [DJ Specialist], DJ Specialist 47680.
Super Hits, Vol. 2, RCA 67758.
Greatest Hits [Columbia River], Columbia River 210000.
Super Hits [1999], Sony 4989662.
Love Songs, BMG International 67440.
La Legende Country, Sony 4913072.
Honky Tonk Angel, Golden Stars 5131.

Legendary Dolly Parton, BMG 753102.
Dolly Parton & Friends at Gold, Goldband 7770.
Dolly Parton, Legend 64020.
Honky Tonk Angel, Pegas 275.
Midnight Country, Dressed to Kill 0815.
The Best of Dolly Parton [Gold Disc], Hot Town Music 102816.
Gold: Greatest Hits, RCA 74321840202.
Jolene/My Tennessee Mountain Home, BMG 82236.
Back to Back, Pegasus 333.
Legends, Camden 74321892502.
Jolene/Coat of Many Colors, BMG International 86964.
Mission Chapel Memories 1971–1975, Raven 121.
Dolly Parton and Kenny Rogers, Golden Stars 5276.
RCA Country Legends, RCA 65101.
All American Country, BMG Special Products 4521.
Best of the Best, Federal 500.
Best of Dolly Parton BMG 37333.
I'll Be Home for Christmas, Sony 467672.
Songs of Love & Heartache, Sony Mid-Price 5100502.
Makin' Believe, Legacy 176.
Greatest Hits, BMG International 98526.
Ultimate Dolly Parton [1-CD], RCA 52008.
The Bluegrass Collection, Camden 82876567282.
Dolly Parton and Kenny Rogers, Goldies 25178.
The Very Best of Love, Madacy 50251.
Platinum & Gold Collection, RCA Nashville/BMG Heritage 57229.
The Great, Import 50213.
The Only Dolly Parton Album You'll Ever Need, BMG 82876626282.
Puppy Love, Air 603.
The Early Years, Xtra 26450.
Artist Collection: Dolly Parton, BMG International 63626.
The Collection [universal International], 9820143.
The Essential Dolly Parton, RCA 69240.
Country Legends, Country Legends 76670.
Love Songs, RLG/Legacy 76176.
Covered by Dolly, Sterling Ent 35272.
Best of Dolly Parton: Original Hits, Paradiso 750.
Collection, Sony International 678153.
Ultimate Dolly Parton [2-CD], Sony International 50389.
Puppy Love, Pazzazz 079.
Puppy Love and Ruby, Pazzazz 079.
The Acoustic Collection: 1999–2002, Sugar Hill 4008.
Country Hit Parade, Direct Source 70542.
All I Can Do/New Harvest ... First Gathering, BMG 88697061082.
Burlap & Satin/Real Love , BMG 88697061132.
Great Balls of Fire/Dolly Dolly Dolly, BMG 88697061162.
The Very Best of Dolly Parton [2007], BMG 88697060742.
16 Top Tracks, RCA 90108.
Great Dolly Parton, Rajon CDR0296.

Barbara Mandrell (1948–)

Midnight Angel

The contribution of female artists in country has a long, colorful history that stretches from the efforts of the Carter women in the early 1920s to the greatness of Patsy Cline, the superstardom of Dolly Parton, Loretta Lynn and Tammy Wynette, to today's sterling lineup. There was also the lady singer who began as a child prodigy and eventually dominated the industry as the Midnight Angel. Her name is Barbara Mandrell.

Barbara Mandrell was born on December 25, 1948, in Houston, Texas, into a musical family; her father owned a music store and her mother taught piano lessons. Barbara began her music lessons at a very early age and made her debut playing the accordion at her church at five. By age ten, Mandrell had made so much progress on the pedal steel guitar that she appeared on television and radio in Bakersfield, California.

One year later her father thought so much of her blossoming talent that he took his eleven-year-old daughter to a music trade show in the Windy City. The appearance in Chicago was a seminal event in her career because it was there that she met Joe Maphis and Chet Atkins. Both were greatly impressed, and the former took her on his tour at the Showboat Hotel in Las Vegas. This concert performance led to a regular spot on the local television program *Town Hall Party*, in Los Angeles. Johnny Cash spotted her and took her along on his traveling show, which also featured June Carter, Patsy Cline and George Jones.

The Mandrells decided to form their own family band in order to tour the West Coast. By this time, two more family members augmented the lineup: sisters Louise and Irlene, who were musically gifted like their oldest sibling. The band also included a young drummer named Ken Dudney, whom Barbara would later marry. The group performed in Southeast Asia, a rarity for country music acts at the time.

Barbara begin her recording career in the early 1960s and had her first regional hit with "Queen for a Day." After a few years on the circuit, she married Ken Dudney and quit the music industry to raise her young family. She grew restless since it was obvious that someone with her talent was not destined to stay at home but to entertain the masses. She returned to the music world at a favorable time when female singers were beginning to make a real impact on the industry.

In 1969, she signed with CBS records and enjoyed her first national hit, "I've Been Loving You Too Long (To Stop Now)." The Otis Redding classic proved she could handle material outside the country parameters. The song "Playin' Around with Love" was another early nugget in her blossoming career. In 1970, she began performing with singer David Houston, and their partnership also generated considerable chart success.

In 1975, she decided that a change was necessary and moved to ABC Records, where she came under the guidance of producer Tom Collins. It was from this point on that she began a run at the charts, which would include eighteen recorded albums and a number of hit singles. Mandrell built up momentum with numbers like "Sleeping Single in a Double Bed," "Woman to Woman," "If Loving You Is Wrong (I Don't Want to Be Right)," "Standing Room Only," "Years," "I Was Country When Country Wasn't Cool," "'Till You're Gone," and "One of a Kind Pair of Fools." In a few short years she rose to a postition among the elite of the country music circuit.

By 1979, she had reached the height of her powers. She won the CMA Female Vocalist award against such heavy competition as Dolly Parton, Loretta Lynn, Tammy Wynette and Crystal Gayle. A year later, Barbara, along with Louise and Irlene, enjoyed their own television variety show. It was a slick program with exceptional musicianship, famous guests, some comedy skits and a spiritual song at the end of each episode, which led to Barbara releasing an album of religious material. After a very successful two-year run, Barbara, suffering from exhaustion and vocal strain, was forced to end her television program. In 1981, she won another CMA Female Vocalist award and starred on the HBO special *The Lady Is a Champ.* She also appeared in *Burning Rage,* a television movie.

On September 11, 1984, tragedy struck hard when she and two of her children were involved in a horrible car accident that nearly killed her. It would take years to regain her health, and she never recovered her lost momentum. To complicate matters Tennessee law forced her and her husband to file a lawsuit, making it appear that rich and famous Barbara Mandrell was suing the estate of a penniless, dead young man. A lurid picture was painted for the public to consume.

After a full two years of recovery Mandrell was physically, mentally and emotionally ready to pick up the threads of her once blossoming career. The songs "There's No Love in Tennessee," "Get to the Heart," "Fast Lanes and Country Roads," "Angel in Your Arms," "No One Mends a Broken Heart Like You," and "Child Support" returned her to favor. But the New Traditionalists had taken over the radio airwaves, and her career waned. The last three singles to chart were "I Wish That I Could Fall in Love Today," "My Train of Thought,"and "Mirror Mirror" in 1988–1989.

However, from the late 1980s to the 1990s she extended her career with live appearances, including two very successful tours, titled No Nonsense and Stepping Out, the latter recorded as a highly rated TNN special. There was still magic in her ability to deliver hits with an unmistakable style. With the car accident behind her, fans flocked to see her perform live.

She expanded her career to include more acting roles. She appeared on *Empty Nest, Diagnosis Murder, Dr. Quinn Medicine Woman, The Commish* and *Walker, Texas Ranger.* She would also have a solid part in the daytime drama *Sunset Beach.* Her television show ten years before had given her solid experience. In 1990, she released the autobiography *Get to the Heart: My Story* that included the real truth of the aftermath of that terrible crash in 1984, and she did a talk show tour to promote the book.

In 1997, she shocked the country community world when she left music in order to concentrate on her acting career. In October of that year she performed on the Grand Ole Opry one final time. That was televised on TNN and received excellent ratings. She starred in the made-for-television movies *The Wrong Girl* and *Stolen from the Heart.* She also made several appearances in a number of television series.

In 2006, a special CD was put together entitled *She Was Country When Country Wasn't Cool: A Tribute to Barbara Mandrell.* It reached the Top Forty. It featured a number of stars, including Reba McEntire, Kenny Chesney, Sara Evans and LeAnn Rimes, among others. The Great American Country channel promoted the record with several specials that took a look at her fabulous career. Later that year, she appeared at the CMA Awards. She continues to retain a fan base as companies keep gaining mileage out of her catalog.

Barbara Mandrell is a country music survivor, a talented individual who displayed her immense abilities as a child prodigy. It took her some time to achieve the success that many predicted she would enjoy. If she had not suffered that horrible accident, she might have become the greatest female country music star, even surpassing Patsy Cline. At the time of the crash she was at the height of her creative powers.

Although known best as a singer, Mandrell is also an outstanding instrumentalist. As a young prodigy on the pedal steel guitar she was holding her own as a ten-year-old against much older and experienced competition. She is a musician with a soft touch on many instruments, and that is one side of her career that has been underappreciated. It seems that once she displayed her intense vocal powers, her other abilities were quickly forgotten.

Barbara Mandrell's voice is a special one. It contains many shades that can color a song lyric with specific emphasis in a flash. In her vocal style there is a hint of a woman who has seen much in life. The country queen's vocal delivery can also be bright and expressive, a take-charge element that guarantees better times are ahead.

But the instrumental and vocal talent are only part of the Mandrell package. With the wealth of performance experience to her credit, she always delivered a first-rate live concert. She displayed this vast ability on stages around the world, in small honky tonks as well as huge arenas, and on her short-lived but extremely popular television show.

Her recorded material offers another glimpse of her many abilities. Every record boasts at least one or two real nuggets, songs that the listener could wrap themselves around and adopt as their own. Once she began her run of number one hits, there was no stopping her, and Mandrell delivered them with relative ease.

She gave the world a number of great songs including "Treat Him Right," "Midnight Oil," "This Time I Almost Made It," "Love's Ups and Downs," "Midnight Angel," "Moods," "I Was Country When Country Wasn't Cool" and "Sleeping Single in a Double Bed." Whether singing original material or a cover version, she spun gold with her special musical talent.

She was an important cog in the country-pop movement of the late 1970s and early 1980s, influencing a number of current artists including Shania Twain, Martina McBride, Reba McEntire, Garth Brooks, Faith Hill, Tim McGraw, Kenny Chesney, Trace Adkins, Carrie Underwood, and Miley Cyrus. She blazed a trail during her reign that Olivia Newton-John, Kenny Rogers, John Denver, Alabama and Anne Murray followed.

Mandrell shared the stage with many artists, including her family and her husband, among others. A short list includes Waylon Jennings, Brent Rowan, Michael Rhodes, Eddie Bayers, Steve Gibson, Lee Greenwood, Mike Ragogna, Tanya Tucker, Diane Tidwell, Lisa Silver, Terry McMillan, John Jarvis, David Hungate, Jerry Crutchfield, Jimmy Bowen, Pete Bordonali, the Branson Brothers, David Briggs and Ray Price, among others. The list also includes country singers who guested on her television show, such as Johnny Cash, Alabama, Marty Robbins, Kenny Rogers, Dolly Parton, the Statler Brothers, Ray Charles, John Schneider, Glen Campbell and comedians such as Bob Hope, Phyllis Diller and Andy Kaufman.

Barbara Mandrell is one of the most successful female country artists of all time. Her dominance in the industry from the 1970s to the early 1980s has been rarely matched. She is the only person to win back-to-back CMA Entertainer of the Year Awards. There are many who believe that if she had not suffered that career changing accident in 1984, she could have become the best in the history of the genre.

Despite having her career shortened, she won many awards including those two prestigious CMA awards mentioned above. As well, there are the two Female Vocalist of the Year awards in 1979 and 1981. She amassed nine People's Choice awards for Favorite Female Country Music Vocalist and the Living Legend Award given only to entertainers who have been in the business for at least twenty-five years. She has also been able to claim the Tex Ritter Award and a Grammy for Best Inspirational Album of the Year.

The Barbara Mandrell story is a heartwarming tale of a child prodigy who managed to parlay that promising talent into a successful career as she raced to the very top of the heap only to have it cruelly destroyed in a fraction of a second. But true to her spirit she recovered and forged a new identity proving the Midnight Angel has always been a special country personality.

DISCOGRAPHY:

Treat Him Right, Columbia 30967.
Midnight Oil, Columbia 32743.
This Time I Almost Made It, Columbia 32959.
This is... ABC/Dot 2045.
Lovers, Friends & Strangers, Universal Special Products MCAC-673.
Midnight Angel, ABC/Dot 2067.
Love's Ups and Downs, ABC/Dot 2098.
Moods, MCA 1677.
Just for the Record, MCA 3165.
Love Is Fair, MCA 5136.
Barbara Mandrell Live, MCA 1697.
Looking Back, Columbia 37437.
He Set My Life to Music, MCA 1492.
In Black & White, MCA 5295.
Spun Gold, MCA 5377.
Barbara Mandrell, MCA 20150.
Christmas At Our House, MCA 5519.
Meant for Each Other, MCA 31231.
Get to the Heart, MCA 5619.
Moments, MCA 5769.
Sure Feels Good, Capitol 46956.
I'll Be Your Jukebox Tonight, Capitol C2-90416.
Morning Sun, Capitol 91977.
Key's in the Mailbox, Capitol 96794.
Nonsense, Capitol 94426.
Standing Room Only, Pair 1323.
Fooled by a Feeling, Universal Special Products 20860.
It Works for Me, Razor & Tie 2828.
Branson City Limits, Unison 9017.
Sisters in Song, Sony 34978.
My Train of Thought, Capitol 4BX-44276.
The Best of Barbara Mandrell CBS 34876.
The Best of Barbara Mandrell, Pair/ABC 1119.
The Best of Barbara Mandrell, Universal Special Products 31107.
Greatest Hits, MCA 5566.
Greatest Country Hits, Curb 77363.MCA 170160.
Love's Ups and Downs/Lovers, Friends & Strangers, MCA 38030.
This Is ... Midnight Angel, MCA 28025.
The Best of Barbara Mandrell, Hollywood 713.
The Collection, Capitol 31921.

Ultimate, Brainsounds 5919.
Entertainer of the Year, Madacy 833.
In the Name of Love, Sony Special Products 16553.
Super Hits, Columbia 68507.
Collection, EMI-Capitol Special Markets 98225.
Country Spotlight, Direct Source 6167.
Dueling Country, Direct source 9017.
Good Ole Country, St. Clair 78242.
20th Century Masters — The Millennium Collection: The Best of Barbara Madrell, MCA 170160.
The Midnight Oil/Treat Him Right, Collectables 6459.
Ultimate Collection, Hip-O 556524.
Columbia/Epic Singles 1969–75, WestSide 503916.
The Ten Commandments of Love, Bitz 303.
Best of Barbara Mandrell, Universal International 170058.
Back in the Saddle, Legacy 175.

Crystal Gayle (1951–)

Family Tradition

In the first fifty years of country music there were numerous family acts, including the Carters, the Stonemans, the Tanners and the Cashes, among others. One of the more modern familial connections involves Loretta Lynn, who hit the charts in the 1960s and 1970s on the road to superstardom. A few years later, her kid sister appeared on the scene ready to carry on the family tradition. Her name was Crystal Gayle.

Crystal Gayle was born Brenda Gail Webb on January 9, 1951, in Paintsville, Kentucky. Although they shared the same father, each girl would be raised quite differently. When Brenda was four, the family moved to Wabash, Indiana, and it was here that she began to sing in the church and aspired to be a professional entertainer like her older sister. She continued to hone her skills developing her blossoming talent at many different venues.

Crystal's big break came when she turned sixteen and toured with her older sister. Eventually the association would lead to a contract with Decca Records in 1970 and a first single, "I've Cried the Blue Right out of My Eyes," which made the Top Forty of the country charts. Although Lynn's fame was something that could help Gayle out, it also hindered her. Crystal was encouraged to sing and act like her sister, and the first song she waxed was from her sibling's catalog.

In an effort to move out from under her sister's shadow, she changed her name to Crystal Gayle. She drew the first part of the name from a love for Krystal hamburgers as a child. She also appeared regularly on *Jim Ed Brown's Country Place* television show in 1972 for greater exposure. She then signed to United Artists Records and worked with producer Allen Reynolds, who helped her develop a distinct style.

In 1975, the release of her self-titled debut album yielded the single "Wrong Road Again," which climbed to the Top Ten of the country charts. A second album, *Somebody Loves You,* appeared the same year and was another positive building block in her ambition to cultivate her own following. In some ways it was more challenging to build a career with certain expectations rather than having none to live up to.

In 1976, she recorded "I'll Get Over You," which made it into the pop charts and became her first number one single. "You Never Miss a Real Good Thing (Till He Says Goodbye)" gave her a second number one single. After years of struggling, she was finally reaping the benefits of hard work and the good strategy of moving away from sister Loretta Lynn's shadow.

In the summer of 1977 she made giant strides in carving out her own musical niche with the smash hit "Don't It Make My Brown Eyes Blue." It was a number one country hit and peaked at number two on the pop charts, but more importantly it defined her sound. The album *We Must Believe in Magic*, which contained her breakthrough effort, went platinum, and Gayle had finally, completely emerged from her sister's shadow.

She would place three more number one hits on the charts: "Ready for the Times to Get Better," "Talking in Your Sleep," and "Why Have You Left the One You Left Me For." In 1979, she became the first country artist to visit China as part of a Bob Hope television special. She entered the 1980s with much anticipation.

The first part of the decade was a good one. She signed with Columbia Records in 1980 and scored a string of Top Ten hits for the next seven years. However, in 1987, her popularity began to decline like other veteran country artists. She rebounded with the *Ain't Gonna Worry* album reuniting with producer Allen Reynolds, who had been responsible for her breakthrough success in the late 1970s.

Throughout the 1990s her recording career took different paths, with much of it concentrated on speciality projects done for small, independent labels. She also recorded two gospel albums, *Someday* and *He Is Beautiful*. In 1999, she dedicated herself to a tribute project: *Crystal Gayle Sings the Heart & Soul of Hoagy Carmichael*. In 2000, she cut *In My Arms*, an album of children's songs. Outside the music business she ran a fine jewelry and crystal shop in Nashville.

Although the recording side of her career declined, as a performer she flourished in America and Europe. Long before she became a star, Gayle knew how to work a crowd by watching her sister do so for years. After living in her older sister's musical circle, Crystal had carved out her own niche. She continues to record and perform.

Crystal Gayle is a country music delight. Since her breakthrough in the late 1970s she has managed to build a strong career with her undeniable talents. Although she spent years being compared to her more famous sister, Gayle eventually was able to cultivate her own fan base. With her trademark hair and rich voice she became a mainstay of the mainstream country set.

She has a very commercial voice. A keen student of singing styles, she learned how to phrase well-crafted words with a particular attention to detail. Her vocal delivery allowed her to explore several different routes and was tailor-made for the country-pop genre.

Along with Tammy Wynette, Barbara Mandrell, Dolly Parton, Loretta Lynn, and Tanya Tucker, Gayle was one of the leading figures of the country-pop movement during the 1970s and 1980s. Although unable to continue the momentum created with the release of "Don't It Make My Brown Eyes Blue," the long-haired singer maintained a strong career and remained a popular concert attraction. Like the aforementioned singers, she paved the way for later artists in the same vein, such as Shania Twain, Faith Hill, Trisha Yearwood and Tim McGraw.

She gave the world many great songs. A partial list includes "Somebody Loves You," "High Time," "I'll Get Over You," "A Woman's Heart (Is a Handy Place to Be)," "Restless," "You," "Wrong Road Again," "Beyond You," "Don't It Make My Brown Eyes Blue," "One More Time," "Dreaming My Dreams with You," "You Never Miss a Real Good Thing (Till He Says Goodbye)," "I'll Do It All over Again," "Make a Dream Come True," "Cry Me a River," "Ready for the Times to Get Better," "Paintin' This Old Town Blue," "Time Will Prove I'm Right," "Too Deep for Tears," "We Should Be Together," "Never Ending Song of Love," and "Faithless Love." Whether it was a straight country tune or pop-flavored material or some other song in a different style, she injected her personal touch every time, creating magic.

Gayle's biggest influence was her older sister Loretta Lynn. That relationship was a mixed blessing; it certainly opened doors for her being related to such a famous country music singer. However, it was obvious that Crystal had her own style and struggled hard to distance herself from the long shadow that her sibling cast. In the end, she succeeded in creating her own body of work, which made its own impact.

Gayle has in turn influenced a number of young country stars, including Sara Evans, Miranda Lambert, LeAnn Rimes, Martina McBride, Lindsey Haun, Shania Twain, Terri Clark, Lorrie Morgan, Gretchen Wilson, Meredith Edwards, Mindy McCready, Mindy Smith, Lila McCann, Megan Mullins and Julie Roberts, among others. Any singer who has claimed country roots and attempted crossover appeal in the past thirty years owes Crystal a debt.

The Crystal Gayle story is that of a young chanteuse who had an incredible range that allowed her to delve in any style. It is also the tale of an artist who benefited from having a famous sibling but at the same time struggled to get out from under the increased expectations. With her trademark long hair and gifted vocal delivery, she carved her own niche while maintaining a family tradition.

DISCOGRAPHY:

Crystal Gayle [1975], MCA 20167.
Somebody Loves You, EMI America E2-48382.
Crystal, EMI America E2-48381.
We Must Believe in Magic, Razor & Tie 2044.
When I Dream, Razor & Tie 2045.
Miss the Mississippi, Capitol C2-95563.
We Should Be Together, United Artists 969.
These Days, Columbia CK-36512.
Hollywood, Tennessee, Capitol C2-95564.
True Love, Elektra 60200.
Cage the Songbird, Warner Bros. 23958.
Nobody Wants to Be Alone, Warner Bros. 4-25154.
Crystal Gayle [1986], Capitol 4X 9019.
Straight to the Heart, Warner Bros. 1-25405.
What If We Fall in Love, Warner Bros. 2-25507.
Nobody's Angel, Warner Bros. 2-25506.
Ain't Gonna Worry, Capitol C2-94301.
A Crystal Christmas, Warner Bros. 25508.
Three Good Reasons, Liberty C2-96507.
Crystal Gayle [1978], EMI America E2-48383.
Someday, Intersound 9315.
Walk with Me, Audio K-7 1565.
Mountain Christmas, Intersound 9185.
Sings the Heart & Soul of Hoagy Carmichael, Intersound 9362.
In My Arms, Madacy 599.
Collection: 20 Songs from the Heart, Music Club International 477.
Crystal Gayle Christmas, Direct Source 2009.
All My Tomorrows. Southpaw 1535.
Heart & Soul, Southpaw 1546.
We Praise! He Is Lord, Braun Media 4122.
Country Pure, Pair 1083.
I've Cried the Blue Right Out of My Eyes, MCA 2334.
Classic Crystal, EMI E2-46549.
A Woman's Heart, Liberty 00-1080.
Favorites, EMI America E2-46582.
Crystal Gayle's Greatest Hits, Columbia CK-38803.
Musical Jewels, Pair 1126.

The Best of Crystal Gayle, Warner Bros. 2-25622.
Singles Album, EMI 7926122.
All-Time Greatest hits, Curb D2-77360.
The Very Best of Crystal Gayle, Vol. 1, EMI America E2-94826.
Greatest Hits, Capitol C2-95886.
50 Original Tracks, EMI Country 7894672.
Best Always, Branson Entertainment 9307.
The Best of Crystal Gayle, Curb 77644.
Best of Crystal Gayle, EMI 6790.
20 Great Love Songs, Disky 866612.
Straight to the Heart, Castle 554.
Super Hits, 69098.
Best of Crystal Gayle: Talking in Your Sleep, Castle 122.
Blue: All Her Greatest Hits, Hallmark 30864.
Certified Hits, Capitol 34449.
Christmas with Crystal Gayle, Music Club 026.
The Best of Crystal Gayle, Rhino 78282.
20 Love Songs, EMI Gold 5629.
Country Classics, EMI Gold 6324.
Country Legends, Disky 85738.
Country Greatest: EMI Years, EMI 576046.
Love Songs, EMI Gold 538770.
Crystal: The Crystal Gayle Collection, Crimson Productions 317.
Inspiration, Evosound 028.
Talking in Your Sleep, Pegasus 587.
Great hits, Collectables 8653.
Best of Crystal Gayle, EMI 33567.
The Ultimate Collection: Live [Bonus DVD], Madacy 52310.
A Crystal Christmas, Laserlight 32817.
We Must Believe in Magic/When I Dream, EMI/Collectables 2908.
Crystal Gayle, KRB Music 5409.
Greatest Hits, Capitol 02459.

Tanya Tucker (1958–)

Texas Prodigy

There have been many young stars throughout the history of country music. The practice of passing down the basic rudiments of instruments and the lyrics to traditional songs often began at a tender age. In modern times, a number of artists turned professional while still children, including Barbara Mandrell, Ricky Skaggs, Crystal Gayle, Reba McEntire, as well as the performer known as the Texas prodigy. Her name is Tanya Tucker.

Tanya Tucker was born on October 10, 1958, in Seminole, Texas. It was a childhood of constant packing and repacking as her father moved the family throughout the Southwest in pursuit of construction jobs. At six, she started on the saxophone and a couple of years later decided that she wanted to be a singer. The youngster debuted with Mel Tillis who was so awestruck by her control and maturity that he invited the little chanteuse up on stage. At nine, Tucker was a regular on the Las Vegas circuit.

The wheels had been set in motion for her to launch a recording career when her demo tape fell into the hands of Dolores Fuller, a songwriter. She sent it to Billy Sherrill, the country music A&R man at CBS Records, who was very impressed. He signed the teenage vocalist to a recording contract with the Columbia label, and the Tanya Tucker ship was ready to be launched.

She cut "Delta Dawn," instead of "The Happiest Girl in the Whole U.S.A.," the initial song that was chosen to be her debut single. It was a good move because "Delta Dawn," released in 1972, became a Top Ten hit and placed on the pop charts. Her age — a factor that the record company attempted to hide from the public — was leaked and turned into positive publicity. She enjoyed a second Top Ten hit with "Love's the Answer."

Her debut album, *Delta Dawn*, proved a phenomenal start for someone so young in the music industry. With the title cut and "New York City Song," she demonstrated a firm control of vocal power. A cover of Hank Williams Sr.'s "I'm So Lonesome I Could Cry" was a tip to the old school and proved that she could handle classic material. Her third single, "Jamestown Ferry," was also on this work, as well as the Jerry Reed tune "Smell the Flowers."

The release of her fourth single, "What's Your Mama's Name," gave Tucker her first number one hit. She proved her staying power with the release of the *What's Your Mama's Name* album. Producer Billy Sherrill utilized the songwriting talents of Earl Montgomery and Dallas Frazier, who provided the title cut as well as "California Cotton Fields." Other highlights included "Horseshoe Bend," "Blood Red and Goin' Down," "Song Man," and "Teddy Bear Song." The latter foreshadowed her adventures into country-rock that would occur a few years down the road.

A year later, she emerged with "Would You Lay With Me (in a Field of Stone)," a major hit that was another song juxtaposing her innocence with a more mature subject matter. The fifteen-year-old knew how to craft a successful album (credit also goes to Sherrill). The effort also included "Bed of Roses," "The Man Who Turned My Mama On," "How Can I Tell Him," and "Why Me Lord?"

Even a change in record companies to MCA in 1975 didn't slow her momentum. *Tanya Tucker*, her next album, was another example of how a teenager could deliver classic country, displaying a maturity beyond her years. "Lizzie and the Rainman" and "San Antonio Stroll" were major hits. Other highlights included "I'm Not Lisa," "Son of a Preacher Man," "When Will I

Be Loved," and "The King of Country Music." At this point, despite her tender age, she was one of the most important country music artists of the day, and her performances were events.

In 1978, now a veteran on the music scene at age twenty, she adopted a more contemporary image and desired crossover power. In order to achieve her goal she recorded the rock-oriented *T.N.T.* album, complete with provocative cover; the effort eventually went gold. Highlights included cover versions of the Everly brothers' "Lover Goodbye," John Prine's "Angel from Montgomery," Chuck Berry's "Brown Eyed Handsome Man," and the Elvis Presley chestnut "Heartbreak Hotel." In pursuing this path, Tucker alienated her country music audience but gained a new one.

For someone who had shot across the musical landscape like a rocket, her sudden decline was a surprise. Her sales fell in the late 1970s because she was no longer a teenage sensation. Although *Ridin' Rainbows, Tear Me Apart, Dream Lovers* and *Should I Do It* were all solid album efforts, they did little to promote her career. By the early 1980s, the well had run dry as she scored only a couple of minor hits. In order to boost her sagging career she recorded with Glen Campbell, with the tabloids linking the pair romantically.

In an effort to expand her star power she appeared in her first feature film, *Hard Country*. She switched to Arista Reocrds in 1982, and had a moderate hit with "Feel Right," found on the album *Changes*. A live set gave fans an idea of the passion and first-class performance skills that she had developed on the concert stage.

By the mid–1980s her career seemed to be back on track as she scored with "One Love at a Time," found on the record *Girls Like Me*. The momentum carried her into the next decade. "I Won't Take Less Than Your Love" (a trio recording with Paul Davis and Paul Overstreet), "If It Don't Come Easy," "Strong Enough to Bend" and "Two Sparrows in a Hurricane" brought her back into the spotlight.

Tennessee Woman was a strong album as was *What Do I Do with Me*, which contained the ballads "Down to My Last Teardrop" and "Trail of Tears." She remained a powerful live attraction and toured regularly. But her strength was always her albums, and *Can't Run from Yourself* was another example of the range of her abilities. It contained some slow blues like the title track, ballads like "Half the Moon," and a country-rock piece, a duet with Delbert McClinton, "Tell Me About It."

In the latter part of her career she suffered another dry spell. Although *Complicated* (her thirtieth release), *Tanya, Live at Billy Bob's Texas,* and *Tanya Tucker Live! You Are So Beautiful* were all solid efforts, the wave of new country-pop vocalists had taken over the charts.

Despite an uneven recording career, she remained popular on tour. A constant stream of greatest hits collections was released to satisfy her hard-core fans. In 2005, she starred in her own reality show, *Tuckerville*, on The Learning Channel. She continues to record and perform.

Tanya Tucker is a country music survivor. The initial explosion of her career was ignited when she was barely into her teens. Her perseverance over the dry spells she has endured is a tribute to her spirit. She has never lost her grit, her passion to entertain, and, most importantly, her talent.

Tucker's voice chronicles the history of her entire professional career. In the beginning, she stunned everyone with the passion of her vocal delivery. At just thirteen, she possessed the raw power of a much older artist. As she matured, her voice became less of a novelty yet never lost its strength.

She boasts an impressive catalog of songs. A partial list includes "Delta Dawn," "Jamestown Ferry," "What's Your Mama's Name," "Would You Lay with Me (In a Field of Stone)," "Don't Believe My Heart Can Stand Another You," "Texas (When I Die)," "I'm in Love and He's in Dallas," "I'll Come Back As Another Woman," "It's Only Over for You," "If It Don't Come Easy," "I Won't Take Less Than Your Love," "Daddy and Home," "Call on Me," "Same Old Story," "As Long As There's a Heartbeat," "Don't Go Out," "Oh What It Did to Me," "Memories We Still Haven't Made," "Some Kind of Trouble," "Trail of Tears," "Time and Distance," "It's a Little Too Late," "Cashing the American Dream," "Two Sparrows in a Hurricane," and "Half the Moon."

From the start of her career, Tucker was classified as a country-pop diva and despite forays into rock and roll she remains in her initial mold. Today, she might be classified as adult contemporary. More importantly, thirty years after she first recorded her first song she continues to forge ahead as a mature, creative artist.

Her longevity has ensured that she influenced a number of artists including Stephanie Bentley, Trick Pony, Clarice Rose, Lindsey Haun, LeAnn Rimes, Shania Twain, Terri Clark, Miranda Lambert, Ashley Monroe, Danielle Peck, Catherine Britt, Sara Evans, Carrie Underwood, Taylor Swift and Mindy McCready, among others. In the beginning, Tucker made very few mistakes in the recording industry. The fact that her career fizzled later on never diminished her overall popularity.

The Tanya Tucker story is that of a young girl who possessed the voice of a woman. Although her career shot off like a rocket and seemed to level off later on, she remained a solid name in the industry. Now a mature singer, her concerts are still events, and her records still sell, proving that the Texas prodigy was not a one-hit wonder.

Discography:

Delta Dawn, Columbia 31742.66.
The Sound of Tanya Tucker, CBS 3010.
What's Your Mama's Name, CBS 32272.
Would You Lay with Me (In a Field of Stone), CBS 32744.
Tanya Tucker, MCA 2141.
Here's Some Love, MCA 2722.
Lovin' and Learnin', MCA 2167.
You Are So Beautiful, Embassy 31568.
T.N.T., MCA 3530.
Ridin' Rainbows, MCA 3066.
Tear Me Apart, MCA 5106.
Dream Lovers, MCA 3109.
Should I Do It, MCA 5228.
Live, MCA 22039.
Changes, Arista ALB6-6381.
Girls Like Me, Capitol ST-12474.
Love Me Like You Used To, Liberty C2-46870.
Strong Enough to Bend, Liberty C2-48865.
Tennessee Woman, Liberty C2-91821.
What Do I Do with Me, Liberty C2-95562.
Can't Run From Yourself, Liberty C2-98987.
Lizzie & the Rain Man, University Special Products 20219.
Country Queen, PCD-2-1258.
Soon, Liberty C2-89048.
Fire to Fire, Liberty 28943.
Christmas with Tanya Tucker and Suzy Bogguss, CEMA Special Markets 18275.
Complicated, Capitol 36885.
Tanya, Capitol 38827.
Live at Billy Bob's Texas, Smith Music Group 5039.
Tanya Tucker Live! You Are So Beautiful, Infosound 6532.
Lonesome Town, MCA 20219.
Tanya Tucker's Greatest Hits, Columbia 33355.
Greatest Hits Encore, Liberty C4-94252.
Greatest Hits, MCA 31153.
The Best of Tanya Tucker, Universal Special Products 31156.
Greatest Hits, Liberty C2-91814.
Lovin' and Learnin'/Tanya Tucker MCA 38028.
Ridin' Rainbows/Here's Some Love, MCA 38029.
Greatest Country Hits, Curb D2-77429.
Collection, MCAD-10583.
The Best of Tanya Tucker, Tee Vee 6008.
Hits, EMI 7990592.
Greatest Hits, Capitol 56836.
Greatest Hits, CEMA 17976.
Greatest Hits, 1990–1992, Liberty 81367.
Tanya Tucker, Capitol 28822.
The Best of My Love, Sony Special Products 21126.

Love Songs, Capitol 52809.

Super Hits, Sony 69065.

What's Your Mama's Name/Would You Lay with Me (In a Field of Stone), Collectables 6097.

Best of My Love, Platinum Disc 1500.

Sisters: An Anthology, Renaissance 205.

Country Classics, Vol. 2, EMI 527034.

20 Greatest Hits, Capitol 22093.

20th Century Masters — The Millennium Collection: The Best of Tanya Tucker, MCA 170159.

Tanya Tucker Anthology, Disky Communications 645542.

The Dresden Dolls, Universal 1125772.

Tanya Tucker Country Classics, EMI 856030.

The Upper 48 Hits: 1972–1997, Raven 143.

Country Classics, EMI 6323.

Very Best of Tanya Tucker, Disky 85022.

Country Greatest: EMI Years, EMI 576042.

Country Divas, Dynamic (Emp 520), 2135.

16 Biggest Hits, Legacy 94561.

Country Hit Parade, Direct Source 58992.

The Definitive Collection, Hip-O 0006968.

The Best of Tanya Tucker, Pegasus 633.

Nothin' but the Best, Vol. 3, MCA Special Products MCAC-22093.

Garth Brooks (1962–)

No Fences

Mainstream country music is the sound of the purists, those who have always strongly insisted that the tradition should remain untainted by elements of pop, rock, and other styles. Others believed that in order for country to expand its appeal it needed to meld with different ideas. One individual proved that the latter theory could be very successful. His philosophy was that music has no fences. His name is Garth Brooks.

Garth Brooks was born on February 7, 1962, in Tulsa, Oklahoma. His mother had cut a handful of records for Capitol in the mid–1950s that had never charted. Although music was one of his boyhood interests, he was more devoted to sports and earned a partial athletic scholarship at Oklahoma State University as a javelin thrower, but an injury curtailed any dreams of participating in the Olympics.

He turned to his other interest — music — while in college. He began to sing in local Oklahoma clubs with his partner, lead guitarist Ty England. It was a good break from studying and earned him some pocket money. At this point he was strictly an amateur, and the idea of turning professional seemed a far away dream.

In 1984, he graduated with an advertising degree, but decided to pursue his true love, music. He moved to Nashville but was soon back home due to his frustration with the business. He continued to perform in Oklahoma clubs and later married his college girlfriend putting musical aspirations in jeopardy.

In 1987, he decided to try Nashville a second time and moved there with his wife. He had a better understanding of how the music industry worked. He began to connect with various people in the business, including songwriters and producers, eventually acquiring a powerful management team but was still unable to garner a recording contract. Despite the many quality demo tapes he put together, no label was interested in signing him.

It took a live performance for an executive at Capitol Records, a company that had passed on his demo at least once, to finally sign him. He cut his first album with producer Allen Reynolds at the controls, and the self-titled debut effort was released in 1989. The years he had spent honing his skills in small clubs were about to pay off handsomely.

The album was a success; it spawned four singles, including "Much Too Young (To Feel This Damn Old)," the number one hits "If Tomorrow Never Comes" and "The Dance," as well as "Not Counting You," which peaked at number two in the charts. Despite the appeal of his music, fellow newcomers Clint Black, Travis Tritt and Alan Jackson were more established as country male vocalists. Within a year, Brooks would overshadow all of them on his way to becoming the best-selling country music artist in history.

Although his first effort had been a solid one, it was his sophomore release, *No Fences*, which made him a true superstar. It appeared in the fall of 1990, and shot up the country charts where it remained number one for twenty-three weeks. The single "Friends in Low Places" had preceded the milestone-setting album. The CD boasted the hit songs "Unanswered Prayers," "Two of a Kind, Workin' on a Full House," and "The Thunder Rolls." Two years later, the record had sold over ten million copies.

Brooks, with his tour de force *No Fences*, had shattered all accepted country conventions. The mania swept through into his live shows as he broke attendance records, selling out stadiums within minutes of ticket availability. The hysteria was due to the quality of his music, his swelling popularity, and his 1970s rock-style performances.

He used a cordless, headset microphone that allowed him the freedom to roam the large stadium. He basked in soft glowing spotlight colors, adding an extra dimension to his visual show. There were also explosions, the smashing of guitars, as well as a harness that enabled Brooks to swing out high above the crowd. His performances were influenced by the Rolling Stones, Kiss, Aerosmith and other arena rockers of the 1970s. No country artist had ever incorporated rock and roll techniques of that magnitude into their stage performances.

In 1991, his third album, *Ropin' the Wind*, was released and earned accolades as being the first country disc to debut at the top of the pop charts. It sold over ten million copies and included the number one hit singles "Shameless," "What She's Doing Now," and "The River." At this point in his career, Brooks seemingly could do no wrong as the top draw in country music.

His 1992 Christmas offering, *Beyond the Season*, went multi-platinum, and Brooks's domination of the industry started to attract negative attention. Before his fourth album, *The Chase*, appeared, an advance single, "We Shall Be Free," became available. With this effort he was trying too hard to push the boundaries of contemporary country, and many radio stations refused to play it. The CD debuted at number one, but it sold half of what his two previous records had.

In 1993, he returned with *In Pieces*, a more straightforward country album that saw him regain his hard-core fan base. Although he would never reach the same commercial peaks as he enjoyed with *No Fences* and *Ropin' the Wind*, he was still a superstar capable of selling out concert stadiums and doing a brisk business in the record stores.

The Hits, a collection of his best up to that time, sold eight million copies. *Fresh Horses*, his fifth studio album, kicked off with the same power as previous multi-platinum releases, but it tailed off after hitting the three million mark. Most artists would have been ecstatic with such a record, but for Brooks it was a slight disappointment, considering what his previous efforts had sold.

In a marketing ploy that backfired, Brooks wanted to promote his seventh album, *Sevens*, in a unique way. The record was supposed to be released in 1997 to coincide with a huge concert in Central Park in New York City. But a major management shakeup at Capitol Records left him upset because many of his contacts had been fired. He held back the release of the album and performed the concert in Central Park ahead of time. The new executives decided to concede to his demands, and the album shot straight to number one upon its release and sold well.

In another marketing strategy, he pulled his first six albums out of print and issued *The Limited Series*, a box set that contained the first six efforts and some bonus tracks. The original recordings were kept off the market until their tenth anniversary, when they were released only as a DVD audio. In 1998, a concert set, *Double Live*, appeared but didn't sell as well as projected.

It was at this point in his career that he began to devote his energies to other pursuits, namely baseball and movies. He tried out for the San Diego

Padres baseball team, failed, and retreated to film. He was slated to star in a thriller titled *The Lamb*, playing the main character named Chris Gaines. Over time he created an elaborate biography for the fictional character, complete with invented material and a musical history. He recorded a full album of songs — as Chris Gaines — that flopped as audiences were not willing to accept a slimmed-down, shaggy-haired, soulful pop crooner in place of the genuine singer. The confusion over the entire Chris Gaines persona hurt sales of his *Magic of Christmas,* a traditional Garth Brooks album. The film was never made.

By 2000, Brooks's personal life was in turmoil as his wife sought a divorce. Brooks quit the music business after his next solo project in order to maintain his family life. He had talked of retiring from performing in 1992 and again in 1995 but had gone back on tour each time. In 1999, he and his wife separated, and two years later the couple divorced.

In 2001, Brooks officially announced his retirement. At the end of the year, his last album, *Scarecrow*, was released. He performed a few times in order to promote the album but had for all intents and purposes retired. The album didn't sell as well as previous releases, but it reached number one on both the pop and country charts. Although he had finished recording, some of his previously unrecorded material surfaced and charted including the single "Why Ain't I Running," in 2003.

In December 2005, Brooks married longtime friend and fellow country music star Trisha Yearwood. There had been rumors for years that the pair were having an affair, although both vehemently denied the accusations. He retired to a ranch in Oklahoma with his new wife.

Since then he has made brief appearances. In September 2005, he performed John Fogerty's "Who'll Stop the Rain" with Yearwood on the *Shelter from the Storm: A Concert for the Gulf Coast* telethon for Hurricane Katrina relief. He appeared at the Grand Ole Opry's 80th birthday celebration in a duet with Steve Wariner on "Long Neck Bottle," and with legends Bill Anderson, Porter Wagoner and Little Jimmy Dickens. He also performed "The Dance" as a solo guitar piece. Some time later he sang "Good Ride Cowboy" at a Country Music Association Awards Show in Times Square, a performance that was very well received.

Perhaps the biggest news during his retirement years has been the contractual agreement with Wal-Mart to lease the rights to his back catalog. It was the first time in history that a musician had signed a deal to allow a single retailer to peddle his music. The move did little to hurt his sales, and he continued to push product on regular basis. For example, the single "Good Ride Cowboy" would eventually go to number one upon its release, proving that he still possessed a magic touch. But Brooks, the best selling country music artist of all time, remains retired.

Garth Brooks is a country music mega-superstar. He single handedly made it possible for anyone in the industry to sell millions of copies of their CD, when before his arrival it was inconceivable for anyone to go multi-platinum. He did it with his fusion of Merle Haggard country, honky tonk, 1970s singer-songwriter sensitivities and arena rock theatrics. There are many sides to his appeal that led to his phenomenal success.

The voice of a generation was a key to his huge record sales. Brooks's vocal style was soothing, exciting, contemporary, self-reflective and good-natured. There was never an overexuberance in his delivery but a reassurance and sincerity in his words that appealed to a cross-section of listeners, an essential element in his popularity. He didn't reach out to just one section of the populace but to everyone as individuals.

The lyrics to his songs were also important in his rise from obscurity to superstardom. The words spoke directly to people about their lives, dreams, relationships, failures and triumphs. He reached back into the 1970s and took a page from the crop of folk-rock singer-songwriters with his sensitive lyrics and music. But he did it better than any of them, improving on the technique and setting the bar higher than few could ever hope to match.

Although his musical abilities were never outstanding, there was always a solid accompaniment to his vocal delivery, another essential element to his success. There was nothing very flashy about the instruments or musicianship in his backup band, but it was the type of sound that appealed to a diversity of the music-buying public. He was in many ways an every person's musician, lyrically and musically, but at the same time he possessed his own unique, irresistible style.

The one area that Brooks differed from all of his contemporaries and anyone else in country music history was the execution of his concerts. Once again he dipped back into the 1970s and incorporated rock and roll theatrics in his live shows. He drove the audiences wild with his antics, which in turn spurred on his astronomical record sales.

His marketing savvy was another key element. Never before in the history of the genre had one performer channelled his work to the public to suit his particular tastes as Brooks did. He had a marketing vision, and it was a major reason why his records became monster sellers. He had complete control over his product and often demonstrated more common sense than many executives in the record company.

Garth Brooks gave the world a number of treasures, including "Much Too Young (To Feel This Damn Old)," "If Tomorrow Never Comes," "The Dance," "Not Counting You," "Friends in Low Places," "Unanswered Prayers," "Two of a Kind, Workin' on a Full House," "The Thunder Rolls," "Shameless," "What She's Doing Now," "The River," "We Shall Be Free," "Why Ain't I Running" and "Good Ride Cowboy." The material was usually first rate, and each song was injected with his particular stamp, a magical element that made him famous.

He was one of the most influential country figures of all time and the most important in the contemporary era. Every country artist in the past decade has stolen at least one page from the Garth Brooks notebook. He has passed on the wisdom of those who influenced him. These influences include Journey, Billy Joel, Conway Twitty, George Jones, George Strait, the Eagles, and especially Merle Haggard.

A partial list of those he influenced includes Billy Ray Cyrus, Emilio Navaira, Chad Brock, Colors, Brother Johnson, Trace Adkins, Vince Gill, Travis Tritt, Toby Keith, Keith Urban, Jason Aldean, Pat Green, and Brad Paisley, to name a few. In short, any country singer who has heard Brooks cannot help but follow the trail he blazed.

The Garth Brooks story is that of a very clever and gifted individual who utilized every advantage he possessed to carve out a niche in country music history that will never be duplicated. Every aspect of his career — the marketing strategy, the live performance theatrics, the singer-songwriter sensitivity and the abundant talents — proved that the music of Garth Brooks is an international language that has no fences.

DISCOGRAPHY:

Garth Brooks, Capitol 40023.
No Fences, Capitol 93866.
Ropin' the Wind, Capitol 96330.
Beyond the Season, Capitol 98472.
The Chase, Capitol 98473.
In Pieces, Capitol 80857.
Fresh Horses, Capitol 32080.
Sevens, Capitol 56599.
Double Live, Capitol 97424.
In the Life of Chris Gaines, Capitol 20051.
Garth Brooks & the Magic of Christmas, Capitol 23550.
The Magic of Christmas: Songs From Call Me Claus, Capitol 35624.
Scarecrow, Capitol 31330.
The Hits, Liberty 29689.
Unlimited Series, Capitol 94572.
No Fences/Garth Brooks EMI 796241.
Complete Set, Chrome Talk 13215.
The Lost Sessions, Pearl 1084.
The Limited Series [CD/DVD], Sony/BMG 88697027402.
Garth Brooks, Pearl 6001102.

Trisha Yearwood (1964–)

The Sweetest Gift

The contribution of females in country music is well established and runs throughout the history of the genre. Many of these performers enjoyed major crossover success due to the wide range of their incredible talent. In the mid–1990s the country-pop explosion was in full bloom and featured a number of talented artists including the singer with the sweetest gift. Her name is Trisha Yearwood.

Trisha Yearwood was born on September 19, 1964, in Monticello, Georgia. She started to sing from an early age and honed her skills participating in talent shows and jammed with local club bands. Her biggest influences were country music divas Patsy Cline and Emmylou Harris, rock/pop star Linda Ronstadt and Elvis Presley. Yearwood studied the music business in college and then served an internship for MTM Records where she gained invaluable experience.

In 1985, she moved to Nashville to pursue a full-fledged country music career. She cut a few demos and then later sang backup on Garth Brooks's tour. The friendship between the two future stars would take an extraordinary twist ten years down the road. Later, she performed with songwriter Pat Alger in a local bar where a producer for MCA Records discovered Yearwood and signed her to a recording contract.

In 1991, her self-titled debut reached number two on the C&W charts and contained a good number of hits, including "She's in Love with the Boy," "Like We Never Had a Broken Heart," "That's What I Like About You," and "The Woman Before Me," which went to number four. The latter song earned her the ACM Top New Female Vocalist Award in 1992. Her behind-the-scenes team featured the savvy producer Garth Fundis, who smartly chose the type of material that Yearwood excelled at. This included in particular, songs written by Garth Brooks, Pat McLaughlin, Carl Jackson, Kostas and Hal Ketchum.

She opened shows for Garth Brooks, a huge opportunity since he was the hottest ticket in country music. When Yearwood first moved to Nashville, she had met Brooks, and the two made a musician's pact, promising to help one another out if the other became a big star. Trisha's exposure as an act on the most crucial tour on the country circuit greatly enhanced her burgeoning status.

Her second album, *Hearts in Armor*, released just after her divorce to Christopher Latham, was a masterpiece and broke Yearwood worldwide.

Themes of love, heartbreak and cheating ran throughout the record and were best illustrated on the gritty "Woman Walk the Line" (an Emmylou Harris cover), "You Say You Will," "Down on My Knees," and a duet with Don Henley of the Eagles, "Walkaway Joe." With excellent production from Fundis and a host of top-notch songwriting as well as musicianship, it was no surprise that her sophomore effort was so successful.

Yearwood expanded on her new success with a variety of activities including a new perfume called Wild Heart (made by Revlon). She appeared in the film *The Thing Called Love* and was the subject of a biography, *Get Hot or Go Home—Trisha Yearwood: The Making of a Nashville Star.* Suddenly, she was everywhere, performing at large outdoor concert festivals, on the talk show circuit and featured in magazines.

Her third effort, *The Song Remembers When*, received a lot of attention and was featured as a cable television special. The singles "You Say You Will," "Down on My Knees," and the title track were more gems to add to her catalog. In an era when there were many strong female country artists, including Shania Twain, Faith Hill, and Reba McEntire, Yearwood was a standout. She sold millions of records and became an in-demand concert attraction.

She continued to build her career by releasing one solid album after another. *The Sweetest Gift* was a countrified collection of Christmas classics sung only as Yearwood could with her full-throated, beautiful voice. Although the album *Thinkin' About You* was a disappointment, she rebounded with *Everybody Knows,* a stronger effort that was pure country-pop. The working-person ballads, her forte as a singer, were in abundance, including "Believe Me Baby (I Lied)," "Maybe It's Love," "I Want to Live Again," and "A Lover Is Forever."

Songbook: A Collection of Hits was nestled in between the previous and next album effort, *Where Your Road Leads,* which saw her move more towards a pop music style. Although she had not totally abandoned her country roots, Yearwood demonstrated that her considerable vocal talent was an instrument that could play any style. "Powerful Thing," "Bring Me All Your Lovin'," "I Don't Want to Be the One," and "I'll Still Love You More" were the album highlights.

With *Real Live Woman* she managed to attain the balance between mainstream country and melodic pop satisfying her diverse fan base. She covered Bruce Springsteen's "Sad Eyes" and Linda Ronstadt's "Try Me Again." It was a professional album delivered by a professional singer with enough experience in her second decade of recording to know how to deliver satisfaction.

Inside Out was very much a collection of love songs and featured duets with Don Henley (the title track), Rosanne Cash (Cash's self-penned "Seven Year Ache)," and Vince Gill ("I Don't Paint Myself into Corners"). It would be another four years before she released her next effort, *Jasper County*, and the interval was a good respite. She was reunited with Fundis, and they put a collection together that sparkled with country grit and emotional toughness.

The biggest news of her career was a personal note as she married Garth Brooks on December 10, 2005. The two were longtime friends dating back to when they were just aspiring singers. It was the third marriage for her since she had wedded Robert Reynolds, the bass player for the Mavericks, on May 21, 1994, but divorced him in 1999. She continues to record and perform.

Trisha Yearwood is a country music treasure. Once her professional career began, she proved to be a genuine jewel with supreme vocal talent, excellent choice of material, and magnetic live presence. During her reign, the singer has dominated the country charts for over a decade, releasing a number of quality albums.

She possesses a remarkable voice. Her vocal delivery is superb with a wide range that can go from a whisper to a full-throated wail in an instant. Her ability to accent a syllable or note creates tension and drama, a trait that is an essential ingredient to her success. Her exact pitch and precise lyrical pronunciation separate Yearwood from the other country-pop divas.

Although she is talented enough to sing in any style, her principal material has always been working-class love songs. She is also comfortable with bluesy, up-tempo tunes as well as rockers. Because Yearwood has the vocal ability to make most material work, she has strayed from her country roots and settled into more of a pop-friendly environment.

Yearwood is a country-pop singer and one of the finest artists plying her trade in that vein. However, there has always been one very interesting fact that has made her stand out from the rest of the country-pop divas. Although she is a beautiful woman, she has never projected herself to be some kind of sex symbol and has always been interested in being known as a good singer. She has exceeded this humble goal and is now known as a great singer.

While growing up, Yearwood was a huge Elvis fan and incorporated some of his pop sensibility into her developing style. But it is the 1970s crossover sensation Linda Ronstadt whom most fans compare Trisha to. She has the same powerful voice and has chosen her material carefully to appeal to the right audience, much the same way Ronstadt did in the 1970s.

For someone as young as Yearwood it is surprising that she has such a loyal following. Her disciples include Shania Twain, LeAnn Rimes, Mindy McCready, Bobbie Cryner, Mandy Barnett, Allison Moorer, Meredith Edwards and Cyndi Thomson. Her list of followers continues to grow.

Like Twain, Rimes, McCready, Reba McEntire, Patty Loveless, and Faith Hill, Yearwood has mixed country roots with a strong dose of 1970s pop. The result has been huge success and many awards. She has expanded the parameters of country music to appeal to a larger audience with winning results.

She has captured numerous awards. For example, in 1994, a duet with Aaron Neville on "I Fall to Pieces" earned her a Grammy for Best Country Vocal Collaboration. In 1997, she was nominated for an Oscar for the Grammy Award-winning "How Do I Live," featured in the film *Con Air*. Although she has never won an Emmy for her television work, she has acted on different shows, including a role as a forensic pathologist on the popular series *Jag*.

The Trisha Yearwood story is that of a young girl who had big dreams on the Georgia farm where she grew up and was determined to make those dreams come true. She succeeded in doing so because of her sheer talent, grit and determination.

DISCOGRAPHY:

Trisha Yearwood, MCA 10297.
Hearts in Armor, MCA 10641.
The Song Remembers When, MCA 10911.
The Sweetest Gift, MCA 11091.
Thinkin' About You, MCA 11201.
Everybody Knows, MCA 11477.
Where Your Road Leads, MCA 70023.
Real Live Woman, MCA Nashville 170102.
Inside Out, MCA Nashville 0881702002.
Jasper County, MCA Nashville 3226.
Live in Concert Big Bang, MCA 77408.
Songbook: A Collection of Hits, MCA 70011.
Everybody Knows/Thinking of You, MCA 1701622.
Songbook: A Collection of Hits [Australian Bonus Tracks], MCA 11707.
The Collection, Madacy 52136.
Greatest Hits, MCA Nashville 000877602.

Shania Twain (1965–)
Twang-Pop

In the first generation of country musicians there were two outstanding Canadians who made a large impact on the U.S. market: Wilf Carter and Hank Snow. In the modern era there have been many more cross border artists who invaded the American charts. In the 1990s, one Canadian female rose to prominence with her sassy twang-pop. Her name is Shania Twain.

Shania Twain was born on August 28, 1965, in Windsor, Ontario, but raised in the small, rural northern town of Timmins, Ontario. Her musical career began with the guitar at an early age, and she honed her singing, writing and playing skills. Her parents encouraged her ambitions and spent considerable time and energy to make sure that she appreciated her special talent.

She sang on local radio and television stations as well as at community events. Because she was underage, her parents would take her to the bars in the wee hours of the morning to sing after the establishments had stopped serving alcohol. The dedication and fortitude of her parents helped shape her future. Tragically when Shania was 21, both were killed in an automobile accident.

Twain was immediately thrust into a role of responsibility, charged with taking care of her four younger brothers. She used her musical talents to survive by taking a job singing at a resort in nearby Deerhurst. She bought a house and provided her brothers with a stable home life.

In a way, the job at the resort in Deerhurst was a blessing because it allowed Twain to woodshed, harnessing her talent and working up material. She was capable of singing a variety of tunes that ranged from George Gershwin to Andrew Lloyd Webber, as well as other pop songs and some country bits as well. There was even some rock and roll injected into her repertoire. It was this period that enabled her to develop the stage stamina she would need in a few short years and to learn how to take an audience's musical pulse.

Once her brothers were able to take care of themselves, she forged ahead with her music career. She recorded a strong demo tape and performed in a showcase concert that caught the attention of executives from Mercury Nashville. In 1993, her self-titled debut album was released and spawned two minor singles, "What Made You Say That" and "Dance with the One That Brought You." Although Twain made a few ripples in the U.S. market, she was much more appreciated in Europe where her video earned her the Rising Video Star of the Year award.

It was about this time that she found true love. Robert John "Mutt" Lange, a hard-rock producer of albums by AC/DC, Def Leppard, Foreigner and the Cars, had heard Twain's debut effort and wanted to work with her. They fell in love, married, and together wrote or co-wrote all the material that would be found on her second effort.

In 1995, *The Woman in Me* was released, and it catapulted her to stardom. "Any Man of Mine," "(If You're Not in It for Love) I'm Outta Here!," and "No One Needs to Know" all became number one hits. The first single, "Whose Bed Have Your Boots Been Under," peaked at number eleven, and "The Woman in Me" reached position fourteen on the charts. By 1996, the album had sold over six million copies and broken the record for the most weeks spent at number one on the country charts. More importantly, it signified a resurgence in the country-pop movement and made Shania the queen of the style.

That status was reinforced with the release of *Come On Over,* which followed the successful formula of writing and producing songs built for the AOR crowd. She demonstrated that countrified mainstream pop was her strong suit. "Man! I Feel Like a Woman," "Love Gets Me Every Time," and "Come on Over" were successful products of the Lange–Twain songwriting team. She would be on the road for two years promoting the disc that would sell a whopping sixteen million copies by the end of the tour.

The always savvy husband-wife team, plotting each step of her career with care and precision, decided that the mega-star singer needed some down time. They retreated to their Swiss home and started a family. Their first child, a boy, was born in the summer of 2001. During this period of juggling domestic life and planning the next move, they were writing new material.

In 2002, *Up!* was released to great anticipation considering how well the last two albums had done. Although it boasted a couple of huge hits in "I'm Gonna Getcha Good!" and "Forever and for Always," it didn't have the staying power of previous efforts. It still was a multi-platinum seller and certainly didn't hurt her career. The era of multi-platinum CDs seemed to be over in country music circles.

In 2004, a *Greatest Hits* package was released and raced up the charts as expected. The first single, the duet song "Party for Two" with Billy Currington, made the country Top Ten, while a pop version with Sugar Ray lead singer Mark McGrath made the Pop Top Ten in the United Kingdom and Germany. She continues to record and perform.

Shania Twain is a country music queen. She has cleverly built a strong career with the help of her husband and in the process became a superstar. The combination of her talent, sophisticated marketing techniques, wholesome good looks and songwriting ability add up to one explosive and successful package.

Twain has a magical voice designed for the country-pop songs that have made her famous. It is an accessible style, one that can handle up-tempo material as well as slow, tender ballads. The recognizable element in her vocals only enhances her appeal. There are others with wider range and perhaps more ability, but few possess Shania's savvy and precise delivery.

She has built a career on mostly original material, which is quite remarkable considering many artists construct their catalog on the songwriting of others. It is a side of her musical personality that doesn't always get enough recognition. Of course, she has an excellent partner in husband Lange, and they have proven to be a formidable team, able to pen massive country-pop smash hits.

Twain is the complete artist and has utilized her singing success to conquer other mediums. She appeared at Super Bowl XXXVII and performed two songs, "Man! I Feel Like a Woman!" and "Up!" One of her songs, "Shoes," was included on the television show *Desperate Housewives* soundtrack. In November 2005, she appeared on an episode of the television reality show *The Apprentice*. She has also released two fragrances, one for Revlon and the other for Stetson.

She has won many awards, including several Grammys. Some of her personal honors include the 1999 Entertainer of the Year by both the ACM and the CMA, making her the first non–U.S. citizen to win the latter. She was inducted into Canada's Walk of Fame, had a street named after her in Timmins, as well as the Shania Twain Center. In 2005, she was also made an Officer of the Order of Canada.

Twain is one of many current female country artists with a definite pop side to her material. Along with Faith Hill, Martina McBride, and Trisha Yearwood, among others, the Canadian girl has managed to meld her traditional roots with various elements. Of the many women singers in country music none have benefited more from the marriage of the two styles than Shania.

She is the queen of country in her native land. She is also one of many Canadian country entertainers, including Terri Clark, Lisa Brokop, Lorna Lyns, Jess Lee, Jason Lines, the Cowboy Junkies, George Canyon, Oh Susanna, Anne Murray, Stompin' Tom Connors, Fred Eaglesmith, George Fox, Colleen Peterson, Justin Rutledge, Michelle Wright, Adam Gregory, Carolyn Dawn Johnson, Rita McNeil and Kate Maki.

She has given the world a number of great tunes. A partial list includes "What Made You Say That," "Dance With the One That Brought You," "Any Man of Mine," "(If You're Not in It for Love) I'm Outta Here," "No One Needs to Know," "Whose Bed Have Your Boots Been Under," "The Woman in Me," "Man! I Feel Like a Woman," "Love Gets Me Every Time," "Come on Over," "Shoes," "I'm Gonna Getcha Good," "Forever and for Always," and "Party for Two." Her catalog is an impressive list of country-pop songs that are internationally known.

The Shania Twain story is a heartwarming tale of a small-town girl who became an international star. She overcame personal tragedy and many obstacles in order to achieve superstardom. With the help of her husband, she has harnessed her talent to race to the top of the country music world with her smart, snappy and swinging quality twang-pop.

Discography:

Shania Twain, Mercury 514422.
The Woman in Me, Mercury 522886.
Come on Over, Mercury 5360003.
On the Way, New Millennium 940008.
Come on Over [International], Mercury 170123.

Beginnings: 1989–1990, Jonato 1001.
Wild and Wicked, Neon De Lite 34701.
Up!, Universal 170314.
For the Love of Him, Laserlight 21592.
In the Beginning, Music Club 475.
The Complete Limelight Sessions, Limelight 8140.
The Complete Set: Shania Twain, Griffin Music 3052.
For the Love of Him, Falcone Music 3612.
Greatest Hits, Mercury Nashville 000307202.
Send It with Love, Renaissance 1108.
Beginnings, Brentwood 40953.
All Fired Up, No Place to Go, Pickwick 751392.

Martina McBride (1966–)

Timeless Country

In the 1990s, country-pop became the dominant strain of the genre as a new crop of singers, mostly female, burst upon the scene. Some, like Shania Twain and Faith Hill, became superstars, selling massive numbers of records and performing at sell-out concerts. There was another chanteuse who made a significant impact with her timeless country. Her name is Martina McBride.

Martina McBride was born Martina Mariea Schiff on July 29, 1966, in Medicine Lodge, Kansas, into a musical family. Her father led a local band called the Schifters, and at the tender age of seven she joined the group as did her brother. She honed her singing and instrumental skills (keyboards) and by her teens was making significant contributions to the outfit. It appeared that she would embark on a musical career.

After high school graduation, Schiff played with different groups around the Medicine Lodge area, but her musical aspirations were stifled. In 1990, she married soundman John McBride, and they moved to Nashville. He worked with Charlie Daniels and Ricky Van Shelton, while she concentrated on preparing a first-rate demo that would interest a recording company. In 1991, RCA Records signed her.

The demo that both had worked so hard on was a polished and marketable product. They also caught a break when John was hired as Garth Brooks's production manager. It enabled Martina to open for the most popular singer on the circuit and gave her career a major boost.

In 1992, her debut album, *The Time Has Come*, was released, a traditional honky tonk set mixed with progressive country-folk. It was an odd combination, but it gained critical and fan attention. Like all other beginners, McBride was learning how to make records and with the second effort demonstrated that she had quickly found the right formula.

The more pop-inflected *The Way That I Am* was a major commercial breakthrough as it spawned three memorable singles: "My Baby Loves Me," which raced up the country charts to number two; "Independence Day," which became her signature tune and a much requested number during her live performances; and "Life #9," which reached the Top Ten, securing her position as a powerful new and rising star. Despite adding a different element to her traditional sound, she had not totally abandoned her roots.

She continued her successful ascent with the next album release, *Wild Angels,* which contained two major hits: the title track, her first number one; and "Safe in the Arms of Love," which peaked in the Top Five. By this time she was also a major concert draw and no longer needed to open up for Garth Brooks; McBride had developed her own loyal fan base.

In 1997, *Evolution* became her first Top Ten album and yielded two number one hits, "A Broken Wing" and "Wrong Again," as well as a couple of number two hits "Happy Girl" and "Whatever You Say." A duet with Jim Brickman, "Valentine," went Top Ten and crossed over to the adult contemporary charts, marking the first time she had accomplished that feat. The CD would go on to sell over two million copies, and, more importantly, firmly established her as one of the top female country artists.

Martina McBride Christmas was sandwiched between her previous album and next release, *Emotion.* The single "I Love You" became a number one hit and crossed over to the adult contemporary stations. "Love's the Only House," "There You Are," and "It's My Time" enhanced her growing reputation as one of the finest singers on the circuit. She took time off from recording and toured the CD to enthusiastic audiences.

In 2001, a greatest hits compilation was released and became her first to top the country charts. It contained four new tracks that were eventually available as singles. "Blessed" hit number one, while "When God-Fearin' Women Get the Blues" and "Where Would You Be" reached the Top Ten. By this point in her career it was evident that she was a special talent.

Martina, released in 2003, was dedicated to the female portion of her audience. "In My Daughter's Eyes" was a touching tune that won her more fans from all directions. It was the type of classic song that forced no boundaries and appealed to a broad section of the populace. "How Far," "God's Will" and "Trip Around the Sun" (recorded with Jimmy Buffett) all managed to place on the charts.

In 2005, *Timeless,* a collection of country classics, reached number one on the country charts. It was a mature effort from a seasoned veteran who knew how to deliver a professional work. As well, she recorded "I Still Miss

Someone" with Dolly Parton, indicating the respect that McBride commanded in the musical community and which she gave back to those that blazed the path for her to follow.

In 2007, she released her ninth album, *Waking Up Laughing*. It yielded the Top Five hit "Anyway" and the Top Forty hit "How I Feel." It marked a changed of methods, since she solo-produced and co-wrote the songs. McBride went on tour to promote the effort; Rodney Atkins and Little Big Town opened for her. Martina continues to record and perform.

Martina McBride is a country music jewel. She has established herself as one of the top female acts on the circuit with her golden voice, choice of material, enthusiasm and determination. There are many positive characteristics that make up her musical personality, and they are the major reasons why she rose from obscurity to prominence in a very short amount of time.

McBride possesses a soprano voice, an oddity in country music, but it has allowed her to achieve crossover success. She has been compared to Celine Dion, the French Canadian adult contemporary singer. Both possess an exciting vocal range and power. Both employ melisma, in which a singer strings several notes into one syllable. It is a technique that Martina has perfected and one which separates her from the other female artists on the current scene.

Although McBride began recording traditional honky tonk songs, she eventually switched to country-pop. With the range of her dynamic soprano voice, Martina was better suited to pop-flavored material and has earned great success following this path. Because of her immense talent she could perform in any branch of country with winning results.

She has given the world a number of great songs. A partial list includes "The Time Has Come," "That's Me," "Cheap Whiskey," "My Baby Loves Me," "Life #9," "Heart Trouble," "Safe in the Arms of Love," "Wild Angels," "A Broken Wing," "Happy Girl," "Wrong Again," "Whatever You Say," "I Love You," "Love's the Only House," "When God-Fearin' Women Get the Blues," "Blessed," "Where Would You Be," "Concrete Angel, "This One's for the Girls," "In My Daughter's Eyes," and "Anyway." Of the many songs, "Independence Day" deserves special attention because it was a tune that became an anti-domestic violence anthem. It also earned McBride special status among her peers and the listening public.

The popular vocalist has won many awards, including four CMA Female Vocalist of the Year trophies and three ACM Female Vocalist of the Year Awards. She has expanded her appeal by singing "The Star-Spangled Banner" at Game Three of the 2004 World Series. She has also been associated with the television show *American Idol*. When Carrie Underwood won *American Idol*, she cited McBride as her biggest influence and performed a stunning version of "Independence Day." During the 2006 season, Martina was a guest coach on *Canadian Idol* and took winner Eva Avila on the Canadian leg of her tour.

Like many modern female singers McBride's greatest single influence was Patsy Cline. As well, Martina's father, who introduced his daughter to music, also had a major impact on her career. She has also benefited from listening to Dolly Parton, Barbara Mandrell, Crystal Gayle, Loretta Lynn, Lynn Anderson, Tammy Wynette, Reba McEntire, June Carter Cash, and Emmylou Harris.

In turn, she has had a large impact on a variety of young singers, including Danni Leigh, Meredith Edwards, Carmen Rasmusen, Ashley Monroe, Sara Evans, Terri Clark, Catherine Britt, Miranda Lambert, Taylor Swift and LeAnn Rimes. However, McBride's biggest fan is Carrie Underwood, who has established her own singular musical career patterned on Martina's.

The Martina McBride story is that of a country music winner. She has released top albums and major hit singles with regularity during her distinguished career. Her soprano vocal delivery is instantly recognizable to listeners of different musical tastes. She has entertained millions and influenced many with her timeless country.

DISCOGRAPHY:

The Time Has Come, RCA 66002-2.
The Way That I Am, RCA 66288.
Wild Angels, RCA 66509.
Evolution, RCA 67516.
Martina McBride Christmas, RCA 67654.
Emotion, RCA 67824.
White Christmas, RCA 67842.
Martina, RCA 54207.
Timeless, RCA 72425.
Waking Up Laughing, RCA/BMG/Sony Nashville 03674.
Greatest Hits, RCA 67012.
The Collection, Madacy 52410.
The Collection, Madacy 52492.

Tim McGraw (1967–)

Rise to Prominence

The fluctuation in popularity among country music artists is as old as the genre itself. Some individuals start out like a ball of fire and then fade from the scene just as quickly. At the other end of the spectrum are those who start out slowly and carefully build up momentum on their way to stardom. One such individual after an inauspicious beginning enjoyed a dramatic rise in prominence. His name is Tim McGraw.

Samuel Timothy McGraw was born on May 1, 1967, in Delhi, Louisiana. He was the result of a brief love affair between his mother and prominent baseball player Tug McGraw, a star relief pitcher for the Philadelphia Phillies and New York Mets. However, the future country star wouldn't know the identity of his father until he was eleven years old. Up to that time he was called Tim Smith. Soon after, he adopted the surname McGraw.

Tim grew up in the small town of Start, Louisiana, and was a good athlete like his biological dad. He also listened to a variety of music, including rock, blues, pop, country and jazz. He excelled in sports and attended Northeast Louisiana University on a baseball scholarship with ambitions of one day following in his famous father's footsteps. Another possibility was a career in sports medicine, but the music bug bit and bit hard. He learned how to play the guitar to accompany his singing and set his mind on being a successful recording star.

He honed his skills until he was good enough to perform on the local club circuit and dropped out of school. Despite the myriad of musical styles he had grown up listening to, his favorite was country music, so he decided on that direction. In 1989, he headed to Nashville — ironically, on the same day that his hero Keith Whitley died.

Like all others who arrive in Music City U.S.A. with big dreams and not much else, McGraw struggled. He worked the local club circuit for a couple of years as just another anonymous singer with musical ambitions. It was some three years later that he finally landed a record deal with Curb Records. Not a major label, the company still made good on their promise to record him and released the single "Welcome to the Club," which won over a few fans. His subsequent album didn't even chart.

His fortunes improved slightly when the single "Indian Outlaw" from his second effort, *Not a Moment Too Soon,* was released. The song created controversy because many thought it was disrespectful to Native Americans, while others embraced its novelty appeal. The notoriety enabled the tune to reach the country Top Ten, and it crossed over to the pop Top Twenty.

The controversy enabled his next single, "Don't Take the Girl," to gain much more attention as it moved all the way to the top of the country charts. A second song, "Down on the Farm," from what was shaping up to be a monster album, peaked at number two. The title track, "Not a Moment Too Soon," also made it to number one, and "Refried Dreams" reached the Top Five. The CD would eventually sell over five million copies and top both the country and pop charts, making it the best-selling country album of 1995.

His third effort, *All I Want*, contained the monster smash "I Like It, I Love It." The album raced to the top of the country charts, made the pop Top Five and sold two million copies. Four more singles from the CD were hits including the number one "She Never Lets It Go to Her Heart," the number two "Can't Be Really Gone," and the Top Five "All I Want Is a Life" and "Maybe We Should Just Sleep on It." For someone who had started his career on a low note he was now flying high.

If 1994 and 1995 had been good years, then 1996 was to be a spectacular campaign for a multitude of reasons. McGraw embarked on an extensive tour to support the third album, which saw him greatly enhance his fan base. Everyone wanted to see the man with the cool country hits perform live on stage. The tour's opening act was a pretty belter with a special talent of her owned named Faith Hill. In October, once the tour was over, the two married.

The star magnitude of the union raised Tim's profile even higher. In 1997, McGraw released *Everywhere,* which contained the couple's first duet, "It's Your Love," a number one hit. The CD topped the country charts and peaked at number two on the pop charts. Two more singles from the album went to number one, including "Where the Green Grass Grows," and "Just to See You Smile." "One of These Days" and "For a Little While" peaked at number two.

For nearly a decade Garth Brooks had occupied the throne as the king of contemporary country, but by the end of the 1990s McGraw had unseated him. A 1998 single, "Just to Hear You Say That You Love Me," was another husband and wife duet, this time on Hill's album, *Faith*. The song reached the Top Five.

McGraw helped his cause with another monster seller, the triple platinum *A Place in the Sun*. It went to number one on both the country and pop charts and spawned four top singles including "Please Remember Me," "Something Like That," "My Best Friend," and "My Next Thirty Years." On tour and on recordings, the man who had started out lost in the shuffle was now the reigning country male artist.

In 2000, his first *Greatest Hits* compilation was released and became another best-seller. As well, the single "Let's Make Love," a duet with his wife taken from her *Breathe* album, was another smash. The song proved a true winner as it earned McGraw his first Grammy for Best Country Vocal Collaboration. The only blemish on his record was a scuffle with police during an altercation that involved friend Kenny Chesney. The charges were cleared in time for fans to attend his tour with wife Hill.

In 2001, *Set This Circus Down* was released and went straight to number one on the country charts and peaked at number two on the pop side. It boasted four number one singles, ""Grown Men Don't Cry," "Angry All the

Time," "The Cowboy in Me," and "Unbroken." His golden touch extended to his protégée Jo Dee Messina when their duet "Bring on the Rain" hit number one.

The self-titled *Tim McGraw* album, released a year later, was recorded with his road band, Dancehall Doctors, instead of the standard Nashville session musicians. "Red Rag Top" and "She's My Kind of Rain," as well as a cover of Elton John's classic "Tiny Dancer," hit the charts. The CD debuted at number one on the country chart and proved to be another winner. By this point in his career it seemed as if he could do no wrong.

In 2004, *Live Like You Were Dying* was released and was another chart topper that he co-produced himself. Once again he utilized his road band on the record; it proved to be a very successful formula. The title cut would earn him CMA Single and Song of the Year, ACM Single and Song of the Year, as well as a Grammy.

His next album effort, *Let It Go*, once again debuted at number one on the country charts. The single "Last Dollar (Fly Away)" became another top single to add to his impressive list. It became his ninth number one country album making him a true superstar. He continues to record and perform as a solo artist and with his very talented wife, Faith Hill.

Tim McGraw is a country music mainstay. For over a decade he has topped the charts with regularity and carved a permanent place on the contemporary scene. He is a total package of vocal, instrumental, songwriting and production talent. Tim McGraw and Faith Hill occupy the throne of king and queen of country music.

McGraw has a voice tailor-made for country-pop material, which he has built his career on. There is a husky element in his vocal delivery but also a twang, enabling him to enjoy major crossover success. He is also able to blend his vocal talents with a number of other singers most notably his life partner.

He has also delved into acting. His first appearance was on television on *The Jeff Foxworthy Show*. He later played a sheriff in the film *Black Cloud*. Other movie acting credits include *Friday Night Lights* and *Flicka* in which he played the lead role. His latest acting foray was *The Kingdom*. A well credited actor, he has proven that he possesses a multi-media touch.

But there is more to McGraw than the multi-platinum singles and CDs. Unlike other artists who ignore charity causes as their fame grows, he has donated more of his free time as his star power intensified. He spearheaded the Swampstock event, a softball game and concert, with the proceeds going to Little League baseball. He hosted a New Year's Eve concert in Nashville, with the show raising money for the Country Music Hall of Fame and Museum. Like other artists, he hosted several charity events in the wake of the devastating effects of Hurricane Katrina. Both he and his wife were involved in putting on fund-raising events. He is also a member of the American Red Cross National Celebrity Cabinet and has helped the organization with their important causes.

The Dancehall Doctors serve as McGraw road band as well as the studio musicians on his last two efforts. The band consists of Darran Smith on lead and acoustic guitar; Bob Miner on rhythm, acoustic guitar, banjo and mandolin; Denny Hemingson on steel, electric, baritone and slide guitars, and Dobro; John Marcus on bass; Dean Brown on fiddle and mandolin; Jeff McMahon on keyboards; Bill Mason on drums; and David Dunkley on percussion. Many of them have been with him for over a decade and in some cases even longer.

In 2006, McGraw and his wife embarked on the ambitious Soul2Soul II tour, which was a major commercial success. It was named Major Tour of the Year and outdid the megastar concerts of Madonna and the Rolling Stones. The seventy-plus city adventure became the highest grossing tour in the history of country music.

Tim McGraw has been generously rewarded for his chart success. He has netted three Grammys, eleven ACM awards, ten CMA prizes, and nine American Music Awards. With his ability to spawn number one albums and singles, he will reap more honors in the future. But the best personal honors are those he has received for his charity work in a variety of venues.

At the start of his career few would have predicted that McGraw would someday be the number one male artist on the circuit. Yet, he was determined to make it in the music business and showed all his detractors that he possessed the talent necessary to become a superstar. He has exceeded all expectations with magnificent style and humility during his rise to prominence.

DISCOGRAPHY:

Tim McGraw, Curb 77659.
Not a Moment Too Soon, Curb 77693.
All I Want, Curb 77800.
Everywhere, Curb 77886.
A Place in the Sun, Curb 77942.
Set This Circus Down, Curb 78711.
Tim McGraw and the Dancehall Doctors, Curb 78746.
Live Like You Were Dying, Curb 78858.
Let It Go, Curb 78794.
Greatest Hits, Curb 77978.
Greatest Hits, Vol. 2, Curb 78891.

Faith Hill (1967–)

Mississippi Girl

For many years, when it came to music, Mississippi was considered primarily a blues mecca. However, rock icon Elvis Presley, soul act the Chambers Brothers, country star Conway Twitty, and the king of jazz tenor saxophone Lester Young changed that perspective. In the late 1990s, a female singer known as the Mississippi Girl had an impact on perceptions of the state, putting the Magnolia State on the contemporary country music map. Her name is Faith Hill.

Faith Hill was born Audrey Faith Perry on September 26, 1967, in Jackson, Mississippi. However, she grew up in the small town of Star, an appropriate name for someone who would one day dominate the country music charts. But before she achieved her popularity, she paid her dues like every other artist. She started singing at seven, at local rodeos, churches and school. She attended Hinds Community College but dropped out to pursue a music career.

At nineteen, she moved to Nashville and worked the clubs and bars. She met and married Dan Hill, a music executive in Nashville, but sadly, like a country song, the couple were divorced in 1994. However, by this time the blossoming singer had begun to make a name for herself with a total package of voice, talent, material and looks.

During her stay in Nashville she sold T-shirts at Fan Fair, which provided her excellent connections. One of those individuals who recognized her ambition and talent was singer Gary Morris, who owned a music publinshing company, where she soon worked as a receptionist. Another Gary — songwriter Gary Burr — helped guide her to Warner Brothers Records.

In 1993, she waxed her debut single for Warner Brothers, "Wild One," which became a major hit, reaching the number one spot on the country charts and remained there for four weeks. On the strength of that power single, she released her first album, *Take Me As I Am*, which reached the Top Ten on the country charts and went gold within a year of its release.

Her divorce from Hill fueled the next single, "Piece of My Heart," which also went to number one. Her second album effort, *It Matters to Me*, was released in 1995. At this point, she was one of the rising stars in Nashville; but her greatest success was still to come.

In 1996, she increased her star power with the marriage to country hit machine Tim McGraw after being the opening act on his summer tour. Energized by the union, Hill released her third album, *Faith*, which included a duet "Just to Hear You Say That You Love Me," a number three country hit. Another single, "This Kiss,"a crossover hit, helped the CD reach the Top Five on the country charts. At this point, her rising prominence seemed unstoppable.

In 1999, *Breathe* was released, and it truly broke her career wide open. All the promise that she had displayed on earlier CDs and concerts came into full bloom. A magnificent effort, it yielded the crossover hit singles "The Way You Love Me" and "Breathe." Although her legion of fans considered her a true country queen, Hill's sound also included a strong pop element that endeared the singer to an entirely different audience.

In 2002, her *Cry* album appeared, and it seemed that Hill had inherited her husband's golden touch. The CD contained a number of top singles, including "Back to You," "Baby You Belong," "Free," "This Is Me" and the title song, which earned her a Grammy. She toured with McGraw, and the pair were truly the country music industry's fairy-tale couple, breaking attendance records with their live extravaganza performance.

In 2006, she released *Fireflies,* which proved to be another monster seller on the strength of the singles "Mississippi Girl," "Dearly Beloved," "Stealing Kisses," "The Lucky One," "You Stay with Me," and the duet "Like We Never Loved at All," with her husband. The star power of the McGraw–Hill marital team was one not seen in the annals of country music since George Jones and Tammy Wynette were belting out tunes in the 1970s.

In 2007, she released *The Hits.* Hill also embarked on a reprise of the acclaimed Soul2Soul II Tour with husband McGraw. Faith sang two duets, "I Need You" and "Shotgun Rider," on his *Let It Go* CD. She participated in her idol Reba McEntire's new recording, "Sleeping with the Telephone." Hill continues to record and perform.

Faith Hill is a country music megastar. Her albums and singles continuously chart, and the duets with her husband have all been major hits. She is one of the most recognized names within and outside the industry. In an era when celebrity marriages are put under a microscope and heavily scrutinized, McGraw and Hill have managed to keep it all together.

Faith Hill has the voice of a country music angel. It certainly contains stylistic nuances of her heroine, Reba McEntire, but it is a unique vocal delivery. To listen to Hill's voice is to listen to the past, the current, and future sound of the genre.

There is a sincerity and honesty in the songs that grace her CDs. She pours a lot of herself into each track, and the result is a strong, cohesive catalog that has won her countless awards and major recognition. The choice of her material is a strong reason why she has managed to reach the top of the country music world and remain there for some time.

With her abundance of talent she has given the world a treasure trove of songs. A partial list includes "Breathe," "Cry," "Fireflies," "If My Heart Had Wings," "It Matters to Me," "I Want You," "Let Me Let Go," "Let's Make Love," "Like We Never Loved at All," "Love Ain't Like That," "Lucky One," "Mississippi Girl," "Paris," "Stealing Kisses," "The Secret of Life," "There You'll Be," "The Way You Love Me," "This Kiss," "We've Got Nothing but Love to Prove," "Where Are You Christmas" and "Wish for You." Whether as a solo artist or teamed with her husband, she crafts each song with the special Hill touch.

She has won countless awards and received many special recognitions. She was the Academy of Country Music's Favorite New Female in 1994. In 1996, Faith performed in the ceremonies for the close of the Summer Olympic Games in Atlanta. The song "Cry" won the award for the best Female Vocal Performance in 2003. In 2004, the singer expanded her fame with a movie role in the *The Stepford Wives*, which also included Nicole Kidman and Bette Midler. She has also been a champion for many causes, including support for the Arts and Entertainment Center in Mississippi, which is being built in 2007.

However, she also made headlines for an award that she did not win. In 2006, backstage at the CMA show, Hill seemed perturbed that Carrie Underwood had won Female Vocalist of the Year honors. Her negative reaction was caught on camera for the world to see. Faith insisted that it was all a misunderstanding and was proud of the winner, even going as far as calling Underwood up and congratulating her. It was a blemish on an otherwise very clean record.

She has worked with a number of producers and studio musicians, including Byron Gallimore, Dann Huff, Lonnie Wilson, Steve Nathan, Brent Mason, Julian King, Paul Franklin, Curtis Young, Glenn Worf, Mike Brignardello, Erik Lutkins, Aubrey Haynie, Kristin Wilkinson, Gene Miller, Terry McMillan, B. James Lowry, Michael Landau, Sonny Garrish and John Catchings. Of course, her greatest partner has been Tim McGraw.

Together, McGraw and Hill are currently the most visible couple in country music. They are an award-winning, chart-topping celebrity twosome, who have built a private life for themselves outside of the glamor of the music industry and are the proud parents of three beautiful girls.

Hill, with her special vocal talents, is one of the major country-pop acts of the era. Like Shania Twain, Trisha Yearwood and Martina McBride, Faith has charged her roots with a heavy dose of pop elements, giving the sound a balance and a contemporary edge.

The greatest single influence on Hill was Reba McEntire. Although Faith has emulated her idol, the Mississippi Girl has displayed a distinct musical style that has catapulted her to the top of the charts. Like her idol, Faith has dominated the charts with million-selling singles and records.

Arguably, the second most important influence on Hill has been Tim McGraw. They met while both were on the ascent, and since then they have achieved superstardom together. Although they have sung a few duets together, there is a healthy competition between the two as they spur each other on to greater heights.

In turn, Hill has influenced a number of young singers. A partial list includes Taylor Swift, Sara Evans, Ashley Monroe, Meredith Edwards, Miranda Lambert, Lindsay Haun, Beverley Mitchell, Jesse Sheely, Victoria Boland, Ilse DeLange, Danni Leigh, and Julie Roberts. Each aspiring female country artist can certainly borrow a page from the Mississippi Girl's career sheet on how to succeed in the music business.

The Faith Hill story is about the girl next door who achieved success in her chosen profession. She was a determined young lady who paid her dues from an early age and stayed focus throughout the tough times to build a solid career. The Mississippi Girl is a special talent who has written her own chapter in country music.

DISCOGRAPHY:

Take Me As I Am, Warner Bros. 45389-2.
It Matters to Me, Warner Bros. 45872.
Faith, Warner Bros. 46790.
Love Will Always Win, Warner Bros. 9362473312.
Breathe, Warner Bros. 47373.
Cry, Warner Bros. 48001.
Sunshine and Summertime, Warner Bros. 101813.
Fireflies, Warner Bros. 48794.
There You'll Be: The Best of Faith Hill [Bonus Track], WEA International 48241.
Greatest Hits, Warner Bros. 133052.
The Hits, Warner Bros. 184380.

PART FIVE

Contemporary Country

Contemporary country is a term that encompasses many different themes and ideas. Since country music respects tradition and boasts a simple form, it has allowed for the creation of sub-genres as well as revival of old styles updated with slicker production techniques. Like other types of music, country continues to reinvent itself.

One of the main branches of contemporary country is so-called New Country. It blends the hard, traditional honky tonk roots with a slick, pop-sensibility and crossover appeal. There are also elements of mainstream rock and roll, boogie and twang welded to the roots base. Garth Brooks ignited the trend, and others such as Shania Twain, LeAnn Rimes and Faith Hill benefited from his successes.

But the term contemporary country also covers the revival and continuation of standard sub-genres, such as bluegrass, western swing and honky tonk. Contemporary country also includes alternative, progressive, folk-country, country-rock, neo-traditional, and countrypolitan. Under the current framework there is something for every country music fan.

Contemporary country also includes practitioners outside of America. Since county music's commerical inception, the dominant performers have been mainly from the United States; however, the sound of American country music on the rest of the world influenced performers around the globe. The impact stretches from the very beginning, with pioneers like Jimmie Rodgers and the Carter Family, to today's modern artists like Garth Brooks, Trisha Yearwood, Faith Hill and Tim McGraw. Others performers from the past — such as Roy Acuff, Tex Ritter, Gene Autry, Roy Rogers, Bob Wills, Bill Monroe, Hank Williams, Sr., George Jones, Kitty Wells, Patsy Cline, Loretta Lynn, Buck Owens, Johnny Cash, Willie Nelson, Waylon Jennings and Merle Haggard — continue to guide singers around the world.

Country music, like blues and jazz, is an international music with singers in every corner of the planet. Australia, Japan, the United Kingdom, Germany, India, New Zealand, Canada, Ireland, and Russia boast vibrant country music colonies. A few examples include Adam Harvey, Morgan Evans,

Kasey Chambers, and Travis Collins (Australia); Gord Bamford and Shane Yellowbird (Canada); Lucie Diamond (United Kingdom); Bering Strait (Russia); John McNicholl (Ireland); Charlie Nagatani (Japan); and Bobby Cash (India).

Despite the many performers who ply their trade around the world, the U.S.A. remains the leader and greatest producer of country singers. A partial list of the present and future stars in contemporary country includes Ryan Adams, Trace Adkins, Gary Allan, John Anderson, Rodney Atkins, Dierks Bentley, Suzy Bogguss, Iris DeMent, Guy Clark, Tracy Byrd, Chris Cagle, Carlene Carter, Deanna Carter, Mark Chesnutt, Donovan Chapman, Joe Diffie, Katrina Elam, Sara Evans, Carolyn Dawn Johnson, Tracy Lawrence, Kathy Mattea, Lila McCann, Joe Nichols, Brad Paisley, Kellie Pickler, Blake Shelton, Marty Stuart, Josh Turner, Lindsey Haun and Gretchen Wilson.

With more than eighty years of country music recordings to draw upon, the contemporary set have a vast and rich history to build their careers on. The old songs never grow tired, and with fresh production technology the new singers will continue to keep the genre strong and proud.

This section of the book covers a wide range of locations, ages and styles. Included are artists from the United States, Canada, New Zealand and Australia. Half of the ten singers profiled in this section were born from 1967 through 1970, while the others were all born during the 1980s. They represent traditional, country-pop, alternative, adult contemporary, and country-rock. However, the common thread throughout the contemporary country category is they are an integral part of the contemporary country scene. Included here are the following performers:

- Keith Urban, born in New Zealand, combined rock and roll outlaw image and highly respected guitar skills to find success in Nashville.
- Kenny Chesney was a late bloomer who struggled for years until he blossomed into one of the top male country stars.
- Terri Clark is a Canadian who delivered a more traditional style rather than pop or rock tinged material.
- Jo Dee Messina is a fiery singer who overcame many obstacles in order to achieve recognition.
- Alison Krauss has dedicated her career to bluegrass and to delivering it to a wider audience.
- LeAnn Rimes burst out of the scene with a smash hit and album before drifting to more contemporary album-oriented material.
- Carrie Underwood is a winner of the television reality show *American Idol,* which served as a launching pad for her career.
- Miranda Lambert was a teenage singer when she hit the big time following in the footsteps of Brenda Lee, Tanya Tucker and LeAnn Rimes.

- Catherine Britt is an Australian country music singer who has made an impact on Nashville.
- Taylor Swift is a teenage sensation and one of the fresh faces of New Country.

Keith Urban (1967–)
New Zealand Cowboy

As with blues, jazz and rock, the appeal of country music has spread around the globe. A couple of generations have grown up listening to Jimmie Rodgers, Hank Williams, Sr., Patsy Cline, Johnny Cash, Dolly Parton, and Garth Brooks. In an effort to emulate their heroes, many youngsters have picked up a guitar and started to play and sing. One of these young boys fell in love with the twangy sounds he heard from America to become the New Zealand Cowboy. His name is Keith Urban.

Keith Urban was born on October 26, 1967, in Whangarei, New Zealand. He was the son of shop owners in Australia. It was Keith's parents' shop that led to their son's musical career. They allowed a patron one day to place an ad in their store window on the promise that the person would teach young Keith how to play guitar. The boy was a natural and two years later was winning contests.

When not practicing his instrument, Keith worked in a youth acting company where he was required to sing, dance and memorize lines. It was perfect grooming for the musical career he would later pursue. At home, his father, a country music buff, played the records of Glen Campbell, Dolly Parton, Don Williams and Jimmy Webb. The young Urban, a keen student of all types of music, studied the guitar techniques of Mark Knopfler of Dire Straits and Lindsey Buckingham of Fleetwood Mac fame.

By his teens he had already decided on a musical career and quit school to pursue his dreams. He scuffled around for a few years before the winds of change turned in his favor. The Australian music business was primed for change and Urban was one of the driving forces with his brash, rocking country style. He recorded a self-titled album that would win him a few honors. Despite the success and popularity in his homeland, he had always cast an eye towards Nashville.

Urban made a few trips to Nashville building bridges and finally, in 1997, he moved to Music City, U.S.A., with an Australian bandmate, drummer Peter Clarke. The duo added bass player Jerry Flowers, an American from

West Virginia, to fill out a trio and formed a band called the Ranch. They landed a record deal with Capitol Records and released a self-titled debut album to intense critical acclaim. Despite the promise the Ranch held, Urban departed for a solo career.

Since he had garnered such high praise for his unique take on country music and outstanding guitar playing, he drew attention from many different corners. He guested on Garth Brooks's *Double Live* and contributed other session work with the Dixie Chicks. He met Matt Rollings, a formidable musician and producer, who worked the controls of Urban's next album.

Sadly, Urban had developed a cocaine habit, and before he could resume his promising career he needed to clean up his act, so he checked into rehab. Once he was given a clean bill of health, he returned with his self-titled debut album. The CD yielded three Top Five hits: "But For the Grace of God," "Your Everything," and "Where the Blacktop Ends." It earned him Top New Male Vocalist Award at the ACM Ceremonies and the CMA Horizon Award, in 2001.

A year later, *Golden Road* was released and boasted three number one singles, "Somebody Like You," "Who Wouldn't Wanna Be Me," and "You'll Think of Me." The song "Raining on Sunday" peaked in the Top Five. He would later tour with Brooks & Dunn and Kenny Chesney, exposing him to a wider audience. At this point, Urban was one of the best-known and popular singers on the circuit with his rock and roll image and hard-driving approach.

In 2004, he released *Be Here,* which contained four number one singles: "Days Go By," "You're My Better Half," "Making Memories of Us," and "Better Life." The single "Tonight I Wanna Cry" peaked at number two. But the songs were only part of the success. His high-powered tours, session work and extensive media exposure went a long way towards building a Keith Urban mystique.

In 2005, he enjoyed a banner year. He toured with Katrina Elam, performed in the Live Philadelphia concert in July, starred in a Gap commercial, was named CMA's Entertainer of the Year and played in front of a European crowd for the first time in his career. He also toured with Bryan Adams in the UK and Ireland. It was in England that his *Days Go By* album was released, a compilation of songs from *Be Here* and *Golden Road*. At the end of the year he headlined his own tour with support acts Nerina Pallot and Richard Winsland.

In 2006, his single "Once in a Lifetime" was a massive hit, but he made just as many headlines for his marriage to actress Nicole Kidman. He also spent more time in rehab at the famous Betty Ford Center for alcoholism. Once he had cleaned up his act, he resumed his potent career.

In 2007, he released *Love, Pain & the Whole Crazy Thing*. The album would go to number one and yield the singles "Once in a Lifetime," "Stupid Boy," and "I Told You So." As usual he toured in support of the record, this time with the Wreckers as opening act. He continues to record and perform.

Keith Urban is a country music battler. Despite the massive success he has enjoyed, he overcame many obstacles before attaining his fame. He is blessed with excellent talent and has made the most of it to achieve stardom. The New Zealand/Australian singer proved that there was more than enough cowboy in him to make it in Nashville.

Urban is a fine singer, but he is a much better guitarist. He is a modern country musician, and his influences are reflected in his playing. There is something catchy about the riffs he plays, and there is plenty of twang. Yet there is a contemporary sound to his instrumental workouts, and many have utilized those skills on their records.

His talent has not gone unnoticed. He has won many awards, not just in Nashville, but around the world. CMA and CMT have both honored him, while back in Australia they have not forgotten his achievements. Other honors include the French Association of Country Music Artist of the Year, Country Music's Hottest Bachelor, CMA Golden Guitar Instrumentalist, and a Grammy for Best Male Country Vocal Performance for the song "You'll Think of Me."

Another part of the Urban rise to fame has been his music videos. The dramatic content of his pieces has spurred record sales and fans' desire to see him live on stage. With the many channels that play videos on a regular basis, any artist hoping to make it big in the music industry needs more than a few gold hits under his or her belt. Keith Urban has made the most of his good looks, his sex appeal, and bad boy charm to further his career.

Urban is part of a burgeoning country music movement in Australia and New Zealand. Others in country music from the Land Down Under include Catherine Britt, Slim Dusty, Johnny Ashcroft, Sherrie Austin, Adam Brand, Troy Cassar-Daley, Kasey Chambers, Beccy Cole, Smoky Dawson, Gina Jeffries, Lee Kernaghan, Reg Lindsay, Jamie O'Neal, the Blue Heeler, Deep Creek, Southbound, Karma Country and Tracy Coster. Although he has based his career in Nashville, he is still part of the Australian music scene.

He also shares similarities with many American singers, including Rockie Lynne, Brad Paisley, LeAnn Rimes, John Williamson, Bryan White, Faith Hill, Tim McGraw, Trisha Yearwood and Patty Loveless, among others. Like the aforementioned artists, Urban mixes his style with various elements of pop and rock. Also, his tours are dynamic, making the most of his individual talents.

There were many influences on Urban. Certainly, Garth Brooks — with his country-pop, 1970s singer-songwriter touch and rock and roll concert techniques — made an impact. The guitar stylings of Mark Knopfler and Chet

Atkins also made a profound impression on Keith's touch. The New Zealand Cowboy even borrowed from the vocabulary of Jimi Hendrix. But, like all other successful artists, he was able to assemble the myriad elements into one cohesive sound that he called his own.

The Keith Urban story is that of a controversial and talented individual. In a short time he has catapulted to the top of the country music scene with his undeniable ability. Despite his troubles with substance abuse, the New Zealand Cowboy remains a vital force.

DISCOGRAPHY:

Keith Urban, Capitol 97591.
Golden Road, Capitol 32936.
Be Here, Capitol 77489.
Love, Pain & the Whole Crazy Thing, Capitol 77087.
Keith Urban, EMI 57484.
Keith Urban/The Ranch, WEA International 302086.
Days Go By, EMI 477581.
Keith Urban/Golden Road, Warner Strategic Marketing 303367.

With the Ranch:
The Ranch, WEA 197742.

Kenny Chesney (1968–)
Average Guy

The measure of success is not always how many CDs an artist sells or the size of the crowd they play to. Success is also not measured by how quickly a musician rises from total obscurity to national and international prominence. Instead, it is calculated by the sincerity, quality and depth of their music. Such is the case of the average guy whose name is Kenny Chesney.

Kenny Chesney was born on March 26, 1968, in Knoxville, Tennessee, but grew up in the small town of Luttrell, the home of Chet Atkins, the famous picker, producer and country artist. Although Chesney listened to both country and rock and roll, he harbored no musical ambitions until his college years. While at East Tennessee State University, he deviated from marketing studies to practice his guitar and play in a bluegrass outfit.

The long road to stardom began with performances at local venues — including Mexican restaurants — as well as playing for tips at other locales. He started to write songs and eventually put enough of them together for a self-produced demo tape that sold a few copies mostly through word of mouth.

Unfortunately, there were no major labels ready to sign the talented, average country music guy.

In 1991, he graduated and moved to Nashville. Chesney was just another anonymous singer with big dreams in a city full of aspiring musicians with the same ambitions. He found work at a rough honky tonk bar, where he gained invaluable experience, but his career seemed stalled. Kenny made progress when he signed a music publishing deal with Acuff-Rose publications and finally after much effort was awarded a recording contract with Capricorn Records.

In 1993, his debut album, *In My Wildest Dreams,* was released and showed much promise, but a lack of promotion and a company shakedown hurt chances of it making a major breakthrough. Eventually, he moved over to BNA Records, one of RCA's subsidiaries.

He had been writing songs for some time, and many of them appeared on his first album for his new label. *All I Need to Know* was released and contained his first two Top Ten hits, the title track and "Fall in Love." It seemed after years of hard work and just missing the mark he was on his way to true stardom.

Chesney began to perform in better venues than the honky tonk dives that he had started out in, and continued to build up his popularity. There was something about his average guy looks and manner that connected with audiences. There was no pretense about Kenny's music, and this sincere quality enabled him to enthrall a special segment of the public.

The recording side of his career was also gaining momentum. The second BNA album, *Me and You,* went gold and yielded two singles that peaked in the Top Five: "When I Close My Eyes," and the title track, both of which narrowly missed becoming his first number one hits. Chesney was moving closer to the fame that had eluded him for so long and that he had strived very hard to achieve.

In 1997, he scored his first number one hit, "She's Got It All," one of the many outstanding songs on his fourth full-length CD, *I Will Stand.* As well, "That's Why I'm Here" peaked at number two. After eight years in the music business and overcoming many obstacles, Chesney was finally ready for his major breakthrough.

The 1999 album *Everywhere We Go* would go double platinum and boast two number one hits, "You Had Me from Hello," and "How Forever Feels." It also contained the Top Ten singles "What I Need to Do" and "She Thinks My Tractor's Sexy." His concert reviews improved, and now most of the crowd was there to see him not as an opening act but as a star.

A *Greatest Hits* package became another double platinum seller and included two new songs, "I Lost It," and "Don't Happen Twice." While the former peaked at number three on the country charts, the latter went all the way to the top. The fact that he was able to put together a successful "best of" package after only five studio albums spoke volumes about his overall ability.

In 2002, he returned with the excellent *No Shoes, No Shirt, No Problems* album. It was his second offering to top the charts on the strength of four major singles: "Young," "The Good Stuff," "A Lot of Things Different," and "Big Star." He had become one of the top country artists on the circuit and didn't appear ready to relinquish the title.

His 2004 album, *When the Sun Goes Down*, won the Album of the Year at the Country Music Awards. The single "Anything but Mine" was a number one hit, while "I Go Back" and "The Woman with You" peaked at number two on the country charts. The charmer "Keg in the Closet" finished in the Top Ten. At this point, Chesney's success was measured on his consistent ability to record top hits and CDs.

In 2006, he was named CMA Entertainer of the Year on the strength of the two CDs he released: *Be As You Are (Song from an Old Blue Chair)* and *The Road and the Radio,* another winning collection. The singles "Summertime" and "Living in Fast Forward," pulled from the latter effort, both reached the number one spot. "Who You'd Be Today" and "You Save Me" peaked at number two and three respectively.

By 2007, he was an established entertainer and one of the top country male performers on the circuit. The sixth single from *The Road and the Radio,* "Beer in Mexico," became his third number one from the monster CD. Chesney also toured to enthusiastic crowds and critical reviews, often headlining over such acts as Sara Evans, Brooks & Dunn and others. He continues to record and tour.

Kenny Chesney is a late bloomer. Although it took him some time to achieve the success that he now enjoys, through perseverance and hard work the goal was attained. He always possessed the necessary tools to attain stardom, but it took a major effort to align everything together before it happened.

Chesney has one of the finest voices in contemporary country, but there is nothing really spectacular about it. His vocal delivery contains a husky tone, with a strong male timbre that has allowed him to excel in mainstream and honky tonk, as well as enjoy crossover success on the pop charts. The range enables him to sing any type of material.

In a short time, he has recorded an impressive body of work, and his catalog contains many interesting songs. For example, "Young" harkens back to vivid images of his childhood. On "She Thinks My Tractor's Sexy," Chesney gets down with simple country music and has fun with it. Other treasures in his catalog include "Fall in Love," "Me and You," "When I Close My Eyes," "She's Got It All," "That's Why I'm Here," "How Forever Feels," "You

Had Me from Hello," "What I Need to Do," "I Lost It," "Don't Happen Twice," "Young," "The Good Stuff," "A Lot of Things Different," "Big Star," "No Shoes, No Shirt, No Problems," "There Goes My Life," "I Go Back," "Anything but Mine," "Who You'd Be Today," "Living in Fast Forward," "Summertime," and "You Save Me."

He has remained in the public eye for more than just his music. In May 2005, he married actress Renee Zellweger in the Virgin Islands. She was the star of the movie *Jerry McGuire* and one of the top draws in Hollywood. Unfortunately, the marriage ended four months later, and Chesney was the subject of much magazine gossip.

Chesney is one of the new breed singers. His studio work sells well, and his singles consistently reach the top of the charts. His live performances are events as legions of his devoted fans can't seem to get enough of his down home, friendly style.

He has been rewarded for his achievements. In 1997, the ACM voted him New Male Vocalist of the Year. Five years later, they cited him as Top Male Vocalist of the Year. He would go on to win three Entertainer of the Year Awards, in 2004, 2006 and 2007. The CMT gave him three consecutive Male Video of the Year prizes from 2005 to 2007.

The Kenny Chesney story is that of a nice guy who had to work very hard to gain the success that he now enjoys. As one of the most popular and exciting country acts on the circuit, Chesney appears to have a very bright future. He achieved this stardom through hard work, perseverance and his average guy image.

DISCOGRAPHY:

In My Wildest Dreams, Capricorn 42023.
All I Need to Know, BNA 66562.
Me and You, BNA 66908.
I Will Stand, BNA 67498.
Everywhere We Go, BNA 67655.
No Shoes, No Shirt, No Problems, BNA 67038.
All I Want for Christmas Is a Real Good Tan, BNA 51808.
When the Sun Goes Down, BNA 56609.
Be As You Are (Songs from an Old Blue Chair), BNA 61530.
The Road and the Radio, BNA 72960.
Live: Live Those Songs Again, BNA 86578.
Just Who I Am: Poets & Pirates, RCA 711457.
Greatest Hits, BNA 67976.
The Best of Kenny Chesney, BNA 74321792492.
The Collection, Madacy 53446.

Terri Clark (1968–)

New Country Canadian

Canada has produced a number of first-rate country musicians. Wilf Carter and Hank Snow were mainstays during the early days of the genre. Anne Murray, known more as a popular singer than one with twang, enjoyed some crossover success. Later on, in the 1980s and 1990s, k.d. lang and Shania Twain continued the Canadian tradition. There was another noted singer from the Great White North who captured the attention of the industry with her New Country Canadian sound. Her name is Terri Clark.

Terri Clark was born on August 5, 1968, in Montreal, Quebec, but spent her childhood thousands of miles away in Medicine Hat, Alberta. Her grandparents, Ray and Betty Gauthier, were stars in Canada, and at different times they opened for George Jones and Little Jimmy Dickens, among others. The popular country music duo greatly influenced their granddaughter's future direction. Clark's mother was also an entertainer, mainly a folk singer, working the local coffeehouse circuit.

Clark taught herself how to play guitar at an early age and decided on a future path during a childhood that was filled with music. The records of Reba McEntire, the Judds and Linda Ronstadt had a special influence on her developing skills. In her teens, she performed at various venues and was only biding her time before she could relocate to Nashville.

In 1987, she moved to Music City, U.S.A. Like so many others before her, Terri was just another aspiring singer who arrived in the town unemployed with big dreams. However, Clark decided that she wouldn't be without a job for long and marched into Tootsie's Orchid Lounge to ask for an audition. Surprisingly, they allowed the plucky girl to play a set that impressed the manager into hiring her as the house singer.

The initial burst of achievement was followed by a long period of struggle and dues paying. For seven years she played the clubs and worked odd jobs to support herself. The long wait did give her time to accumulate first-rate material. Despite a frustrating search for a recording contract, she did find love in the big city when she married fiddler Ted Stevenson.

Finally, in 1994, she signed to a major label, Mercury Records. A year later, her self-titled debut album appeared and was a smash hit, yielding three Top Ten songs, "Better Things to Do," "When Boy Meets Girl," and "If I Were You." The album went gold, and Clark supported the CD with a tour, opening for mainstream star George Strait.

In 1996, *Just the Same* proved that she was no one-hit wonder but possessed some staying power. The CD outsold her first effort and went platinum on both sides of the northern border. "Poor, Poor Pitiful Me" and "Emotional Girl" did well in the U.S. reaching the Top Ten, but in Canada they went all the way to number one. The dual success gave her career more balance and power.

Two years later, she offered her third major studio work, *How I Feel*, featured her first U.S. number one single, "You're Easy on the Eyes," a feat duplicated in Canada. She was not only a solid recording artist in both nations, but also a strong concert draw as her career gained momentum.

Terri continued to add fuel to an accelerated career with her fourth album, *Fearless*, released in 2000. Although the CD gained a higher chart position in Canada than it did in the United States, the single "A Little Gasoline" peaked in the Top Twenty. Of course, in Canada, it was another smash hit. Clark had surpassed the success her grandparents had enjoyed as she carried on the family tradition.

By this point in her career, Clark was one of the main singers with a large fan base in both Canada and the United States. Few acts enjoyed a dual popularity on both sides of the border. She solidified this fame with a fifth studio album, *Pain to Kill*, which produced two Top Five singles, "I Wanna Do It All" and "I Just Wanna Be Mad," as well as the Top Forty hit "Three Mississippi."

Like most other artists, she released a greatest hits collection that included a new song, "Girls Lie Too," which raced to number one in the U.S. and surprisingly stalled at number two in Canada. A "best of" set is a good indication of a singer's level of stardom, and it seemed that Clark had achieved a very high status.

In 2005, *Life Goes On*, a CD of new material, faired poorly. Only one song, "She Didn't Have Time," reached the U.S. country charts. Clark also took the marriage plunge a second time that year, exchanging vows with tour manager Greg Kaczor. (She had divorced Ted Stevenson in 1991.) Later, when her contract with Mercury Records expired, Terri signed with BNA Records.

Clark's first album for her new label was *My Next Life*, which yielded the single "Dirty Girl." After a decade as a recording artist, she had accumulated a loyal following, and her concerts were sold out events in Canada as well as the United States. Terri is one of a handful of Canadian artists to break so wide open in the American market. She continues to record and perform.

Terri Clark is a country music powerhouse. From her first self-titled CD, which featured only self-penned material, she proved herself to be star. She has continued to deliver top songs and exciting concert performances. Her emotive style has captured the imagination and ears of a generation of fans.

Terri Clark has a voice that can cover a wide range of material, including hard honky tonk, ballads, rock and roll, and pop-flavored tunes. She sings like an angel with a voice that is as big as Canada. There is a reassuring element in the vocal delivery that is the basis of her sound.

She is a formidable songwriter with heart, insight and grit. Very few new country artists are allowed to write all of the songs on their debut CD, but Clark did just that. She has continued to dispense one gem after another on each subsequent release.

Terri has given the world a number of great songs. A partial list includes "Better Things to Do," "When Boy Meets Girl," "If I Were You," "Poor, Poor Pitiful Me," "Emotional Girl," "How I Feel," "You're Easy on the Eyes," "A Little Gasoline," "I Wanna Do It All," "I Just Wanna Be Mad," "Three Mississippi," "Girls Lie Too," "She Didn't Have Time," and "Dirty Girl." Her ability to deliver these tunes in the studio or live in concert with equal power is a tribute to her talent.

Her concerts display a multi-sided country personality. She is a glamor queen with plenty of high style and flash but is also a powerful singer with excellent taste. Clark's expansive voice can fill an arena, sweeping through the crowd like a musical missile that makes a direct hit. There is a tender side to Terri's stage persona as well as the gritty, sassy side.

Clark is a new breed country artist. Although she has often been compared to fellow Canadian Shania Twain, they took different paths on the road to success. Twain followed the country-pop route, while Clark remained embedded in the traditional honky tonk style. Each created music on her own terms and found success.

Clark is one of the top Canadians on the country music scene. Others include Shania Twain, Carolyn Dawn Johnson, Rita McNeil, the Rankins, Michelle Wright, George Canyon, the Wilkinsons, Prairie Oyster, Brad Johner, Jason McCoy, Paul Brandt, Emerson Drive, the Road Hammers, and Shane Yellowbird, among others.

Clark has also won many honors, including seven Canadian Country Music Fan's Choice Awards. She has also captured Album of the Year and single of the year for "Better Things to Do" in 1996. Terri was named Female Vocalist of the Year by the CCMA in 1997 and then back-to-back in 2004 and 2005. With her supreme talent there are many more prizes to be won in the future.

One of the biggest influences on Clark was 1970s pop diva Linda Ronstadt, who enjoyed crossover success. A talented individual, Ronstadt had an impeccable ability to pick the right material to sing and never tried anything she couldn't conquer. Reba McEntire also made an impact on Terri. There was always a dual attack from the most successful female country star in her ability to deliver hard country and tender ballads.

The Terri Clark story is that of a young prairie girl who paid heavy dues to become an international country song queen. She has proven herself to be an exceptional talent throughout her career and after a decade on the scene has never shown any signs of slowing down. The songbird with the huge voice, right looks, and fiery spirit is truly a winner with her Canadian New Country.

DISCOGRAPHY:

Terri Clark, Mercury Nashville 526991.
Just the Same, Mercury Nashville 532879.
How I Feel, Mercury Nashville 558211.
Fearless, Mercury Nashville 170157.
Autographed Jacket, N-Tunes Syndicate 0100080.
Life Goes On, Mercury Nashville 000257902.
Pain to Kill, Mercury Nashville 170325.
My Next Life, RCA 708072.
Greatest Hits 1994–2004, Mercury 000190602.
20th Century Masters — The Millennium Collection, Mercury 7009.

Jo Dee Messina (1970–)
Dared to Dream

Nashville is a city of hard knocks, a tough place for an aspiring singer to make it. But it is also a town of opportunity, the hub of country music, and the home where aspirations may come true. Many promising individuals have sung in the various establishments only to have their ambitions cruelly destroyed. However, one artist from the East Coast dared to dream and was determined to see her ambitions realized. Her name is Jo Dee Messina.

Jo Dee Messina was born August 25, 1970, in Framingham, Massachusetts, not exactly a center for country music. She began her singing career performing in musicals before her tenth birthday. Later, her attention turned to the polished styles of the Judds, Reba McEntire and Dolly Parton. In her teens, she gigged in local clubs often accompanied by a sister and brother.

At nineteen, she realized that the chances of ever reaching the stardom of one of her idols in the small, remote Massachusetts town were slim, so like hundreds of singers before her, Messina relocated to Nashville. She worked menial jobs to keep body and soul together and survived the cutthroat music industry by entering local talent competitions, where she held her own. Her big break came when she won a contest that led to the Nashville radio show *Live at Libby's*. Producer Byron Gallimore was impressed and helped her record a proper demo.

At the time, Gallimore was working with another young, unknown country singer named Tim McGraw. At one of McGraw's concerts, Messina met a label executive from Curb Records, who was astonished by her vocal style and excellent phrasing, and the company signed her to a recording contract. The dream that she had nurtured since a youngster now seemed within reach.

In 1996, her self-titled debut was released and gave her two Top Ten hits, "Heads Carolina, Tails California" and "You're Not in Kansas Anymore." Although it was a solid start, careers in Nashville are not built on one CD. She needed to prove that she was no flash in the pan and did so with her sophomore effort.

Two years later, *I'm Alright* was released and it proved to be everything an aspiring singer could want for his or her second CD to be and more; it demonstrated that she had staying power. The recording yielded three number one hits that reached the top of the charts on the same week: "Bye-Bye," "I'm Alright," and "Stand Beside Me." A fourth, "Lesson in Leavin'," peaked at number two. She was the only person in history to have three singles reach the top position during the same week. As a result, Messina won the CMA Horizon Award and ACM honored her as the Top New Female Artist in 1999; she was suddenly one of the hottest properties in country music.

She had displayed her ability to cover the songs of past great singers with her version of legend Dottie West's "Lesson in Leavin'," which turned out to be a major hit that stayed high on the charts for two months. It would become the third highest-ranked country song of the year behind Lonestar's "Amazed" and Kenny Chesney's "How Forever Feels." Messina toured with George Strait and finished the year off with another Top Ten hit, "Because You Love Me." Even before the next year had started she was chosen as the opening act for the Judds' Reunion tour, exposing her to a wider audience.

In 2000, *Burn*, her much anticipated third album, was released and boasted four top singles, including two number one hits, "That's the Way" and "Bring on the Rain," a duet with Tim McGraw, a blossoming star. There were two more hit songs, the title track and "Downtime." As well, "Dare to Dream" would make it to the Top Forty. It was her first album to sit at the top of the charts, and it featured more of a pop element than previous efforts.

It seemed that at the turn of the new millennium Messina was everywhere. She headlined her first tour with Rascal Flatts as the opening act. She appeared on the television shows *Nash Bridges* and *Touched by an Angel*. The single "Dare to Dream" was part of the soundtrack for the movie *Driven*. A Christmas album, *A Joyful Noise,* and a greatest hits package followed. The hits album debuted at number one on the country album chart. A single, "I Wish," peaked in the country Top Twenty.

On the surface it seemed that her career was flourishing, but the pressures of stardom were beginning to take their toll. Messina entered a dark stage when, like many other country artists before her, she battled the bottle. In an effort to regain control of her life, Jo Dee checked into a rehab program. An engagement to road manager Don Muzquiz was negated. A legion of fans waited to see if she was washed up.

But true to her fiery spirit, she rebounded in late 2004 with the single "My Give a Damn's Busted," which signaled a comeback when it went to number one and stayed at the top for two weeks. The song was released in advance of a fresh record of studio material.

In 2005, *Delicious Surprise* was released and three singles, "Not Going Down," "Delicious Surprise (I Believe It)," and "It's Too Late to Worry," all made the country Top Twenty. It was a solid effort and proved that Messina had put past troubles behind and was ready to resume her career.

The performance side of her career flourished with shows in support of the troops. The USO/Armed Forces Entertainment Tour took her to Naples, Venice and Vicenza in Italy. Later Jo Dee performed back in the U.S.A. with opening acts Tim Murphy and Tracy Byrd. The concerts were a welcome sight for fans who still believed that she possessed a special talent. Messina continues to record and perform.

Jo Dee Messina is a country music survivor. She struggled hard before landing her first recording contract and faced different obstacles during the rest of her career. But her fire, passion and talent enabled the talented singer to bounce back and pick up the threads of a once successful career.

Messina has a cheerful, confident voice. She has the ability to be passionate and bittersweet with the same note. There is also a laid-back/mellow side to her sometimes hard-edged delivery, allowing the singer to cover a wider range of material. Jo Dee is capable of pushing a song forward with vigor without sounding forced. There are many dimensions to her vocal delivery, but it all rings true country.

She has given the world a number of treasures. A partial list includes "Heads Carolina, Tails California," "You're Not in Kansas Anymore," "Bye-Bye," "I'm Alright," "Stand Beside Me," "Lesson in Leavin'," "Because You Love Me," "That's the Way," "Burn," "Downtime," "Bring on the Rain," "I Wish," "My Give a Damn's Busted," and "Dare to Dream." With a fine voice and an ability to chose quality material she will provide more gems in the future.

Messina is part of the new breed. She is slightly older than LeAnn Rimes, Ashley Monroe, Carrie Underwood, Catherine Britt, Erika Jo Herigen, Miranda Lambert, Lindsey Haun and Taylor Swift, but has enjoyed terrific success in this millennium, outshining many of her contemporaries.

Unlike many other modern female country singers, Patsy Cline was not Messina's major influence. Instead, the combination of Dolly Parton with her pop-flavored material, the Judds with their sass and smooth delivery, and

Reba McEntire with her determined spirit had a strong impact on Jo Dee's musical personality. She took key elements from all three and created her own winning sound.

Messina represents an interesting trend in contemporary country. At the birth of the industry, a majority of the singers were from the Appalachian region. Today, artists are from around the globe as well as all over the map of the United States. For instance, Anita Cochran and Larry Ballard hail from South Lyon and Bay City, Michigan, respectively; Dierks Bentley calls Phoenix, Arizona, home; Clint Black was born in Long Branch, New Jersey; Gary Allan is a native of Southern California; Jann Browne is an artist from Anderson, Indiana; and Lila McCann was born in Stelacoom, Washington. Although not the only country personality from Massachusetts, Messina is certainly the most famous.

The Jo Dee Messina story is that of a fiery country star who has proven herself in a very tough industry. Despite the obstacles in her way she has managed to continue building a strong career. Like every other singer to arrive in Nashville, she dared to dream; Messina made that dream come true.

DISCOGRAPHY:

Jo Dee Messina, Curb 77820.
I'm Alright, Curb 77904.
Burn, Curb 77977.
Delicious Surprise, Curb 78770.
A Joyful Noise, WEA 78755.
Greatest Hits, Curb 78790.
Live in Concert, Big Band Concert 77402.

Alison Krauss (1971–)

Bluegrass Propagator

In the 1940s, Bill Monroe, the Father of Bluegrass, assembled all of the various elements of the bluegrass sound — the fast paced tempos, intricate rhythms and innovative effects — to form one cohesive style. Today this unique branch of country music continues in two different forms: traditional and progressive. Of the hundreds of acts who have dedicated their careers to keeping the flame burning, the bluegrass propagator stands out in the modern era. Her name is Alison Krauss.

Alison Krauss was born on July 23, 1971, in Champaign, Illinois. At the age of five, she started taking classical violin lessons but soon abandoned the music of the great composers for bluegrass. She honed her skills quickly and before her teens won the state fiddling championship prompting the Preservation of Bluegrass in America Society to name her the Most Promising Fiddler in the Midwest. By fourteen, she had been performing for six years and joined a local outfit called Union Station.

She assumed leadership of the group sometime after joining and proved her mettle at the Newport Folk Festival, where Krauss delivered a dynamic set that resulted in a recording contract. In 1985, Alison made her recording debut on the album *Different Strokes* with her brother Viktor, Jim Hoiles, and Bruce Weiss. The CD was released on the independent Fiddle Tunes label. Although a positive experience, the fiddle champ yearned to record material of her own choosing and received that opportunity when she signed a contract with Rounder Records.

Her first solo album, *Too Late to Cry*, featured the efforts of her backing band, Union Station, which consisted of guitarists Jeff White, banjoist Alison Brown and bassist Viktor Krauss. The group would undergo several changes throughout the years, and eventually legends Jerry Douglas on Dobro, Sam Bush on mandolin and Tony Trischka on banjo joined the ranks. Although her initial effort received solid reviews, it was evident that the budding star needed time to mature before she could truly make an assault on country music.

With each successive album, she displayed a maturity, developing as an artist and creating stronger efforts. In 1989, Krauss and Union Station released the album *Two Highways,* which was nominated for a Grammy. Although the album didn't win the prestigious award, it proved that she was on the threshold of the greatness that had been predicted of her when at twelve Alison claimed the title of state fiddling champion.

In 1990, *I've Got That Old Feeling* was released and won the Grammy for Best Bluegrass Recording. More importantly, it was this album that laid the groundwork for all bluegrass acts of the 1980s and 1990s; Krauss and Union Station had set the bar. Although recognized among her many peers and throughout the country music community, true mainstream stardom continued to elude her.

Union Station solidified its lineup in the early 1990s around mandolinist Adam Steffey, banjoist-guitarist Ron Block, bassist Barry Bales, and guitarist Tim Stafford; Stafford later left the group and was replaced by Dan Tyminski. It was this latter version of the band that recorded her next album, *Every Time You Say Goodbye*, which featured Shawn Colvin's "I Don't Know Why." The CD graced the country charts thanks in large part to the videos that were shown regularly on Country Music Television.

In 1994, *I Know Who Holds Tomorrow* was released. It was a solid album effort that brought her closer to the recognition that she deserved. For seven years, Krauss had championed bluegrass along with Union Station. After a long period of paying dues, she was finally ready to receive the credit she was due.

In 1995, *Now That I've Found You: A Collection* was released and made Krauss a star. It raced all the way to number two on the country music charts and placed at the Top Ten of the pop charts. It sold a million copies and brought her the mainstream popularity that had eluded her for so long. From this point on, she became the prime exponent of the bluegrass tradition and sparked a renewed interest in the style that hadn't been seen in many years.

In 1997, she won another Grammy for *So Long So Wrong*. It contained the songs "So Long, So Wrong," "No Place to Hide," "Looking in the Eyes of Love," and "Blue Trail of Sorrow." Bluegrass had enjoyed a renaissance, and many pointed to Krauss as the most important single factor in this new rise in popularity. The combination of solid recordings, outstanding live performances and the proper media exposure catapulted her to the forefront.

In 1999, *Forget About It* appeared. Another solid effort, it demonstrated her insight into bluegrass and ability to deliver the music in a fresh way so that it would appeal to a contemporary audience. By this point in her career, she was forever linked with the country music sub-genre, but in order to achieve a higher plateau Krauss needed to break out of the mundane cycle of recording and touring her own work.

Krauss climbed that mountain in 2000 when she and Union Station participated in a new project. They joined John Hartford, Ralph Stanley and others on the multimillion selling soundtrack of the film *O Brother, Where Art Thou?* A later tour enhanced her reputation. Always a champion of bluegrass, she was now acknowledged as the true queen of the style throughout the entire musical community.

In 2001, *New Favorite* appeared, and the album soared to the top of the charts, reaching gold status in four months. Some of the highlights included "The Lucky One," "I'm Gone," "Boy Who Wouldn't Hoe Corn," "New Favorite," and "Daylight." Later, the album *Live* captured the group dynamics of one of their concert performances. The CD raced to number one on the U.S. bluegrass charts and eventually went platinum. Krauss now possessed an incredible amount of momentum in her favor.

In 2004, *Lonely Runs Both Ways* was released, and the album quickly raced up the country chart on the strength of two number one singles, "Restless" and "If I Didn't Know Any Better." It would eventually settle in the top position on the bluegrass charts and go double platinum. At this point she alternated between solo and band projects.

In 2007, she released *A Hundred Miles or More: A Collection,* which topped the U.S. bluegrass charts and peaked at number two on the country charts. The album wasn't so much a greatest hits package as a compilation of collaborations, soundtrack appearances and non-band endeavors. It included "Whiskey Lullaby" with Brad Paisley, "How's the World Treating You" with James Taylor, "Molly Ban" with the Chieftains, and other tracks. There were five new songs: "You're Just a Country Boy," "Simple Love," "Jacob's Dream," "Away Down the River," and "Sawing on the Strings." She continues to record and perform.

Alison Krauss is a modern bluegrass jewel. She has continued with pride and distinction the tradition that Bill Monroe established. She has skillfully carried the bluegrass flag, acting as the main exponent of the style for more than twenty years. There are many sides to her illustrious career.

Krauss is a superior musician, something that has been evident for many years. As a child prodigy she amazed anyone that was fortunate enough to witness her incredible talent. Over the years she has never stopped progressing on the fiddle, and her current sound is that of a diverse, mature and incredible player. The fiddle player developed into a first-rate all-around performer and carved out a legendary niche for herself in country music circles.

Krauss has a soprano voice that is truly angelic. Her vocal range is suited to the material that she often sings, which is about lost love. Although noted for her bluegrass and country style, she has also dabbled in rock, pop and adult contemporary, with a strong enough voice to pull it off. Her vocal talents only strengthen and complement her instrumental skills.

Her style is a combination of influences that have allowed her to meld the traditional with the new, thus solidifying her role as one of the major ambassadors of the genre. Alison's major influence was Bill Monroe, but there have been others, including Lester Flatt & Earl Scruggs, as well as the Stanley Brothers. There is a distinct quality to her playing that has enabled Krauss to claim a unique voice in bluegrass and country music.

She is a solid bandleader and has been the focus of Union Station, one of the prime modern bluegrass outfits on the scene, for a very long time. Her ability to assemble a top-notch outfit and to keep it together speaks volume of her strong leadership qualities. Krauss has displayed these attributes in every project she participated in, including session work with Vince Gill, Michael McDonald, Dolly Parton, Phish and Kenny Rogers.

Union Station has played a large part in her rise from child prodigy to queen of bluegrass. The current lineup includes Dan Tyminski, an acoustic guitarist as well as lead and harmony vocalist. A talented performer, he has been a mainstay on the bluegrass front for years and came into his own on the soundtrack for *O Brother, Where Art Thou?* His recordings on that project won him many awards, including a Grammy. Jerry Douglas, the Dobro player, boasts nine Grammy Awards, a National Heritage Award and a *Life* Magazine article that recognized him as one of the ten best country musicians of all time. Ron Block, the banjoist and guitarist in the group, is also a main songwriter of religious and devotional material, giving the band an extra dimension. Aside from his contributions to Union Station, he has done studio work for Susan Ashton, the Cox Family, Clint Black, Dolly Parton and Vince Gill, among others. Barry Bales, the bassist, also provides harmony vocals. The talented musician has worked with Reba McEntire, Susan Ashton, Merle Haggard, Ronnie Bowman, the Cox Family, Vince Gill, Dolly Parton and many others.

Krauss has worked with a number of other artists outside Union Station. The wide range includes Willie Nelson, Dolly Parton, Robert Plant, and the rock group Phish, among others. She recorded a duet, "You Will Be My Ain True Love," with Sting for the soundtrack of the film *Cold Mountain*. In 2003, Alison won a Grammy with James Taylor for the song "How's the World Treating You." She has also produced CDs by Nickel Creek, the Cox Family, Reba McEntire, and Alan Jackson.

During her career, Krauss has earned numerous Grammy Awards; in fact, she has won more than any other female artist in history. She has also captured multiple Country Music Association Awards and International Bluegrass Music Association Awards. Her session credits include instrumental and vocals on a variety of albums featuring myriad styles.

The Alison Krauss story is one of triumph, talent, determination and perseverance. The bluegrass propagator has carried on a tribute to Bill Monroe with true class.

DISCOGRAPHY:

Too Late To Cry, Rounder 0235.
Two Highways, Rounder 0265.
I've Got That Old Feeling, Rounder 0275.
Every Time You Say Goodbye, Rounder 0285.
I Know Who Holds Tomorrow, Rounder 610307.
So Long So Wrong, Rounder 0365.
Forget About It, Rounder 0465.
New Favorite, Rounder 0495.
Live, Rounder 610515.
Lonely Runs Both Ways, Rounder 610525.
Now That I've Found You: A Collection, Rounder 0325.
Home on the Highways: Band Picked Favorites, Rounder/Cracker Barrel 13.
A Hundred Miles or More: A Collection, Rounder 11610555.
Raising Sand (with Robert Plant), Rounder 619075.

LeAnn Rimes (1982–)

Teenage Sensation

There are essentially two types of country music artists. The first is the one-hit wonder, a drifter who scores great success with a song only to just as quickly disappear from the public eye. The second is an anonymous singer who enjoys success with their first hit single but demonstrates staying power as they forge a long career. The teenage sensation who stunned the country music world with her monster hit falls into the latter category and remains a dominant force in the music today. Her name is LeAnn Rimes.

LeAnn Rimes was born on August 28, 1982, in Jackson, Mississippi, but was raised in Garland, Texas. She began to sing as a young child and performed at local talent contests. At eleven, she released her first album, *Nor Va Jak*, recorded on an independent label. The record did nothing to advance her career, but she was not to be deterred.

She caught her first big break when Bill Mack, a Dallas disc jockey and record promoter who liked what he heard, took the promising star under his tutelage. He had a plan that included the waxing of the single "Blue," a song he had written for the immortal Patsy Cline, but which she never cut because of her untimely death. Rimes, like many other aspiring female country singers, was a huge fan of the divine Miss Cline.

In 1995, buoyed by the fact that Mack was in her corner, Rimes performed over one hundred concerts and even appeared on television. The young singer landed a record contract with Curb Records and recorded the single "Blue," which was a stone classic. It received considerable radio airplay on country as well as pop stations, catapulting her to stardom. The ensuing CD debuted at number three on the pop charts and earned nominations for the Country Music Association Horizon Award and Best Female Vocalist Award. Other album highlights included "The Light in Your Eyes," "Cattle Call," "Fade to Blue," and "Talk to Me," which earned LeAnn songwriting credits.

Her sophomore album release, *You Light Up My Life: Inspirational Songs,* was not the logical extension of *Blue.* It contained more pop material than country but remained a solid effort because of Rimes's natural ability. The CD showed that she was capable of handling more than just mainstream material.

In 1997, she released *Sittin' on Top of the World* which was, once again, more of an adult contemporary album than a pure country record. While fans waited for a genuine follow-up to her initial album, they received a collection of songs that included Prince's "Purple Rain." Although established as a successful performer, she needed to find more suitable material if she was to continue a solid country recording career.

Rimes's next offering was a self-titled record and an obvious attempt to return back to country's roots and the style of her main influence, Patsy Cline. There were five cover tunes, including "Crazy," which the young singer performed in perfect imitation of her idol. It was more of a countrified effort than her previous releases, with the only truly exciting track being "Big Deal."

In 2001, *I Need You* was a pure pop album and seemed far removed from her countrified debut effort. However, Rimes remained a solid concert attraction, delivering a catalog of songs with the conviction of someone much older than nineteen. On stage, LeAnn sang her country material like a performer of that vein and not like a pop diva. However, the move to adult contemporary had gained the singer a new audience at the cost of the initial fan base.

God Bless America was an album of classic songs, including the title song, "The Lord's Prayer," "Amazing Grace," and a version of the national anthem. Although it was a wholeheartedly patriotic effort the singer who performed on this CD and the one who had stunned the country music world with her debut record seemed like two totally different performers.

The follow-up album, *Twisted Angel*, was even more of a pop effort than anything else that she had released up to this time. It seemed that Rimes had shed her country crooner image, which was unfortunate for fans and the genre. Although she was a gifted singer who was very capable of having crossover appeal, one can only wonder how much more successful her career would have been if she had remained in the traditional vein.

She tested this hypothesis with the release of *This Woman*. Although not a pure, traditional album, it did contain a balance between adult contemporary and contemporary country. It returned her a portion of the fan base that she had lost in the past few years. Highlights included "Some People," "I Dare You," and "Something's Gotta Give."

In 2006, *Whatever We Wanna* was another pop-oriented album. Some of the highlights included "And It Feels Like," "A Little More Time," "Everybody's Someone," and "This Is Life." She co-wrote six of the fifteen tracks on the work, which was only released in Europe. Because of her previous release, the somewhat countrified *This Woman*, had done well in the marketplace, Rimes decided to continue along this path.

Her next CD, *Family*, featured Rimes the songwriter more than ever before as she had a hand in penning every tune. While there was still some pop gloss, songs such as "Good Friend and a Glass of Wine," "Nothing Wrong," and "One Day Too Long" displayed her country side. She continues to record and perform.

LeAnn Rimes seems like a lost country music star. Like k.d. lang, Lyle

Lovett and others, she has drifted from her roots after such a promising debut. Recent recording have straddled the line between dance-pop, adult contemporary and mainstream country. Despite her seeming lack of interest in recording country material, her great voice remains intact.

Like Brenda Lee and Tanya Tucker, Rimes possessed an adult voice while still in her early teens. The sheer range and power of LeAnn's vocal delivery earned her immediate attention and accolades. However, like the aforementioned artists, once the talented singer grew up, the excitement at the novelty of someone so young with a mature, throaty voice had evaporated.

Rimes has won numerous awards. In 1996, she won a Grammy for Best New Artist and Best Female Country Vocal Performance, as well as the ACM Top New Female Vocalist, Song of the Year and Single of the Year Awards. In 1997, she was named the TNN/Music City News Female Star of Tomorrow and captured the CMA Horizon Award and the American Music Awards Favorite New Artist.

Rimes is one of the new breed artists and is one of the finest vocalists of a generation. Sadly, on many of her CD releases, she relied on her voice to carry the work instead of suitable material. While capable of being a leading light in the new contemporary country movement, LeAnn has chosen a different path. The eclectic nature of her work has split up her fan base and weakened her record sales.

Rimes is one of the most talented singers on the current country-pop circuit; however, she shares the limelight with a number of other performers. Megan Mullins, Erika Jo, the Wreckers, Ashley Gearing, the Lynns, Sherrié Austin, Lila McCann, Mindy McCready, the Moffatts, Wynonna Judd, Kathie Baillie, Faith Hill, Shania Twain and Trisha Yearwood are similar artists.

Like so many other contemporary country artists, LeAnn has been greatly influenced by Patsy Cline. With an uncanny ability to sound like Cline and successful covers of a handful of Cline's songs, the young star has paid a deep homage to her favorite singer. However, Rimes has managed to carve a distinct career instead of remaining in her idol's shadow.

In turn, Rimes has had an influence on a small but dedicated stable of singers, most notably Paula DeAnda and Ilse DeLarge. DeAnda is a Texas-born rhythm & blues vocalist whose major idol growing up was Selena. The young singer cut the singles "What Would It Take" and "Doing Too Much," which cracked the country Top Forty. Ilse DeLarge is a country-pop singer from Holland who enjoyed a strong debut with *World of Hurt*. Her second album release, *Livin' on Love*, was more rock than country. She also cut a version of "Blue," which was a major hit in her native country.

Rimes's career has taken on many different dimensions. She sang the theme song "Light the Fire Within" for the opening ceremony at the 2002

Winter Olympics in Salt Lake City. In 2006, LeAnn became the new host of the U.S.A. Network reality television series *Nashville Star,* a post she held for one season. That same year she sang the theme song "Twinkle in Her Eye" for the cartoon *Holly Hobbie.* Perhaps her most important performance was during a three-hour special on *Larry King Live,* a benefit for the victims of Hurricane Katrina. She also sang "Remember When" for Disneyland's fiftieth anniversary celebration.

The LeAnn Rimes story is one of a very talented artist who possesses the ability to sing in any style and be successful. Although the pop tunes have been a good direction for her career, country music fans yearn for the days when she promised to be a major force in the genre. They hope that the once teenage sensation will take her rightful place as the queen of contemporary country music.

DISCOGRAPHY:

Blue, Curb 77821.
You Light Up My Life: Inspirational Songs, Curb 77885.
Sittin' on Top of the World, Curb 77901.
LeAnn Rimes, Curb 77947.
I Need You, Curb 77979.
God Bless America, Curb 78726.
Twisted Angel, Curb 78747.
What a Wonderful World, Curb 78779.
This Woman, Curb 78859.
Whatever We Want, WEA International 8229.
Unchained Melody, Curb 77856.
Greatest Hits [Japan], Sony/Columbia 53141.
Greatest Hits, Curb 78829.
Greatest Hits [Bonu DVD], Curb 78829.
The Best of LeAnn Rimes, Curb/London 71481.
The Best of LeAnn Rimes, WEA International 79493.
The Best of LeAnn Rimes: Remixed, WEA International 74092.

Carrie Underwood (1983–)

Country Idol

Country music, more than any other style, has produced a great number of teenage sensations. In the 1950s and 1960s, Brenda Lee stunned audiences with her powerful voice. In the 1970s, Tanya Tucker was barely a teen when she hit the top of the charts, sounding like a singer twice her age. In the 1990s, a very young LeAnn Rimes excited the entire industry with "Blue," her breakthrough smash single. In the first decade of the 2000s, there was another name to add to this prestigious list, the young woman known as the Country Idol. Her name is Carrie Underwood.

Carrie Underwood was born March 10, 1983, in Checotah, Oklahoma. She began her musical career at the tender age of three singing in the local church. Her progress was rapid as the talented vocalist displayed her talent at functions for the Lion's Club, as well as Old Settlers Day. Underwood graduated to festivals in her native state and nearby ones where she performed in front of sizeable crowds. It was in this variety of venues where she developed her singing style and instrumental abilities on the guitar and piano.

Throughout her teens Carrie continued to hone those skills and aspired to a musical career. She paid close attention to the meteoric rise of Shania Twain, Faith Hill, Trisha Yearwood and Martina McBride. Carrie dreamed of the day when she would share the stage with those acts, but it seemed like it was too far away.

After high school graduation she majored in mass communication at Northeastern State College, intending to become a journalist but never losing the passion to sing. In 2005, Underwood auditioned for television's *American Idol* and moved up through the ranks — from the initial group, to the twelve finalists, and finally winning the competition. Her victory brought the young singer instant recognition and provided her with a strong fan base because many viewers had sweated it out week after week pulling for the Oklahoma native to win.

Underwood recorded her debut single, "Inside Your Heaven," which was released in the summer of 2005. As victor of *American Idol*, she found new doors were opened for her, including the American Idols Live! tour as well as endorsement deals for Hershey's and Skechers. It was also during this period that she began to record her first album.

Some Hearts was a smash hit and eventually went triple platinum. The monster single, "Jesus, Take the Wheel," won Single of the Year at the Academy of Country Music Awards, and she was also named Top Female Vocalist. She would go on to win a Dove Award from the Gospel Music Association and, later on, Best Female Video at the CMT Awards. The second single from the album, "Don't Forget to Remember Me," peaked at number two on the *Billboard* Hot Country Chart, eventually reaching number one for a week on the *Radio & Records* Country Singles Chart.

A top album, plus two hit singles, only enhanced her blossoming reputation, which was accelerated with an appearance on the 2006 *American Idol* finale. By this time a recognized name in North America, she toured to support the *Some Hearts* CD, expanding on her popularity. Underwood performed the scheduled dates to enthusiastic reviews as the fans of previous contests came out to cheer her on.

She also performed in South Africa as part of the Idol Gives Back Benefit episode during which she sang a cover of the Pretenders' "I'll Stand by You." The fourth single from her debut CD, "Wasted," hit the charts and reached the number one position. It was rare that a debut effort would garner so much staying power on the charts.

In 2007, she scooped up three CMT Awards for Video of the Year, Female Video of the Year, and Video Director of the Year for "Before He Cheats." Later that same year she would capture three more prizes at the ACM Awards for Album of the Year and Top Female Vocalist. Underwood was by now a true celebrity.

Her album, *Some Hearts*, would go on to sextuple-platinum sales; she was the first young female star to achieve such a lofty plateau since LeAnn Rimes's breakthrough a decade before. Fans hoped that Underwood would continue to record in the country music vein and not head off some other direction as the gifted Rimes had done.

Her non-musical activities also gained her recognition: Underwood became a spokesperson of the People for the Ethical Treatment of Animals and did public service announcements for the Humane Society. She would later be named Victoria's Secret's Sexiest Female Musician and voted as one of *People* magazine's Most Beautiful People.

Underwood is a young singer with tremendous talent and a very promising future ahead of her. She has already gathered more awards than some artists earn in a lifetime of music and is definitely one of the brightest stars of the new country group. She continues to record and perform.

Carrie Underwood is a country music jewel. Her vocal and musical talents have been polished with appearances on the *American Idol* series as well as in concert performances to support her breakthrough album. Despite these improvements there remains much untapped potential in the fast-rising female star.

Underwood's voice has unlimited power. She can soar high above the refrain of a song and take it to uncharted territory. Her delivery is a mixture of contemporary country comfort and pop commercialism that enables the young singer to give each song a special treatment. As she matures, the vocal prowess will grow without sacrificing any of its charm or beauty.

With only one album to her credit, her catalog is thin but excellent. Every tune from the debut album, *Some Hearts*, was a possible chart-topper. It ranges from the title song to interesting tunes like "Starts with Goodbye," "The Night Before (Life Goes On)," "Lessons Learned," "We're Young and Beautiful," and "I Ain't in Checotah Anymore," a tribute to her small hometown.

Although there is a pantheon of country female stars to influence the younger artists, it is Martina McBride, one of the younger stars, who has been cited to have the strongest impact on Underwood. Carrie even covered one of her idol's songs, "Independence Day," which appeared on the B-Side of the number one single "Inside Your Heaven."

Carrie Underwood is one of the new breed country artists. Along with Sara Evans, Miranda Lambert, Taylor Swift, Jamie O'Neal, Catherine Britt, Danielle Peck, Lindsey Haun, Ashley Monroe, Meredith Edwards, Jo Dee Messina, Kathy Mattea, and Terri Clark, she represents the future of the genre. Each of the above singers is a unique individual, and a few of them, including Messina and Clark, have been around longer than the rest of the pack.

Underwood is a country-pop singer who has attempted to follow in the footsteps of Tammy Wynette, Barbara Mandrell, Crystal Gayle, Tanya Tucker, and especially Martina McBride. She now has McBride, Shania Twain, Faith Hill, Trisha Yearwood and the rest of the crop of young singers as competition. With her abundant musical gifts, Underwood has the potential to be as successful as any of her role models and even more so.

The Carrie Underwood story is that of a girl who received one break and made the most of it. She has a promising future, based on the release of her first album which was a huge hit. She has quickly become the country idol to her large fan base and to Nashville industry types.

DISCOGRAPHY:

Some Hearts, Arista 71197.

Miranda Lambert (1983–)

Texas Nightingale

In 1972, a young Texas singer took the industry by storm with her powerful voice. Tanya Tucker was a phenomenon who enjoyed incredible success at a very tender age. Thirty years later there was another prodigy from the Lone Star State who wowed audiences as the Texas Nightingale. Her name is Miranda Lambert.

Miranda Lambert was born on November 10, 1983, in Longview, Texas, into a musical family of sorts. Although Miranda's parents ran a private investigation office, her father was an amateur guitarist and songwriter. There was all kinds of music around, and the Lamberts encouraged a love for it.

There is in every singer or musician's life a turning point, a moment of enlightenment where a start in music begins to develop. For many it is the discovery of some past figure like a Jimmie Rodgers, Hank Williams, Sr., Bob Wills, Bill Monroe, Patsy Cline, Johnny Cash, Merle Haggard, Dolly Parton, Loretta Lynn or George Strait. For Lambert, it was a Garth Brooks concert that she attended while a little girl that ignited the spark in her to pursue a country music career.

She started to sing, learn guitar and write her own songs with her father acting as a tutor. At sixteen, she appeared on the *Johnny High Country Music Review* in Arlington, the very same show that helped launch the career of LeAnn Rimes. Lambert continued to enter talent contests, which led to minor success, including a local television commercial and a small part in the teen movie *Slap Her She's French*. She formed the Texas Pride Band and began to perform live around the Dallas area.

She snubbed her initial chance to record in Nashville because, like the members of the alternative country and Outlaw movements, Miranda wanted to sing country on her own terms, not someone else's. Instead she released a self-titled, independent CD, which featured two songs — "Texas Pride," and "Somebody Else"— to enter the Texas charts. Lambert continued to appear live at various venues, including the Rea Palm Isle Ballroom in Longview, Texas, where Elvis Presley and Willie Nelson had once performed.

Lambert entered many contests, including the Texas auditions for Nashville Star where she placed third. Her attempt to portray Tammy Wynette in a musical play was unsuccessful as the young singer finished second in the competition. Despite these setbacks, Sony Music signed her to a contract, and two years later *Kerosene* was released.

Kerosene debuted at number one on the country charts putting Lambert in a select group of artists to have achieved that important distinction. Another significant note was the fact that Miranda wrote or co-wrote eleven of the twelve tracks, which showed a definite maturity and talent. Rarely are young singers allowed to record their own material to the extent that she did. The CD was a hit with both fans and critics who hailed the youngster as one of the bright lights in country music.

In order to promote *Kerosene,* she toured as the opening act for Keith Urban and George Strait. With each new show she gained a few more interested fans, but she really broke it all open with her performance at the 2005 Country Music Association Awards in the Big Apple. Her performance on the show was an electrifying display of controlled emotion and helped pushed the explosive "Kerosene" into the country Top Twenty. A second single, "New Strings," would also hit the charts.

It was with confidence that she entered the studio to record her sophomore album, *Crazy Ex-Girlfriend,* where, once again, Lambert was responsible for writing a large portion of the material, including eight of the eleven songs. The tune "Crazy Ex-Girlfriend" was the unintentional first single, and she performed the song at the CMA Awards; however, "Famous in a Small Town" became the official debut single.

The album was more than just a collection of songs strung together to fill a CD. The theme of a spurned woman looking for revenge and to mend her broken heart ran throughout the entire work and illustrated a sophisticated writing talent. The motif was found in "Crazy Ex-Girlfriend," "Gunpowder and Lead," "Guilty in Here," and "Down." It was a stunning release of pure passion that established her as more than just a one-hit wonder.

While the recording side of her career soared, Lambert's performance opportunities also increased. In 2005 and 2006, she joined Toby Keith's Hookin' Up & Hangin' Out tour to help promote the album. In 2007, Miranda performed with Dierks Bentley on his Live and Loud Tour, which also included Eric Church and Jason Aldean. The young singer has proven that not only is she a strong recording artist, but also a good live attraction. She continues to record and perform. In a very short time she has made a very strong impression with her fine voice, intelligent material and enchanting concert presence.

Lambert possesses a contemporary country music voice. Although rooted in the genre, it also contains dimensions that allows her to inject pop and soft rock elements into her songs. There is a sweetness in her vocal delivery that also contains a polished edge. Her songwriting ability separates her from many other female artists on the scene who rely on outside material.

Lambert is one of a strong group of young female country-pop artists that includes Ashley Monroe, Megan Mullins, LeAnn Rimes, Rebecca Lynn Howard, Catherine Britt, Sara Evans, Carrie Underwood, Taylor Swift, Lindsey Haun, Danielle Peck, Julie Roberts, and Mindy McCready. Each aforementioned singer possesses distinct abilities. What separates Miranda from the rest of the group is her songwriting skill.

Lambert has a strong backup band that consists of Aden Bubeck on bass guitar; Chris Kline on keyboards, jaw harp, and harmonica; Alex Weeden on lead guitar; Scott Wray on rhythm, lap steel guitar, and Dobro; and Keith Zebowski on drums. Miranda is a solid guitarist herself and is able to blend her individual sound with that of her group.

It is understandable that with the success of her first two albums she would gain attention. In 2005, she was nominated for the CMA Horizon Award. In 2007, she won the ACM's award for Best New Female Artist and was nominated for ACM Female Vocalist of the Year. With her special talent and work ethic, Lambert will surely win her fair share of prizes in the future.

Perhaps the single biggest influence on Lambert was Garth Brooks. It was after one of his performances that she focused her energies toward a recording career. However, there are others who made an impact on her. Emmylou Harris and Shania Twain, with their ability to write their own catchy tunes, were important in Miranda's development as an artist.

Although her catalog is slim, it is also excellent. A partial list of her songs includes "Texas Pride," "Somebody Else," "Kerosene," "New Strings," "Crazy Ex-Girlfriend," "Gunpowder and Lead," "Guilty in Here," and "Down." The fact that she has written the majority of her hits is remarkable and is a solid reason why she has already been very successful.

The Miranda Lambert story is that of an ambitious singer with an abundance of talent who made the most of her one big break to forge a winning career. With the release of her first two CDs it appears she has the staying power of a true star. The future appears very bright for the Texas Nightingale.

DISCOGRAPHY:

Kerosene, Epic 92026.
Crazy Ex-Girlfriend, Columbia 78932.

Catherine Britt (1984–)

Aussie Style

The wealth, breadth and depth of country music performers of the past eighty years has sparked interest throughout North America and around the world. Country music's influence has ignited a totally different sound from other parts of the globe, including the continent of Australia. In recent years, one of the most talented female singers emerged from the Land Down Under with a distinctive Aussie style. Her name is Catherine Britt.

Catherine Britt was born on December 31, 1984, in Newcastle, New South Wales, Australia. She developed a love for country music at an early age after watching the movie *Coal Miner's Daughter,* the Loretta Lynn story. Later Britt discovered Jimmie Rodgers, Dolly Parton and Hank Williams, Sr. By her preteens, the young singer was a scholar of the original American style, boasting an extensive knowledge of the legends of the genre. She was finally able to show off all of her country education at a Bill Chambers concert.

Bill Chambers, an Australian singer on tour with his band Dead Ringer, was floored when the pretty, waif-like Britt asked him if he could sing "T.B. Blues" from the catalog of the Father of Country Music, Jimmie Rodgers. In Australia, most people had never heard of the song, much less the famous yodeller. Her boldness earned Catherine a chance to sing during Chambers's performance.

Britt demonstrated her unique talent as she won many hearts that fateful night. Chambers, a man with an eye and ear for talent, became the young singer's mentor. He took her on tour with him around Australia where the young vocalist gained invaluable experience. He produced the EP *In the Pines*, her debut recording, released in 1999, which yielded the single "That Don't Bother Me," a song co-written with Kasey Chambers, Bill's young daughter.

The song raced up the charts and made the Top Ten in her native homeland. Although she hoped for a record deal, none were forthcoming, so she continued to pay dues, touring the Australian countryside and singing at various venues. The teenage sensation had also begun to write songs drawing upon the experiences of her young life.

In 2001, *Dusty Smiles and Heartbreak Cures* was issued privately. It featured a half-dozen originals, as well as covers of her favorite singer Hank Williams, Sr., and Merle Haggard. A year later, ABC Records picked it up and re-released it. It cycled heavily on Australian radio proving there was an audience for Britt in her native country. Interestingly, among the spectators passing through on tour was Elton John. A forty-year veteran of the music business, John was impressed after hearing the phenomenal singer and arranged for a meeting.

The meeting was another turning point in her career. Together with Sir Elton, she recorded "Where We Both Say Goodbye," which brought Britt some major international attention. It is not every unknown singer from Australia who can boast recording a song with one of the most famous names in music. Later, upon John's invitation, she performed at the end of his tour in Sydney. All of this activity foreshadowed the success that she was about to experience.

She was now one step away from an American recording contract, and with John praising her vast talents on television and, more importantly, to record executives in Nashville, it happened quickly. In 2004, Britt signed to RCA Records and sang on the Grand Ole Opry. It had taken many trips back and forth from Australia to Music City, U.S.A., but the dues-paying months had paid off handsomely.

A full-length album followed, *Too Far Gone*, when the young phenom was only nineteen. It featured the services of Elton John, Kenny Chesney and Don Helms, the steel guitarist who had played with the immortal Hank Williams, Sr., giving Britt a connection to the past. "The Upside of Being Down" was the first release and made the U.S. Top Forty. In her native Australia, the album was a smash hit, boasting six Top Five Songs.

A second single, "Where We Both Say Goodbye," the duet with Elton John, was released and cracked the U.S. Top Forty. She moved to Nashville and started to appear on the Grand Ole Opry on a regular basis. Although Britt had a solid following in her native Australia, like so many other aspiring country artists she yearned to be at the center of the action in Nashville.

Her CD *Too Far Gone* continued to yield gold nuggets, including three more solid singles, "Swinging Door," "Too Far Gone," and "What I Did Last Night." The latter song reached the Top Forty, but once again she was unable to crack the Top Twenty. However, she was still a big star in Australia, and the double localities of her career fueled one another.

In 2007, another turning point in her career occurred when she joined a tour in support of superstars Brooks & Dunn and Alan Jackson. Although opening for two such heavy acts was intimidating, the fiery Australian singer gave it her best, earning positive reviews. She continues to record and perform.

In a very short time Catherine Britt has shot across the musical horizon like an extremely bright candle with a burning intensity. Her voice, good looks, choice of material, and demeanor on stage are all part of the package. Although not a possessor of an authentic Nashville birth certificate, Britt sounds as if she has always belonged there.

Her voice is like a musical instrument. It has the range of a cold country mile and the charm of a picture-perfect house with a white picket fence. Her natural phrasing makes her sound like a veteran singer, someone who has been belting out hits for decades instead of a young performer. Although she spent most of her early years in Australia, Britt has not a trace of an accent in her vocal delivery.

Although her catalog is slim, she has already recorded a few gems. The song "Swinging Door" is a rollicking number with a fast rockabilly beat and a plaintive violin. "What You Did Last Night," is a gentle ballad that is balanced with the tinge of melancholy in her voice. "Wrapped" moves along like a quiet, sunny afternoon spent horse riding. "Hillbilly Kickin'" is Britt getting down and having fun with a good country-pop tune.

She is another of the many Australian artists to make it big in Nashville. Along with Keith Urban, Kasey Chambers, and Jamie O'Neal, Britt has honored her roots while pursuing the dream of becoming a successful country music artist. Of the many countries that have embraced country music, the Land Down Under boasts one of the largest contingent of acts.

Catherine Britt is one of the new breed. She was born at about the time that the New Traditionalists were beginning to flex their muscles. Like George Strait, Ricky Skaggs and Randy Travis, the Australian singer has instilled a sense of tradition into her music as an homage to those that established the framework for her career. Along with LeAnn Rimes, Jamie O'Neal, Carrie Underwood, Sara Evans, Keith Urban, Taylor Swift and Miranda Lambert, Catherine has already made a strong impact on the genre.

In interviews, on her CDs and in concert she continues to pay homage to her idols, Hank Williams, Sr., and Loretta Lynn. A chance meeting with the latter was a great thrill and encouraged Britt to continue carving out a special niche in Nashville. Already she has impressed many with her boundless talents.

Britt is one of the most active artists on the circuit. She has performed at many venues, including state fairs, the Grand Ole Opry, and festivals. The enterprising young artist has used video as a tool to boost her career. With her good looks, demeanor and talent she is a natural in front of the camera.

The Catherine Britt story is that of a girl who is a winning package. She has the vocal power to remain on the charts for a long time and has already impressed many with her talent in a very short time. The dynamic singer has made everyone take notice of her Aussie style.

DISCOGRAPHY:

Dusty Smiles and Heartbreak Cures, Universal 12402.
Too Far Gone, ABC Music 5101113472.

Taylor Swift (1989–)
Captured Moments

The story of every branch of country music has always been about songwriting. There could be no industry without people penning songs. It is the backbone of the entire history of the genre. One young female singer who hails from Pennsylvania understands this concept as her material of captured moments attests. Her name is Taylor Swift.

Taylor Swift was born on December 13, 1989, in Wyomissing, Pennsylvania, into a musical family. Her maternal grandmother was a professional opera singer and urged her granddaughter to pursue a career in music. By the age of ten the young Swift was performing at karaoke contests, festivals and fairs. She continued to hone her skills, improving quickly with each new experience.

Before her teens she had cut a few demo tapes, but none of them led her to a recording contract. She took a giant step in achieving her goal when she sang the national anthem at a Philadelphia 76ers basketball game. It was a graduation of sorts from the usual venues she performed at, and she hoped that something positive would emerge from this one concert.

In an effort to develop a more effective act she did three things. First, she taught herself how to play the guitar and developed her ability on the instrument quickly as an accompaniment to her fine voice. Second, she continued to fine tune her vocal delivery, which already possessed a strong, rich texture. Third, Swift also began to write songs, improving her skills with each new piece she composed.

There was an added bonus in her effort to become a successful country music artist. One of the best motivators she received at the time was the family's trips to Nashville, where she performed hoping to get noticed. The enterprising teenager made contacts and developed important industry bridges during the time she spent in Music City, U.S.A.

Eventually, her family decided to move to the country music center, an act that would greatly accelerate her career. Unlike many other singers who arrived in the city with a big dream and not much else, Swift possessed the support of her family, a long apprenticeship in music and some previous contacts with Nashville executives. It was now only a matter of creating effective material that would enable her to receive a recording contract.

Swift had been composing songs for some time and had developed a definite skill. While many singers her age usually relied on outside arrangements, she was determined to write her own ticket to fame. It was only a matter of time before one of her songs was polished enough to be released. The piece was "Tim McGraw," and while she was performing it at one of the cafes in Nashville, the founder of Big Machine Records spotted the talented young singer and signed her to the label.

The single "Tim McGraw" and the accompanying video catapulted Swift to national attention. The single would peak in the Top Ten on the country charts, and the video would become a staple on the Great American Country cable channel. The song was found on her self-titled debut CD, released in the fall of 2006.

The smash hit made her a teenage country music star, like Brenda Lee, Tanya Tucker and LeAnn Rimes before her. However, unlike the others, Swift had written or co-written all of the songs on the debut CD. Although she was in the limelight at a very young age, Taylor had been singing in public for a long time so the talented singer was well prepared for stardom.

Highlights of the album included "Tim McGraw," "The Outside," "Mary's Song (Oh My My My)," "A Place in the World," "Cold As You," "Stay Beautiful," "Should've Said No," and "Tied Together With a Smile." Despite her age, it was a mature effort.

In 2007, she won Breakthrough Video of the Year on the CMT Awards. Unfortunately, at the ACM Awards she lost her bid to win Top New Female Vocalist to Miranda Lambert. But Swift didn't need to win an award to expand on her popularity. Taylor appeared on ABC-television's *Good Morning America*, sang the national anthem at the Thanksgiving Day football game, as well as at halftime. She later guested on *The Tonight Show* with Jay Leno where she sang her signature tune "Tim McGraw."

Although the recording side of her career had been launched quite nicely, she needed to concentrate on the performance part. Appearances on television as well as sporting events were good, but her best exposure occurred when she opened for Rascal Flatts and George Strait on tour. The former was one of the most promising groups on the circuit, while the latter was a country music mainstay.

It was inevitable that she would eventually meet the man who inspired the hit song that launched her career. It was a magical moment when Swift finally met her idol, Tim McGraw. It was a connection between two artists who shared a quiet moment together. Taylor continues to record and perform.

Taylor Swift is a country music sensation. She has quickly raced up the charts and into the hearts of country music fans while still a teenager. The singer with the special talent has made incredible strides in achieving her lifelong ambition to be a successful singer.

She has a contemporary country music voice. There is an element of sweetness to it because of her young age, but also a touch of maturity. There is a slight twang in her vocal delivery and a pop tinge. Despite its sophistication, it is a voice that will grow stronger as she matures.

Unlike other teenage sensations such as Brenda Lee, Tanya Tucker and, most recently, LeAnn Rimes, Swift was not someone with the voice of a mature singer trapped in the body of a young girl. Her vocal sound matched her age, but it was still a powerful tool that she utilized to find fame. The sweet quality in her vocal delivery enabled her to avoid the pressures that others were forced to face.

Despite a slim catalog, she has already provided fans with a solid number of songs. A partial list includes "Tim McGraw," "Picture to Burn," "A Place in the World," "The Outside," "Tied Together with a Smile," "Stay Beautiful," "Our Song," and "Should've Said No." With a proven talent for writing songs, she will deliver many more gems in the future.

Taylor Swift is one of the new breed of artists. Along with Ashley Monroe, Miranda Lambert, LeAnn Rimes, Carrie Underwood, Keith Urban, Sara Evans, Catherine Britt, Kellie Pickler, Danielle Peck, Lindsey Haun, and Gretchen Wilson, she represents the future of country music. In a decade it will be interesting to see which of these artists continue in the current vein.

Another astonishing fact about Swift is her songwriting abilities. At sixteen she proved a maturity far beyond her age in exploring the subject matter of her songs. The hit "Tim McGraw" is more than just a song about a teenage girl crush; it is about associating a moment of one's life with something concrete, thereby freezing the image in memory forever.

The Taylor Swift story is that of a pure singer who has managed to harness, polish and empower her natural talent into a successful career. Most importantly, she has concentrated on developing her songwriting skills to the point that she is an excellent tunesmith. This ability promises a very bright future as she strives for captured moments.

DISCOGRAPHY:

Taylor Swift, Big Machine 120702.
Our Song, Big Machine 0103.

Appendix:
Country Music Associations

This is not a complete list. There are hundreds of country music associations in North America and all over the planet. The following is a sampling of the many caretakers who are dedicated to preserving the rich tradition of American country music, which now belongs to the world.

Adirondack Bluegrass League
129 Jay St.
Schenectady, NY 12305
tcowin9483@aol.com

AEGC Bluegrass Association
10 avenue Foch
92250 La Garenne Colombe, France
01 41 19 64 31
aegc@free.fr

The Alabama Country & Gospel Music Association (ACGMA)
P. O. Box 396
Mentone, AL 35984
acgma@yahoo.com

Alberta Society of Fiddlers
120 Heatherglen Crescent
Spruce Grove, AB, Canada
T7X 3X5
leecousineau@shaw.ca

The Anne Arundel County Bluegrass Association (AACBA)
Ritchie Highway / 6th Ave.
Glen Burnie, MD

Appalachian Cultural Music Association
500 Gate City Highway, Suite 140
Bristol, VA 24201
contact@appalachianculturalmusic.org

Appalachian Fiddle & Bluegrass Association
P.O. Box 507
Wind Gap, PA 18091
afba_admin@ afbawindgap.org

Arizona Bluegrass Association (ABA)
P.O. Box 8139
Glendale, AZ 85312-8139
gstring47@hotmail.com

Arizona Old Time Fiddlers Association
7470 Derryberry Lane
Flagstaff, AZ 86004
cntrump@uwtc.net

Athy Bluegrass Music Association
21 Kilkenny Rd., Ballylinana Atby
Ireland
obientony@eircom.net

Bay Area Bluegrass Association (BABA)
League City, TX
www.bayareabluegrass.org

Birthplace of Country Music Alliance
Box 216
Bristol, TN 37621
510 Cumberland Street, Suite 103
Bristol, VA 24201
http://www.birthplaceofcountrymusic.org

Bluegrass & Old Time Music Association of New Jersey, Inc.
Little Silver, NJ
http://www.newjerseybluegrass.org

Bluegrass & Old Time Music Associations of North Dakota
P.O. Box 101
Litchville, ND 58461
http://www.northdakotabluegrass.org

Bluegrass Anonymous (The Louisville Bluegrass Music Association)
P.O. Box 21281
Louisville, KY
http://www.bluegrass-anonymous.org

Bluegrass Association of Southern California (BASC)
Post Office Box 10885
Canoga Park, CA 91309
http://www.socalbluegrass.org

Bluegrass Music Association of Maine
P.O. Box 154
Troy, ME 04987
http://www.bmam.org

Bluegrass Music Denmark
Ærtebjergvej 53
DK 2650 Hvidovre, Denmark
+45 36 78 97 09

Bluegrass West
Post Office Box 614
Los Olivos, CA 93441
folklife@loc.gov

Boston Bluegrass Union
P.O. Box 650061
West Newton, MA 02465-0061
http://www.bbu.org

Brandywine Friends of Old Time Music
Unitarian Universalist Fellowship Hall
420 Willa Road
Newark, DE
bfotm@dca.ne

British Columbia Country Music Association (BCCMA)
Box 56082
Valley Centre RPO
Langley, B.C. V3A 8B3, Canada

British Country Music Association BCMA
PO Box 240, Harrow, Middlesex HA3 7PH, England
theBCMA@yahoo.com

The Buckeye Country Music Organization of America
4819 Warminister Dr.
Columbus, OH 43232

California Bluegrass Association
3430 Tully Road
Modesto, CA 95350
http://www.cbaontheweb.org

Canadian Country Music Association (CCMA)
626 King Street West, Suite 203
Toronto, ON, Canada
M5V 1M7
admin@thatscountry.com

Cape Breton Fiddler's Association
70 Station Street
Dominion, Cape Breton
Nova Scotia B1G 1W2, Canada
cbfiddlers@seaside.ns.ca

Central New York Bluegrass Association (CNYBA)
P.O. Box 491
Baldwinsville, NY 13027
http://cnyba.com

Central Texas Bluegrass Association, Inc. (CTBA)
P.O. Box 9816
Austin, TX 78766-9816
www.centraltexasbluegrass.org

Colorado Bluegrass Music Society
P.O. Box 406
Wheat Ridge, CO 80034-0406
www.coloradobluegrass.org

Connecticut Bluegrass Music Association (CTBMA)
P.O. Box 2042
Salem, CT 06420
860-859-2696
www.ctbluegrass.org

Cornish Bluegrass Association
28 Fore Street Camborne
Cornwall, England
TR14 8AZ

Country Music Association (CMA)
One Music Circle South
Nashville, TN 37203
www.cmaworld.com

Country Music Association of Australia
P.O. Box 298, Tamworth NSW 2340
Australia
www.country.com.au

Country Music Association of Rhode Island
Post Office Box 966
Bristol, RI 02809
http://www.ribgma.com/

Country Music Singers Association
P.O. Box 19916
Oklahoma City, OK 73144
www.cmsaok.com

DC Bluegrass Union (DCBU)
P.O. Box 903
Warrenton, VA 20188
www.dcbu.org

Desert Bluegrass Association
17247 E. Peach Tree Rd.
Mayer, AZ 86333
www.desertbluegrass.org

European Bluegrass Music Association (EBMA)
Steinenweg, CH-4133
Pratteln, Switzerland

Falmouth Fiddlers Association
P.O. Box 608
North Falmouth, MA 02556-0608
www.schoonerflagpoles.com/falmouthfiddlers.htm

Florida State Fiddlers Association (FSFA)
P.O. Box 713
Micanopy, FL 32667
docs@boothmuseum.org

Foothills Bluegrass Music Society
P.O. Box 70056
Calgary, AB, Canada T3B 5K3
garmstrong@dundeewealth.com.

France Bluegrass Musique Association
Les Moutrets
71440 Juif, France

Great Plains Bluegrass and Old-Time Music Association
Omaha, NE 68112-2025.
www.gpbotma.homestead.com

Green Country Bluegrass Association (GCBA)
P.O. Box 2002
Owasso, Oklahoma 74055-2002
www.gcba.homestead.com/

Gulf Coast Bluegrass Music Association (GCBMA)
841 Aleff Road
Pace, FL 32571
www.gcbma.com/

Hardanger Fiddle Association of America
P.O. Box 23046
Minneapolis, MN 55423-0046
www.hfaa.org

Heart of American Bluegrass and Old Time Music (HABOT)
North Cross United Methodist Church
1321 NE Vivion Road
Kansas City, MO 64118
www.banjonut.com/habot

High Lonesome Strings Bluegrass Association
P.O. Box 482
Pleasant Garden, NC 27313
www.highlonesomestrings.org/

Hudson Valley Bluegrass Association
Poughkeepsie, NY
www.hvbluegrass.org/

Idaho Bluegrass Association (IBA)
P.O. Box 477
Star, ID 83669
www.smithfowler.org/bluegrass/IdahoBGindex.htm

Intermountain Acoustic Music Association (IAMA)
P.O. Box 520521
Salt Lake City, UT 84152
iama@xmission.com

International Bluegrass Music Association (IBMA)
2 Music Circle South, Suite 100
Nashville, TN 37203
www.ibma.org

International Country Music Association
P. O. Box 148227
Nashville, TN 37214

Kansas Bluegrass Association
Derby, KS 67037-9000
www.kansasbluegrass.org

Kansas Prairie Pickers Association (KPPA)
Topeka, KS
www.kppamusic.org/

Kentucky Friends of Bluegrass Music Club (KFBMC)
Meadowgreen Park
Clay City, KY 40312
606-663-9008
www.kyfriends.com

Kings River Bluegrass Association
Fresno, CA 93704-4539
www.krblue.net

Lexington Bluegrass
2250 Regency Road
Lexington, KY 40503
www.lbar.com

Manitoba Fiddle Association
Portage La Prairie, Manitoba, Canada
R1N 3B5
www.riedstrasviolinshop.com

Massachusetts Country Music Awards Association
P.O. Box 2066
Abington, MA 02351
www.mcmaa.net

Memphis Area Bluegrass Association (MABA)
P.O. Box 171152
Memphis, TN 38187-1152
www.memphis-bluegrass.org

Middle Georgia Bluegrass Association
7902 Redding Way
Lizella, GA 31052
www.middlegeorgiabluegrass.org

Minnesota Bluegrass & Old-Time Music Association (MBOTMA)
P.O. Box 16408
Minneapolis, MN 55416
www.minnesotabluegrass.org

Missouri Area Bluegrass Committee (MABC)
St. Charles, MO 63301-034
www.bluegrassamerica.com

Montana Rockies Bluegrass Association (MRBA)
P.O. Box 1220
Hamilton, MT 59840
www.mtbluegrass.com

National Traditional Country Music Association
P.O. Box 492
Anita, IA 50020

New Hampshire Country Music Association
702 White Cedar Blvd
Portsmouth, NH 03801

New York State Old Tyme Fiddlers Association
P. O. Box 24
Redfield, NY 13437
lchereshnoski@twcny.rr.com

The North Florida Bluegrass Association, Inc. (NFBA)
P.O. Box 2830
Orange Park, FL 32067-2830
www.nfbluegrass.org

Northern Indiana Bluegrass Association (NIBGA)
5034 Wapiti Court
Fort Wayne, IN 46804-4946
260-432-4485
www.bluegrassusa.net

Northern Illinois Bluegrass Association (NIBA)
P.O. Box 535
West Dundee, IL 60190
www.nibaweb.org

Northern Kentucky Bluegrass Music Association (NKBMA)
P.O. Box 133
Hebron, KY 41048
www.nkbma.com

Northwest Arkansas Bluegrass Association (NABA)
Hwy 65 N
Harrison, AR 72601
www.arkansasbluegrass.com

Oldtime Country Music Club of Canada
Bob Fuller, Secretary
5140 Wellington St.
Verdun, Quebec, Canada
H4G 1Y3
wwwebmonitor@yahoo.com

Oregon Bluegrass Association
P.O. Box 1115
Portland, OR 07207
www.oregonbluegrass.org

Ossipee Valley Bluegrass Festival
P.O. Box 593
Cornish, ME 04020
www.ossipeevalley.com

Patrick Country Music Association
111A North Main Street
Stuart, VA 24171
www.patrickcountrymusic.com

Piedmont Council of Traditional Music
P.O. Box 28534
Raleigh, NC 27611

Piedmont Folk Music
Troy, VA 22974

Redwood Bluegrass Associates (RBA)
P.O. Box 390515
Mountain View, CA 94039-0515
www.rba.org

Rivertown Bluegrass Society, Inc.
P.O. Box 1921
Conway, SC 29528
www.rivertownbluegrasssociety.com

Roanoke Fiddle and Banjo Club
P.O. Box 13314
Roanoke, VA 24032-3314
va-carolina@cox.net

San Diego Bluegrass Society (SDBS)
P.O. Box 15292
San Diego, CA 92175
www.socalbluegrass.org

Seattle Folklore Flyer
P.O. Box 30141
Seattle, WA 98113
www.seafolklore.org

Scottish Bluegrass Association
43 Forth Park Gardens
Kirkcaldy, Fife KY2 5TD, Scotland
www.scottishbluegrass.com

Seven Mountains Bluegrass Association
827 New Valley Road
Marysville, PA 17053-9716
www.sevenmountainsbluegrass.org

Society for Preservation of Bluegrass Music in America (SPBGMA)
P.O. Box 271
Kirksville, MO 63501
www.spbgma.com

South Dakota Friends of Traditional Music
P.O. Box 901
Sioux Falls, SD 57101-901
www.fotm.org

South Louisiana Bluegrass Association, Inc.
P.O. Box 51672
Lafayette, LA 70505
www.southlouisianabluegrass.org

Southeast Minnesota Bluegrass Association (SEMBA)
Rushford, MN 55971
www.semba.tv

Southeastern Bluegrass Association (SEBA)
P.O. Box 20286
Atlanta, GA 30325
www.sebabluegrass.org

Southern Wisconsin Bluegrass Music Association, Inc. (SWBMAI)
P.O. Box 7761
Madison, WI 53707
www.swbmai.org

Southwest Bluegrass Association
1013 N. Lyman Ave.
Covina, CA 91724
www.s-w-b-a.com

Southwest Florida Bluegrass Association
1030 North Central Avenue
Avon Park, FL
www.southwestfloridabluegrass.org

Strictly Country
Postbus 32
9540 AA Vlagtwedde
The Netherlands

Uptown Bluegrass
P.O. Box 1372
Kamploops, BC V2CBL7, Canada
georgemcknight@telus.net

Virginia Bluegrass & Country Music Foundation, Inc.
Richmond, VA 23260

Virginia Folk Music
P.O. Box 1501
Midlothian, VA 23112
sigridwilliams@comcast.net

West Michigan Bluegrass Music Association
11926 Reed Street
Grand Haven, MI 49417
www.wmbma.org

Yellowstone Bluegrass Association
P.O. Box 23143
Billings, MT
www.yellowstonebluegrass.org

Bibliography

Adkins, Trace. *Personal Stand: Observations and Opinions from a Freethinking Redneck.* New York: Random House, 2007.

Bego, Mark. *Alan Jackson: Gone Country.* Dallas: Taylor Publishing, 1996.

_____. *Country Gals.* Wellington, New Zealand: Pinnacle Books, 1994.

_____. *Country Hunks.* Chicago: Contemporary Books, 1994.

_____. *George Strait: The Story of Country's Living Legend.* New York: Citadel Press, 2001.

_____. *LeAnn Rimes.* New York: St. Martin's Press, 1998.

_____. *Vince Gill: An Unauthorized Biography and Musical Appreciation of the Country Superstar.* Victoria, B.C.: Renaissance Books, 2000.

Brown, Jim. *Emmylou Harris: Angel in Disguise.* New York: Fox Music Books, 2004.

_____. *Shania Twain: Up and Away.* New York: Fox Music Books, 2004.

Brown, Jim, and Susan Sparrow. *Faith Hill & Tim McGraw: Soul 2 Soul.* New York: Quarry Music Books, 2002.

Burgener, Sheila, and Raymond Obstfeld, eds. *Twang! The Ultimate Book of Country Music Quotations.* New York: Henry Holt & Co., 1997.

Byworth, Tony. *The Billboard Illustrated Encyclopedia of Country Music.* New York: Billboard Books, 2007.

Cantwell, David, and Bill Friskics-Warren. *Heartaches by the Number: Country Music's 500 Greatest Singles.* Nashville: Vanderbilt University Press and the Country Music Foundation Press, 2003.

Carlin, Richard. *Country Music.* New York: Black Dog & Leventhal Publishers, 2006.

Catalano, Grace. *LeAnn Rimes—Teen Country Queen.* New York: Laurel-Leaf Books, 1997.

Clark, Terri. *Phases & Stages: The Terri Clark Journals.* Toronto: Insomniac Press, 2003.

Collins, Ace. *The Tanya Tucker Story.* New York: St. Martin's Press, 1995.

Collis, Rose. *K. D. Lang (Outlines).* London: Absolute Press, 1999.

Cusic, Don. *Randy Travis: The King of the New Traditionalists.* New York: St. Martin's Press, 1990.

_____. *Reba: Country Music's Queen.* New York: St. Martin's Press, 1991.

Daley, Jackie, and Tom Carter. *Tammy Wynette: A Daughter Recalls Her Mother's Tragic Life and Death.* New York: Berkley, 2001.

Daniel, Wayne W. *Pickin' on Peachtree: A History of Country Music in Atlanta.* Chicago: University of Illinois Press, 2000.

Dawidoff, Nicholas. *In the Country of Country: People and Places in American Music.* New York: Pantheon, 1997.

Dicaire, David. *The First Generation of Country Music Stars: Biographies of 50 Artists Born Before 1940.* Jefferson, N.C.: McFarland, 2007.

Dickerson, James L. *Faith Hill: Piece of My Heart.* New York: St. Martin's Press, 2001.

Egger, Robin. *Shania Twain: The Biography.* New York: CMT Books, 2005.

Feiler, Bruce. *Dreaming Out Loud: Garth Brooks, Wynonna Judd, Wade Hayes and the Changing Face of Nashville*. New York: HarperCollins, 1999.

Fox, Aaron A. *Real Country: Music and Language in Working-Class Culture*. Durham, N.C.: Duke University Press, 2004.

Gray, Scott. *Chicks Rule*. New York: Ballantine Books, 1999.

_____. *Livin' on Country: The Alan Jackson Story*. New York: Ballantine Books, 2000.

_____. *On Her Way: The Shania Twain Story*. New York: Ballantine Books, 1998.

_____. *Perfect Harmony: The Faith Hill & Tim McGraw Story*. New York: Ballantine Books, 1999.

Gubernick, Lisa Rebecca. *Get Hot or Go Home: Trisha Yearwood — The Making of a Nashville Star*. New York: St. Martin's Press, 1995.

Hager, Andrew C. *Women of Country: Dolly Parton, Patsy Cline, Tammy Wynette and More...* Baltimore: American Literary Express, Inc., 1998.

Hager, Barbara. *The Life and Music of Shania Twain*. New York: Berkley Books, 1998.

Hanny, John R. *Asleep at the Wheel*. Danbury, Conn.: Rutledge Books, 2002.

Haslam, Gerald W. *Workin' Man Blues: Country Music in California*. Berkeley: University of California Press, 1999.

Hinman, Ronnie. *Faith Hill*. New York: Chelsea House Publishers, 2001.

Hundley, Jessica, and Polly Parsons. *Grievous Angel: An Intimate Biography of Gram Parsons*. New York: Thunder's Mouth Press, 2005.

Jackson, Alan. *Precious Memories*. Milwaukee: Hal Leonard, 2006.

Judd, Wynonna, and Patsi Bale Cox. *Coming Home to Myself*. New York: Penguin Group, 2005.

Kruth, John. *To Live's to Fly: The Ballad of the Late, Great Townes Van Zandt*. New York: Da Capo Press, 2007.

Mahoney, Judith Pasternak. *Dolly Parton*. Sierra Madre, Calif.: Friedman Fairfax Publishing, 1999.

Mandrell, Barbara, with George Vecsey. *Get to the Heart: My Story*. New York: Bantam, 1991.

McAleer, Dave. *Hit Singles: Top 20 Charts from 1954 to the Present Day (All Music Book of Hit Singles)*. Milwaukee: Backbeat Books, 2004.

McEntire, Reba, with Tom Carter. *Reba: My Story*. New York: Bantam Books, 1995.

McGee, David, and Steve Earle. *Steve Earle: Fearless Heart, Outlaw Poet*. Milwaukee: Backbeat Books, 2005.

Milsap, Ronnie, with Tom Carter. *Almost Like a Song*. New York: McGraw-Hill, 1990.

Moye, Catherine. *Asleep at the Wheel*. Oxford, England: The Bodley Head, Ltd., 1989.

Nash, Alanna. *Dolly: The Biography, Updated Edition*. New York: Cooper Square Press, 2002.

Oglesby, Christopher J. *Fire in the Water, Earth in the Air: Legends of West Texas Music*. (Brad and Michele Moore Roots Music Series). Austin: University of Texas Press, 2006.

Parton, Dolly. *Dolly: My Life and Other Unfinished Business*. New York: HarperCollins, 1995.

_____. *Dolly Parton: Halos and Horns*. Van Nuys, Calif.: Alfred Publishing Company, 2002.

Pepplatt, Francesca. *Country Music's Most Wanted: The Top 10 Book of Cheating Hearts, Honky Tonk Tragedies, and Music City Oddities (Most Wanted)*. Dulles, Va.: Potomac Books, Inc., 2004.

Rascal Flatts. *Me and My Gang*. Milwaukee: Hal Leonard Corp., 2006.

Rich, John, Big Kenny, and Allen Rucker. *Big & Rich: All Access*. New York: Center Street, 2007.

Robertson, William B. *K.D. Lang: Carrying the Torch: A Biography*. Toronto: ECW Press, 1993.

St. John, Lauren. *Hardcore Troubadour: The Life and Near Death of Steve Earle*. New York: Harper Perennial, 2004.

Sample, Ted. *White Soul: Country Music, the Church, and Working Americans*. Nashville: United Methodist Publishing House, 1996.

Sgammato, Jo. *Dream Come True: The LeAnn Rimes Story*. New York: Ballantine Books, 1997.

_____. *Garth Brooks: American Thunder*. New York: Ballantine Books, 2000.

Starr, Victory. *K.D. Lang: All You Get Is Me*. New York: St. Martin's Mass Market Paper, 1995.

Tichi, Cecelia. *High Lonesome: The American Culture of Country Music*. Rev. ed. Chapel Hill, N.C.: University of North Carolina Press, 2006.

Tritt, Travis, with Michael Bane. *10 Feet Tall and Bulletproof: The Travis Tritt Story*. New York: Warner Books, 1995.

Tucker, Tanya, with Patsi Bale Cox. *Nickel Dreams: My Life*. New York: Hyperion, 1997.

Urban, Keith. *Love, Pain and the Whole Crazy Thing*. New York: Cherry Lane Music, 2007.

Williams, Hank, Jr., with Michael Bane. *Living Proof: An Autobiography*. New York: Putnam, 1979.

Wilson, Gretchen, with Allen Rucker. *Redneck Woman: Stories from My Life*. New York: Grand Central Publishing, 2006.

Wynette, Tammy, with Joan Dew. *Stand by Your Man: An Autobiography*. New York: Pocket Book, 1982.

Index